# Crystal Reports™ 8
# For Dummies

MW00991361

## The Standard Toolbar

| Button | Function |
| --- | --- |
| | Creates a new report. |
| | Opens an existing report. |
| | Saves the report. |
| | Prints the report to a printer. |
| | Previews the report in the Preview tab. |
| | Exports the report to a file or e-mail. |
| | Refreshes the report data. |
| | Cuts text or an object. |
| | Copies text or an object. |
| | Pastes text or an object. |
| | Undoes an action. Use the drop-down list to undo more than one action. |
| | Redoes an action. Use the drop-down list to redo more than one action. |
| | Inserts Hyperlink. |
| | Inserts database, formula, parameter, running totals, and other fields. |
| ab | Inserts a text object. |
| Σ | Inserts a summary. |
| | Activates the Report Expert. |
| | Activates the Section Expert. |
| | Activates the Select Expert. |
| | Sets the record sort order. |
| | Inserts a chart. |
| | Inserts a map. |
| | Finds text or data on the current report. |
| 100% | Zooms in and out on your report. |
| | Gives context-sensitive help. |

## Seeing the Data on the Preview Tab

Crystal Reports has two ways to view a report. One way is the Design tab, on which you see the placeholders for the fields, and the other way is the Preview tab, on which real data is inserted into the report from the source database. When you begin creating a report, only the Design tab is visible. To see the Preview tab:

1. **Click the Print Preview button (or choose File⇨Print Preview).**

   Crystal Reports adds the Preview tab and shows you a WYSIWIG (What You See Is What You Get) view of the report. When you print the report, it should match very closely the Preview tab layout.

## Getting Zoomed!

Zooming in allows you to take a closer look at the formatting of your reports — and to make those teeny-tiny adjustments that make a good report a great one. You can do this in either Design or Preview, but Preview is much more interesting. To take a closer look at your report:

1. **Choose View⇨Zoom to open the Magnification Factor dialog box.**

2. **Type a number greater than 100 in the Magnification Factor dialog box to see more detail (you can enter up to 400 as the zoom factor).**

   You have two other choices:

   • Fit Whole Page, which zooms out the view so that you see the entire page at once.

   • Fit One Dimension, which reformats the view so that the entire width of the report is in view.

   To return the view to normal, click the Reset button in this same dialog box.

# Crystal Reports™ 8 For Dummies®

Cheat Sheet

## The Formatting Toolbar

| Button | Function |
|---|---|
| Times New Roman (Western ▼) | |
| 10 ▼ | Selects the point size of text. |
| A▲ | Increases the font size of the selected data one point each time you click the button. |
| A▼ | Decreases the font size of the selected data one point each time you click the button. |
| B | Changes the selected data to boldface. |
| I | Italicizes the selected data. |
| U | Underlines the selected data. |
| ▤ | Aligns the selected data flush left. |
| ▤ | Centers the selected data. |
| ▤ | Aligns the selected data flush right. |
| $ | Displays a currency symbol with the number, when a number field is selected.* |
| , | Displays a thousands separator in the number, when a number field is selected.* |
| % | Puts a percentage sign with the number, when a number field is selected.* |
| .00→ | Adds one decimal place to the number, when a number field is selected. |
| 00.← | Subtracts one decimal place from the number, when a number field is selected. |
| ⟨⟩ | Activates the Highlighting Expert, when a number field is selected. |
| ▤ | Turns Group Tree on or off. |
| 🔧 | Turns Supplementary toolbar on or off. |

*Note:* The program refers to your setting in the International section of the Control Panel (Windows NT) or the Regional section of the Control Panel (Windows 98).

Copyright © 2000 IDG Books Worldwide, Inc.
All rights reserved.

Cheat Sheet $2.95 value. Item 0642-0.

For more information about IDG Books, call 1-800-762-2974.

IDG BOOKS WORLDWIDE

**For Dummies®: Bestselling Book Series for Beginners**

# Crystal Reports™ 8

## FOR

## DUMMIES®

# by Douglas J. Wolf

IDG Books Worldwide, Inc.
An International Data Group Company

Foster City, CA ◆ Chicago, IL ◆ Indianapolis, IN ◆ New York, NY

**Crystal Reports™ 8 For Dummies®**

Published by
**IDG Books Worldwide, Inc.**
An International Data Group Company
919 E. Hillsdale Blvd.
Suite 400
Foster City, CA 94404
www.idgbooks.com (IDG Books Worldwide Web site)
www.dummies.com (Dummies Press Web site)

Library of Congress Catalog Card No.: 99-67169

ISBN: 0-7645-0642-0

Printed in the United States of America

10 9 8 7 6 5 4 3 2 1

10/QR/QY/QQ/IN

Distributed in the United States by IDG Books Worldwide, Inc.

Distributed by CDG Books Canada Inc. for Canada; by Transworld Publishers Limited in the United Kingdom; by IDG Norge Books for Norway; by IDG Sweden Books for Sweden; by IDG Books Australia Publishing Corporation Pty. Ltd. for Australia and New Zealand; by TransQuest Publishers Pte Ltd. for Singapore, Malaysia, Thailand, Indonesia, and Hong Kong; by Gotop Information Inc. for Taiwan; by ICG Muse, Inc. for Japan; by Intersoft for South Africa; by Eyrolles for France; by International Thomson Publishing for Germany, Austria and Switzerland; by Distribuidora Cuspide for Argentina; by LR International for Brazil; by Galileo Libros for Chile; by Ediciones ZETA S.C.R. Ltda. for Peru; by WS Computer Publishing Corporation, Inc., for the Philippines; by Contemporanea de Ediciones for Venezuela; by Express Computer Distributors for the Caribbean and West Indies; by Micronesia Media Distributor, Inc. for Micronesia; by Chips Computadoras S.A. de C.V. for Mexico; by Editorial Norma de Panama S.A. for Panama; by American Bookshops for Finland.

For general information on IDG Books Worldwide's books in the U.S., please call our Consumer Customer Service department at 800-762-2974. For reseller information, including discounts and premium sales, please call our Reseller Customer Service department at 800-434-3422.

For information on where to purchase IDG Books Worldwide's books outside the U.S., please contact our International Sales department at 317-596-5530 or fax 317-572-4002.

For consumer information on foreign language translations, please contact our Customer Service department at 1-800-434-3422, fax 317-572-4002, or e-mail rights@idgbooks.com.

For information on licensing foreign or domestic rights, please phone +1-650-653-7098.

For sales inquiries and special prices for bulk quantities, please contact our Order Services department at 800-434-3422 or write to the address above.

For information on using IDG Books Worldwide's books in the classroom or for ordering examination copies, please contact our Educational Sales department at 800-434-2086 or fax 317-572-4005.

For press review copies, author interviews, or other publicity information, please contact our Public Relations department at 650-653-7000 or fax 650-653-7500.

For authorization to photocopy items for corporate, personal, or educational use, please contact Copyright Clearance Center, 222 Rosewood Drive, Danvers, MA 01923, or fax 978-750-4470.

 is a registered trademark under exclusive license to IDG Books Worldwide, Inc. from International Data Group, Inc.

# About the Author

**Douglas J. Wolf** has written 32 books, ranging from a 1986 book on Lotus 1-2-3 to ACT! 2000, and was the author of the first *For Dummies* book on Crystal Reports, Version 5, and subsequently Versions 6 and 7. His company, HOW-TOSOFTWARE.COM, Inc., produces training videos and CD-ROMs for ACT! and Crystal Reports. The company's Web site is www.howtosoftware.com. Doug is an ACT! Certified Consultant, talk-show host, football coach, and all-around Renaissance man. He is married to the lovely and talented Gloria, has two above-average children, Alexander and Ilsa, and a killer toy poodle, Nietzsche. He has a Business Degree from the University of Minnesota, Mankato.

# ABOUT IDG BOOKS WORLDWIDE

Welcome to the world of IDG Books Worldwide.

IDG Books Worldwide, Inc., is a subsidiary of International Data Group, the world's largest publisher of computer-related information and the leading global provider of information services on information technology. IDG was founded more than 30 years ago by Patrick J. McGovern and now employs more than 9,000 people worldwide. IDG publishes more than 290 computer publications in over 75 countries. More than 90 million people read one or more IDG publications each month.

Launched in 1990, IDG Books Worldwide is today the #1 publisher of best-selling computer books in the United States. We are proud to have received eight awards from the Computer Press Association in recognition of editorial excellence and three from Computer Currents' First Annual Readers' Choice Awards. Our best-selling ...*For Dummies*® series has more than 50 million copies in print with translations in 31 languages. IDG Books Worldwide, through a joint venture with IDG's Hi-Tech Beijing, became the first U.S. publisher to publish a computer book in the People's Republic of China. In record time, IDG Books Worldwide has become the first choice for millions of readers around the world who want to learn how to better manage their businesses.

Our mission is simple: Every one of our books is designed to bring extra value and skill-building instructions to the reader. Our books are written by experts who understand and care about our readers. The knowledge base of our editorial staff comes from years of experience in publishing, education, and journalism — experience we use to produce books to carry us into the new millennium. In short, we care about books, so we attract the best people. We devote special attention to details such as audience, interior design, use of icons, and illustrations. And because we use an efficient process of authoring, editing, and desktop publishing our books electronically, we can spend more time ensuring superior content and less time on the technicalities of making books.

You can count on our commitment to deliver high-quality books at competitive prices on topics you want to read about. At IDG Books Worldwide, we continue in the IDG tradition of delivering quality for more than 30 years. You'll find no better book on a subject than one from IDG Books Worldwide.

*John Kilcullen*

John Kilcullen
Chairman and CEO
IDG Books Worldwide, Inc.

**VIII**
WINNER

*Eighth Annual
Computer Press
Awards ⪰1992*

**IX**
WINNER

*Ninth Annual
Computer Press
Awards ⪰1993*

WINNER

**X**
WINNER

*Tenth Annual
Computer Press
Awards ⪰1994*

**XI**
WINNER

*Eleventh Annual
Computer Press
Awards ⪰1995*

IDG is the world's leading IT media, research and exposition company. Founded in 1964, IDG had 1997 revenues of $2.05 billion and has more than 9,000 employees worldwide. IDG offers the widest range of media options that reach IT buyers in 75 countries representing 95% of worldwide IT spending. IDG's diverse product and services portfolio spans six key areas including print publishing, online publishing, expositions and conferences, market research, education and training, and global marketing services. More than 90 million people read one or more of IDG's 290 magazines and newspapers, including IDG's leading global brands — Computerworld, PC World, Network World, Macworld and the Channel World family of publications. IDG Books Worldwide is one of the fastest-growing computer book publishers in the world, with more than 700 titles in 36 languages. The "...For Dummies®" series alone has more than 50 million copies in print. IDG offers online users the largest network of technology-specific Web sites around the world through IDG.net (http://www.idg.net), which comprises more than 225 targeted Web sites in 55 countries worldwide. International Data Corporation (IDC) is the world's largest provider of information technology data, analysis and consulting, with research centers in over 41 countries and more than 400 research analysts worldwide. IDG World Expo is a leading producer of more than 168 globally branded conferences and expositions in 35 countries including E3 (Electronic Entertainment Expo), Macworld Expo, ComNet, Windows World Expo, ICE (Internet Commerce Expo), Agenda, DEMO, and Spotlight. IDG's training subsidiary, ExecuTrain, is the world's largest computer training company, with more than 230 locations worldwide and 785 training courses. IDG Marketing Services helps industry-leading IT companies build international brand recognition by developing global integrated marketing programs via IDG's print, online and exposition products worldwide. Further information about the company can be found at www.idg.com.
1/26/00

# Dedication

To my terrific neighbors — the Collins, Lempke, Katzfry, Personius, and Belz families.

# Author's Acknowledgments

Thanks are due to Sherri Morningstar, the Acquisitions Editor, and Jeanne Criswell, the Senior Project Editor, who put up with a curmudgeon like me. Also, to the best Crystal Reports trainer in the world, Jennifer Boyle, the book's technical editor, who made many fine suggestions.

## Publisher's Acknowledgments

We're proud of this book; please register your comments through our IDG Books Worldwide Online Registration Form located at http://my2cents.dummies.com.

Some of the people who helped bring this book to market include the following:

*Acquisitions, Editorial, and
Media Development*

**Senior Project Editor:** Jeanne S. Criswell

(Previous Edition: Kelly Oliver, Rebecca Whitney)

**Acquisitions Editor:** Sherri Morningstar

**Copy Editor:** Pam Wilson-Wykes

**Proof Editor:** Dwight Ramsey

**Technical Editor:** Jennifer Boyle

**Contributor and Editor:** Allan McMordie

**Editorial Manager:** Rev Mengle

**Media Development Manager:**
Heather Heath Dismore

**Editorial Assistant:** Candace Nicholson

*Production*

**Project Coordinator:** Valery Bourke

**Layout and Graphics:** Amy Adrian, Joe Bucki, Jason Guy, Barry Offringa, Tracy K. Oliver, Brent Savage, Jacque Schneider, Erin Zeltner

**Proofreaders:** Rachel Garvey, Susan Moritz, Marianne Santy

**Indexer:** Anne Leach

*Special Help*
Vanessa Au, Diana Conover, Donna Frederick, Tonya Maddox, Allan McMordie

---

*General and Administrative*

**IDG Books Worldwide, Inc.:** John Kilcullen, CEO

**IDG Books Technology Publishing Group:** Richard Swadley, Senior Vice President and Publisher; Walter R. Bruce III, Vice President and Publisher; Joseph Wikert, Vice President and Publisher; Mary Bednarek, Vice President and Director, Product Development; Andy Cummings, Publishing Director, General User Group; Mary C. Corder, Editorial Director; Barry Pruett, Publishing Director

**IDG Books Consumer Publishing Group:** Roland Elgey, Senior Vice President and Publisher; Kathleen A. Welton, Vice President and Publisher; Kevin Thornton, Acquisitions Manager; Kristin A. Cocks, Editorial Director

**IDG Books Internet Publishing Group:** Brenda McLaughlin, Senior Vice President and Publisher; Sofia Marchant, Online Marketing Manager

**IDG Books Production for Branded Press:** Debbie Stailey, Director of Production; Cindy L. Phipps, Manager of Project Coordination, Production Proofreading, and Indexing; Tony Augsburger, Manager of Prepress, Reprints, and Systems; Laura Carpenter, Production Control Manager; Shelley Lea, Supervisor of Graphics and Design; Debbie J. Gates, Production Systems Specialist; Robert Springer, Supervisor of Proofreading; Trudy Coler, Page Layout Manager; Troy Barnes, Page Layout Supervisor, Kathie Schutte, Senior Page Layout Supervisor; Michael Sullivan, Production Supervisor

**Packaging and Book Design:** Patty Page, Manager, Promotions Marketing

◆

The publisher would like to give special thanks to Patrick J. McGovern, without whom this book would not have been possible.

◆

# Contents at a Glance

# Cartoons at a Glance

### By Rich Tennant

page 179

page 229

page 63

page 103

page 307

page 7

page 271

**Fax:** 978-546-7747

**E-mail:** richtennant@the5thwave.com

**World Wide Web:** www.the5thwave.com

# Table of Contents

# Introduction

*W*elcome to *Crystal Reports 8 For Dummies.* This book is about one of the best-kept software secrets. Seagate Crystal Reports has been bundled with a wide variety of other software products for several years, and therefore you haven't seen it on the software best-seller list. Yet it is a best-seller. If you've used Visual Basic or an accounting package, you've probably seen the product and wondered how to get it to work.

This book covers what you need to know to begin creating reports that not only look good but actually have data that make sense to the person reading them. The good news is that it isn't difficult to do. In fact, creating reports is quite easy after you understand a few basic concepts, such as how you lay out a report and where you insert the records, summaries, totals, and headings.

## About This Book

I've written more than 30 books on computer software and have been an ACT! consultant for many years. One constant in my experience is the lack of an easy way to generate reports from the data in databases. Crystal Reports solves that problem.

Most folks, however, don't use a report writer every day. At the end of the month or quarter, all of a sudden the boss or you needs a report on the sales activity of a product or sales force, and you're in crunch time trying to figure out how to get the report you want without that creeping feeling of desperation. So I've designed this book to let you turn easily to the page you need to find the necessary steps for success. Therefore, the book is targeted to beginners and intermediate users. You don't have to read this book cover to cover; just grab the chapter or subject you require and read that information. The structure is such that if you are a true beginner, you can start with the first few chapters and get a report out the door.

You needn't be a database expert to use Crystal Reports. If you understand how to start programs in Windows 98 or NT and know what data you want to use in reports, then you should be in great shape!

# Foolish Assumptions

I've made a few assumptions in this book. First, that you're familiar with the rudiments of using a computer and Windows 98 or NT — such as knowing that a mouse is not an animal and that Windows has nothing to do with panes (although *pains* may be accurate). Second, that you have, or someone has, installed Crystal Reports and that you've worked with some sort of database program from which you want to garner reports. I do not assume that you understand how databases are constructed, so I cover that information in Chapter 1. Last, I trust that you have discovered that a computer is stupid — which is to say that it does only what you ask it to do — and that it requires that you learn a special language to communicate with it. That's why the phrase "user-friendly" ranks up there with "the check's in the mail" on the list of oft-quoted fibs.

# How This Book Is Organized

In this book, I try to present the steps for creating reports and then adding enhancements in the sequence most new users would want. You may find other ideas about the topics you want to approach and the order in which you want to approach them, so glance through the following chapter descriptions and empower yourself.

## Part I: What You Need to Know to Survive

### Chapter 1: Setting the Table

Not everyone comes to the report-creation process skilled at using and understanding databases. So read this chapter if you've never had to create a database but have only entered data into one. This chapter gives you an idea of how the information is stored and why it's done that way.

### Chapter 2: Creating a Simple Report

This chapter takes you through the beginning stages of creating a report, including how to determine the type of report you want and how to start inserting database information into a report. I also introduce you to an easy way to generate reports with the Report Experts.

### Chapter 3: Crystal Reports: Basic Skills

The text in a report refers to the stuff you may add that's separate from the database information, such as headings, titles, and footers. A report is only as good as the information it conveys, and the text objects make the report more easily understood.

# *Part II: Manipulating Records*

### Chapter 4: Selecting Records

When you access a database, you may want all the records that are in the database or just a certain type of record. This chapter shows you how to pick the records you want.

### Chapter 5: Sorting and Grouping Records

You can manipulate the database records that are added to your report in a number of ways. This chapter covers changing the sort order and creating groups.

# *Part III: Formatting and Formulas for Success*

### Chapter 6: Charting and Mapping Data

This chapter gives you more stuff on how to add pizzazz to your reports to make them more readable — and the information more accessible. Plus, you can generate a map of your reports based on the records.

### Chapter 7: Using the Crystal Formula Language

Formulas are the way to convert data, insert data from different tables, and perform calculations on data in tables. After you understand the concept of how to construct and insert formulas into a report, you reach a higher plane of reporting. Seagate also includes numerous example formulas, which are discussed in Chapter 7.

### Chapter 8: Using Conditional Formatting

Want a record (such as one that has negative numbers or is in a group) formatted based on the information contained in the record? This chapter is where you find the steps to use conditional formatting.

### Chapter 9: Creating a Subreport

Find out how to insert one report (a subreport) into another report (a primary report). And find out how beneficial a subreport can be.

# Part IV: Putting On Some Finishing Touches

### Chapter 10: Formatting Sections of a Report

This chapter offers a further look at applying formatting based on the information in a report section, making it easy to highlight good news — or downplay bad news.

### Chapter 11: Creating Presentation-Quality Reports

How about adding pictures, logos, and OLE objects to the report? Find out how in this chapter.

# Part V: Creating Specific Types of Reports

### Chapter 12: Creating a Cross-Tab Report

A cross-tabulation report allows you an entirely different look at your database information. It's used frequently in market research as an adjunct to survey data. A cross tabulation can deliver new insights to your customers and prospects. Crystal Reports makes the process of creating a cross tabulation easy.

### Chapter 13: Creating a Summary Report

A summary report prints or displays only the summary information developed by the report process. In other words, when the boss wants only the bottom line, Crystal Reports can deliver. This chapter shows you how to create such a report.

### Chapter 14: Linking to Other Databases

Links are a way of combining information from a variety of tables, in a variety of ways. In this chapter, I explain the best ways to join data from different tables, including using SQL joins and creating reports directly from Access and Excel.

# Part VI: Disseminating Reports without a Hitch

### Chapter 15: Distributing Reports

This chapter covers mailing and exporting your reports, including posting a report to a Web site.

**Chapter 16: Setting Your Options**

Each time you create a report, you can change some automatic settings that determine the size of text, where files are saved, and so on. Each of the settings can be customized to give you complete control of the look of your reports.

## Part VII: The Part of Tens

**Chapter 17: Ten or So Questions to Ask Before You Create a Report**

Revel in ten questions that — if asked — make creating any report easier.

**Chapter 18: Ten (Okay, Eleven) Tricks to Enhance Reports**

Shine with ten proven means of adding appeal to a report.

# Conventions Used in This Book

Taking a leap by ignoring the Geneva Convention so often invoked on *Hogan's Heroes,* I employ the following:

When an instruction says to choose File⇨Save, it means that you're to use your mouse to click (using the left mouse button) the File menu name and then, from the menu that appears, select the Save option. The underlined letter is also a means of making the choice. For example, pressing the Alt key and holding it down while you press the F key opens the menu, as well.

Occasionally, you're asked to type text or a number to make an example work. Whenever that's the case, the text you are to enter appears in **bold type.**

When you read "select the text," you are to click and hold the left mouse button and drag it over the text until the text is highlighted, and then release the mouse button.

At no point do I ask you to refer to the *Seagate Crystal Reports User's Guide.* The manual is very comprehensive, if a bit dry. After you get the reporting basics down, you can peruse it for the advanced topics that I don't cover.

# Icons Used in This Book

To help you quickly find the information you want to read, or at least to make that information a little more memorable, I strategically scatter icons throughout this book. Here's the lowdown on the little graphics:

The information beside this icon is a good piece of information to know. Save time, avoid delays, get ahead, and prosper with these tidbits.

Not that Crystal Reports is dangerous or anything (unless you drop the official User's Guide on your foot), but this icon warns you about things that keep you out of trouble.

If you're interested in the technical and advanced stuff, this icon is the place to go for such information. But you shouldn't need a Ph.D. from MIT to follow along.

This icon reminds you to remember information that it signals. Keep this stuff somewhere in memory, or at least written down on the back of envelopes in the top-right drawer of your desk.

If you want to appreciate what Crystal Reports can do, this icon points out its features for you. Some things may seem like magic.

The information beside this icon is considered basic, common knowledge to have to function within Crystal Reports. Sort of like the time in fifth grade when you were forced to memorize all the provinces of Canada or the 50 U.S. state capitals so that you could function in life. Basic, common knowledge.

# Where to Go from Here

With a cloud of dust and a hearty "Hi-ho, Silver — away!" you're on your way as a report writer. I promise to make it an easy journey, with few delays and much productivity. My company, Wolf's Byte Productions, also produces Crystal Reports CD-ROM training and holds Web-based classes. To get more information, visit www.howtosoftware.com. Thank you for buying this book!

# Part I

# What You Need to Know to Survive

The 5th Wave — By Rich Tennant

SO POORLY DOCUMENTED IS THE SOFTWARE THAT ROY IS BETA TESTING THAT HE FAILS TO NOTICE THAT THE GAME RULES TO "TWISTER" HAVE ACCIDENTALLY BEEN INCLUDED.

# In this part . . .

You know that sooner or later you have to finish the report your boss asked for. This part shows you how to get something rather quickly into the boss's hands. Really. Even though the IS department bought the program and dropped it in your lap with a slight sneer, using Crystal Reports is fairly easy. Open a report and pop in a few fields, and you're in business. Add a couple of titles, and people will think you're an undiscovered genius. No kidding — it happened to a friend of a relative of a guy my brother knows. He started creating reports with Crystal Reports, and he got a good-paying-annual-raise-three-weeks-off-dental-care-plan-never-get-fired government job. You could be next!

# Chapter 1

# Setting the Table

• • • • • • • • • • • • • • • • • • • • • • • • • • • • • • • • • • • • • • • • • • •

• • • • • • • • • • • • • • • • • • • • • • • • • • • • • • • • • • • • • • • • • • •

*W*hat is life without reports? Every business has a database of some sort, and from that database, people expect reports. The problem is that most of the products, such as Paradox, Access, ACT!, dBASE, and Peachtree (to name a few), have report-creating capabilities that are limited and clumsy. In addition, corporate users want to create reports from data stored in larger, more powerful databases, such as Oracle or Sybase, or even from an older mainframe database. These older databases are respectfully called "legacy systems," and the mainframe computers they run on are "Big Iron." (Picture an old steam locomotive.) Crystal Reports can create terrific-looking reports from all these sources of data in almost any format.

Before starting the program, I want to show you how data is stored in products such as Access, Paradox, or FoxPro so that you have an understanding of how Crystal Reports works with your data.

## In the Beginning, There Was a Table

When you create a database in virtually any program, the program creates a *table* into which you enter data. This is true whether you enter data into a *form screen* (which is a screen resembling an invoice or other paper-type form) or into *tabular fields* (which are like spreadsheets with rows and columns).

What do you see when you look at a real-world table? Food! Me, too. But in a computer, a table is a structure for storing information. You view the table that you sit down to at Thanksgiving from above. You see the turkey, mashed potatoes, gravy, and so on, as individual items *on* the table.

Not so with a database table. You look at computer tables from the *side*. Across the top of the table is a list of fields with the legs (usually more than the four you see at a dinner table) underneath the table top. Figure 1-1 shows a computer table.

**Figure 1-1:**
A computer
table,
set for four.

| Record | Turkey | Mashed Potatoes | Pie |
|--------|--------|-----------------|-----|
| Alex   | 6      | 10              | 6   |
| Ilsa   | 2      | 2               | 1   |
| Gloria | 1      | 3               | 3   |

Because the view is from the side, the top of the table has the column headings, which in Figure 1-1 are Record, Turkey, Mashed Potatoes, and Pie. In a computer database, these are the *field names*.

The names on the left are the individual names (or *records,* in database terms) Alex, Ilsa, and Gloria. In some databases, this column has a unique identifier number, such as the record number or a person's Social Security number.

While legs of some sort hold up a Thanksgiving table, in a computer database, the table legs separate the individual pieces of data. In Figure 1-1, the number of servings of turkey eaten by Alex (6) is separated by table legs from the number of servings of mashed potatoes (10) and the number of pieces of pie (6).

A database record consists of the individual pieces of data that run from left to right across one of the rows underneath the table top. In this example, Alex, Ilsa, and Gloria are individual records.

The field names in your database are more likely to be First Name (Fname), Last Name (Lname), Address 1 (Add1), Address 2 (Add2), City, State, and Zip, as shown in Figure 1-2. The names are shortened for simplicity, although things are actually more confusing if you don't know what the abbreviations stand for.

**Figure 1-2:**
A sample
database
table.

| Record# | Fname  | Lname   | Add1            | Add2   | City | State | Zip   |
|---------|--------|---------|-----------------|--------|------|-------|-------|
| 1       | Doug   | Wolf    | 1 $^{st}$       | Street | NY   | NY    | 10025 |
| 2       | Gloria | Lenares | 2 $^{nd}$       | Place  | SF   | CA    | 90024 |

# Form Follows Function

The database you work with may resemble a form, as shown in Figure 1-3. In this database program, for example, you enter records into a table in which each of the fields is the same as its table heading.

No matter how you enter data into a database, all the information ends up in a table — that's where Crystal Reports comes in.

After you enter thousands of records, any database makes finding and editing those records an easy task. You can even sort the records by postal code — but suppose that you want to send a direct-mail piece to each of your customers via bulk mail. To take advantage of the post office's bulk mail discount, you want to bundle the letters together by postal code before you mail them. Crystal Reports can easily sort your letters and mailing labels by postal code and even give you a report that shows how many customers you have in each postal code. In other words, Crystal Reports starts where the "canned" reports that are built into the program you're using leave off.

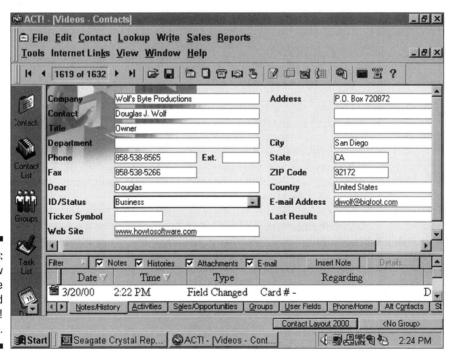

**Figure 1-3:** Form view of a single record in an ACT! database.

# Table for . . . One or More?

Consider for a moment how a real computer database is constituted. Suppose that your company has products with *repeat sales,* meaning you sell the same things over and over to the same customer base. If you were the architect of the company's electronic database (in computer lingo, a *systems design engineer,* harumph), sooner or later you would notice that every time the customer orders, essentially the same data is needed to fill the order. Retyping the customer name, address, and so on for every order (not to mention reentering product information such as price) would be a great waste of time. The solution is to use several tables to hold the data, as follows:

- Customer information
- Product information
- Order information

In the customer-information table, you have the specifics of where to ship, where to bill, and so on. You assign each customer a unique customer number. You also create a product table that has each product listed by name and number, including the price, so that the database can calculate the cost. Then when the customer places an order, you create an order table with the following information:

- Customer number
- Product number
- Product quantity

If you construct your database properly, the correct customer and product information is entered for you, to make the order complete. To get all the information you want on your report, you may need to include one or more tables from a database.

A database can consist of a single table, but it most likely consists of several tables. In this book, I start with a single table, show off the Crystal Reports attributes as best I can, and then move on in Chapter 14 to using multiple tables to make a report.

With some standard PC-type databases (such as dBASE, FoxPro, or Paradox), each table is a separate file stored on a local or network drive. Therefore, each time you need a table for your report, you connect to another physical file — a .dbf file for a dBASE database, for example. Other databases, such as Access or the larger ones like Sybase or Oracle, have all the tables in one file or database connection so that you won't have to make any more connections when you want to add more tables to your report.

# Planning the Report

Before starting Crystal Reports, you must first sit down with a piece of paper and decide what you want in the report. Admittedly, visualizing the report's exact layout at this point may be difficult, but you or the *Dilbert*-like person who's demanding that report should have a clear idea of what you want in the report. Keep in mind that Crystal Reports allows for the creation of myriad mathematical formulas — from simple totals, averages, and maximums and minimums to expressions that Einstein would have admired. You can include charts, footers, headers, and so on. Anticipating computational needs rather than recognizing them only after the report is constructed saves you time — and that's the stuff life is made of.

If you're creating a complex report — one that involves several tables — determine which fields from each table to use and how to link them. In Chapter 14, I show you a terrific Crystal Reports tool for linking disparate tables.

The other benefits of Crystal Reports, such as the nifty text and numbers formatting and company logos, can be added at any time.

## What makes a report?

When you look at a professionally prepared paper report, it usually has a report header, page headings, individual page details, and a report footer. So does Crystal Reports. Every report you create with this program has standard layout sections. The trick to understanding how Crystal Reports transfers the paper world to your computer desktop is to think: *All the parts of a paper report are represented in the Crystal Reports report window.* In other words, Crystal Reports layers the parts of a paper report onto the computer window so that you can see all the parts at the same time — from title section to summary section.

Crystal Reports uses the information in existing databases; neither does it create new databases nor does it affect the data in the source database itself. If you're working on a large database, such as an Oracle database with 2,000,000 records, Crystal Reports can give you a subset of the records in order to easily and efficiently create the report. After the design is finished, the record selection criteria you specify is used to get only the data you need when you run the report.

## Report distribution

The point of creating reports is to distribute the information to all those who need it. You can print, fax, e-mail, or post to a Web site any report you create in Crystal Reports.

# The origin of Crystal Reports (from the book of Relation, Chapter 1, Verse 1)

Now in that time, a mighty tribe of Programmers known as dBASE nerds existed. They dwelt in the land of southern California, known for its fine beaches and beautiful weather. But the dBASE nerds did not surf, nor did they spend much time in the Eden-like climate. Verily, the dBASE nerds were mighty storers of information, creating databases that only the high priests of the tribe could understand. And the people cried out, "You dBASE nerds have created these mighty storehouses of data, but we cry for reports! Reports with cross tabs and charts and lots of fancy fonts." The Programmer High Priests were sore afraid and asked themselves, " What can we do? We have the knowledge of getting data in, but we cannot get it out! We shall be broken into 16 and even 32 bits! Is no one among us able to satisfy the thirst for reports?"

And much lamenting and wailing occurred about their lack of reports. So in this time a small tribe in the northern lands known as Canada had a tribe of Programmers, too. They were known as the *Crystals*. These Crystals were skilled in the ways of the database and had the secret knowledge of reports. And lo and behold, from them sprang forth code that took data to a place it had never been. The code created reports so easily that the people were amazed, and their e-mail and faxes chattered with news. Verily they asked the Crystals for a name for this stupendous code. The wise men of Crystal gathered in council and thought long and hard; much pasta and hops were consumed. Then, after their deliberation, they drew their tribe unto them and declared: "We hereby exclaim the name of our code to be CRYSTAL REPORTS! Go forth from this place and spread the word that a new way of creating reports now exists among us. Truly we have been blessed! And a book shall be struck, so that all the nations, known as *For Dummies* readers, shall come to have knowledge of Crystal Reports and the world shall be made good. So we have said it; so shall it be done."

# Chapter 2

# Creating a Simple Report

· · · · · · · · · · · · · · · · · · · · · · · · · · · · · · · · · · · · · · · · · · · · · · · · · ·

## *In This Chapter*

▶ Starting Crystal Reports

▶ Using Crystal Reports Expert

▶ Saving a Report

▶ Previewing a report

▶ Inserting fields

▶ Moving fields

▶ Using guidelines

· · · · · · · · · · · · · · · · · · · · · · · · · · · · · · · · · · · · · · · · · · · · · · · · · ·

*I*n this chapter, you plumb the depths of opening a database and inserting its fields into a report. You also look at the Crystal Reports Preview as an easy way to see what your report looks like before you print it.

## *Starting Crystal Reports*

When you install Crystal Reports, the computer adds the Seagate Crystal Reports program to the Programs list in your Start menu.

To start Crystal Reports, simply choose Start⇨Programs⇨Seagate Crystal Reports. The Welcome to Seagate Crystal Reports dialog box appears, as shown in Figure 2-1.

**Figure 2-1:**
The
Welcome to
Seagate
Crystal
Reports
dialog box
greets you.

The Welcome to Seagate Crystal Reports dialog box offers you several choices. You can create a new report in two ways — by using the Report Expert or by doing everything yourself, starting from scratch with a blank report. (For more information on these methods, see "Creating a Report with the Report Expert" and "Creating a Report from Scratch" later in this chapter.) You can also open an existing report — one you created previously or one of the demo reports that ships with Crystal Reports.

# Creating a Report with the Report Expert

The Report Expert is an assistant or a wizard that can help you design a report. This means you don't have to be a Report Designing Dynamo to get a great-looking report. By walking you through a series of steps, the Report Expert lets you create a new report quickly and easily. It's also foolproof because you can't forget any major steps. Business users use the Report Expert to quickly start a report that they can then fine-tune later; power users continue to rely on it for the same reason — it's quick.

To see how this expert works, use the Report Expert and the demonstration Access database that come with Crystal Reports to create a new report with two fields. Just follow these steps:

1. **In the Welcome to Seagate Crystal Reports dialog box that appears when you start the program, select the Using the Report Expert radio button and then click OK.**

   The Report Gallery dialog box appears, as shown in Figure 2-2. The Report Gallery offers a collection of report formats from which you can choose.

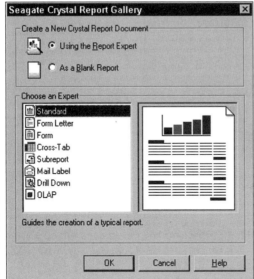

**Figure 2-2:**
The Report
Gallery
dialog box.

2. **In the Choose An Expert box, select Standard and then click OK.**

   The Standard Report Expert dialog box appears, displaying a series of tabs near the top.

3. **In the three sources of report data, click the Database button.**

   The Data Explorer dialog box appears, as shown in Figure 2-3. This feature is new in Crystal Reports Version 8 and makes locating different data sources easy — once you know how it works.

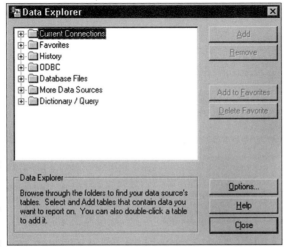

**Figure 2-3:**
The Data
Explorer
dialog box.

When you install Crystal Reports, several sample databases and reports are included. The database you want to use for this example is a Microsoft Access database named *Xtreme,* which consists of multiple tables. You can start by adding a single table and then several fields to the report.

4. **Double-click the Database Files item or click the + sign to the left of the Database Files item.**

   The Find Database File subitem appears.

5. **Double-click the Find Database File item.**

   The Windows Open dialog box appears, as shown in Figure 2-4.

   If you installed Crystal Reports without making any modifications to the file locations (say that three times fast), the folder where the example database is stored is C:\Program Files\Seagate Software\Crystal Reports\Samples\Databases. Figure 2-5 shows the Xtreme database as it appears in the Open dialog box.

**Figure 2-4:**
The
Windows
Open
dialog box.

6. **Double-click the Xtreme.mdb filename.**

   The list of tables in the Xtreme database appears, as shown in Figure 2-6.

   OK, you're doing a lot of clicking to get this far, but Crystal Reports needs to know what database tables to use, and this is the way to locate them. In this example, you use a single table.

7. **Click the Customer table and then click the Add button.**

   A check mark appears on the icon to the left of Customer — the table you just added — indicating that it has become part of the report.

**Figure 2-5:**
Locating the
Xtreme
database
via the Open
dialog box.

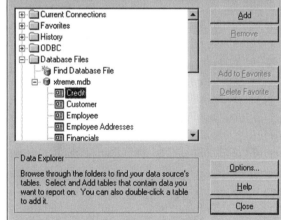

**Figure 2-6:**
Table listing
from the
Xtreme
database.

8. **Click the Close button.**

   You return to the Standard Report Expert dialog box, as shown in Figure 2-7.

9. **To add fields to the report, click the Next button to move to the Fields tab.**

   Crystal Reports shows you the fields that you can add to the report, as shown in Figure 2-8.

   The order in which you select the fields for inclusion in the report is the order in which they're inserted into the report, reading left to right. Even though you can change the field placement afterward, selecting the fields in the order you want is easier at this stage.

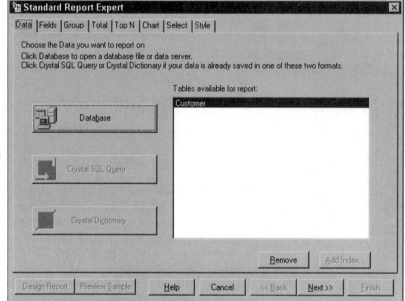

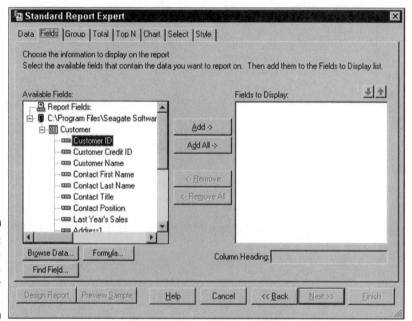

10. **Click the Customer Name field and click the Add button (or double-click the Customer Name field).**

    The Customer Name field appears in the Fields To Display box.

11. **Double-click the City field.**

    You probably have to scroll down the list of fields to find the City field. The City field appears in the Fields To Display box.

    You can see the results of Steps 10 and 11 in Figure 2-9.

    ***Note:*** Near the bottom right corner of the dialog box is the Column Heading text box. If you want, at this step or after you complete the report, you can enter a new name for the column heading in the finished report. You may want to change the column heading if the field name in the database table is obscure, such as Birth date listed as BDATE.

12. **Click the Finish button to see Crystal Reports create the report. It appears automatically in the Preview tab.**

    Crystal Reports inserts the two fields into the Preview window, as shown in Figure 2-10. For more information on the Preview feature, see "Previewing a Report" later in this chapter.

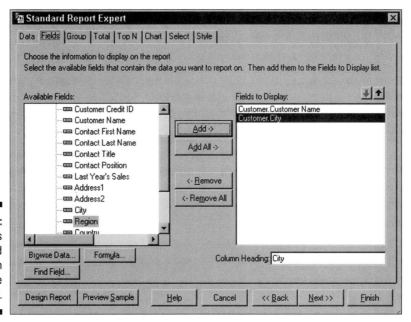

**Figure 2-9:** Two fields are selected for inclusion in the report.

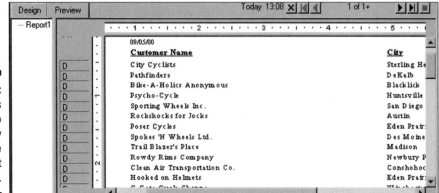

**Figure 2-10:**
Two fields
inserted into
a report by
using the
Report
Expert.

# Saving a Report

Before fiddling around with any report that you've created, you want to save
it. Then you can try all kinds of stuff on your report with no worries. To save
a report, follow these steps:

1. **Choose File⇨Save from the menu bar or click the Save button on the**
   **Standard toolbar.**

   The File menu appears, as shown in Figure 2-11.

2. **Click Save.**

   The Save dialog box appears.

3. **Enter a name for the report in the File name field.**

   Crystal Reports follows the Microsoft convention in that it saves the
   report in the My Documents or your own Personal folder. The reason is
   that all the reports (and whatever else) you create are stored in a single
   folder, to make backing up the reports easy as a precaution in case of
   hard-drive failure. To save the example report in the "Creating a Report
   with the Report Expert" section, use the name Ch2.

4. **Click Save.**

| | |
|---|---|
| ☐ **New...** | Ctrl+N |
| 📂 **Open...** | Ctrl+O |
| **Close** | |
| 💾 **Save** | Ctrl+S |
| **Save As...** | |
| ✓ **Save Data with Report** | |
| **Save Subreport As...** | |
| 🔍 **Print Preview** | |
| **Print** | ▶ |
| **Printer Setup...** | |
| **Page Setup...** | |
| **Options...** | |
| **Report Options...** | |
| **Summary Info...** | |
| **1** C:\WINDOWS\...\Ch2 | |
| **2** C:\WINDOWS\...\gjw | |
| **3** C:\WINDOWS\...\Ch4 | |
| **4** C:\WINDOWS\...\Ch3 | |
| **Exit** | |

**Figure 2-11:**
The File
Menu.

# Viewing a Report in the Report Design Tab

Crystal Reports lets you look at a report in two ways: One way is to use the Preview tab (refer to Figure 2-10) that shows the report with the data; the other way is to use the Design tab, which shows the placeholders for the fields and formatting. These tabs appear on the left side of the screen, just below the menu bars. Just click the one you want to see.

Crystal Reports is an electronic version of a paper report and therefore has the same basic components. Look at the report sections on the Design tab, shown in Figure 2-12.

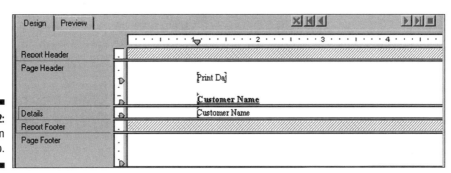

**Figure 2-12:**
The Design
tab.

Along the left side of the Design tab, you see the following report sections:

- **Report Header:** Represents the title or front page of the report. In this section, you can insert a title, perhaps a chart, and maybe even a company logo. This section prints once at the beginning of the report. The Standard Report Expert chooses to hide this section. If you are following along with the exercise, you see the gray shading lines through the section.

- **Page Header:** Represents the header that appears at the top of every page of the report. The header contains field names for the columns of data in the body of the report. In Figure 2-12, the Report Expert shows a field that prints the date the report is printed.

- **Details:** Represents the portion of the report that contains the individual records from the database. Although the section appears small in the Design tab, it holds the most data. This section prints one time for every record retrieved from the database. The Report Expert automatically inserts the fields selected into the Details section of the report.

- **Report Footer:** Represents the portion of the report in which you can print grand totals and other report summary information. It appears once, at the end of the report. The Report Expert has also chosen to hide this section.

- **Page Footer:** Represents the portion of the report that prints at the bottom of every page. It can contain page numbers, the report name, and so on. In the example report, the Page Number field has been inserted on the right side of the page. If you print the report, the number is printed in the bottom right corner of each page.

After you get comfortable with simple reports, you may want to sort or group your records to make a report more useful (see Chapter 5). In this example, grouping your Customers by City puts everyone from the same city together on the report. Whenever you create groups of data, Crystal Reports adds two more sections in the Design tab.

- **Group Header:** Usually contains a field that names the group, and you can insert summary values, charts, and cross-tabulations. The section prints once at the beginning of each group.

- **Group Footer:** Usually contains the summary values for the group and can contain the group name, charts, and cross tabulations. (In fact almost anything the Group Header can do, the Footer can do also!) This section prints at the end of each group.

*Note:* I try to give you some examples of what you can place in various sections, but you can be quite creative. For example, Crystal Reports puts the Group Name in the Group Header and the group totals in the Group Footer, but you can do just the opposite if you want.

# Creating a Report from Scratch

Crystal Reports offers you two ways to create a new report. You can follow the bouncing Report Expert (see "Creating a Report with the Report Expert"), or you can do it all yourself by starting with a blank report. Until you're comfortable constructing reports, or whenever you want to quickly create a report that you can subsequently fine-tune, the Report Expert is generally the way to go.

However, if you want more control over the process and are willing to do more of the work yourself, you can create a new report from scratch, starting with the minimum outline that Crystal Reports provides: sections for headers, details, and footers. Creating an example report from this blank can help you understand how to use this feature and gain some comfort with various aspects of report building. (Before you begin this process, close any previously created report that is still on your screen by choosing File⇨Close.)

To create a sample new report from a blank, complete the following steps:

1. **Choose File⇨New.**

    The Crystal Reports Gallery dialog box appears.

2. **Select the As a Blank Report radio button.**

3. **Click OK.**

    The Data Explorer dialog box appears. If you followed the steps in the "Creating a Report with the Report Expert" section earlier in this chapter, you see the Xtreme database and its tables already listed, so you can skip ahead to Step 6.

4. **Double-click the Database Files item or click the + sign to the left of the Database Files item, and then double-click the Find Database File item.**

    The Open dialog box appears. Assuming that you installed Crystal Reports without changing its suggestions for file locations, you can find the Xtreme database in C:\Program Files\Seagate Software\Crystal Reports\Samples\Databases.

5. **Click the Xtreme filename and then click Open.**

    The names of the tables in the database appear.

6. **Click the Customer table name and then click the Add button.**

    A check mark appears on the icon to the left of Customer — the table you just added — indicating that it has become part of the report.

7. **Click Close.**

    The Crystal Reports Design tab opens, and the Field Explorer dialog box appears, as shown in Figure 2-13.

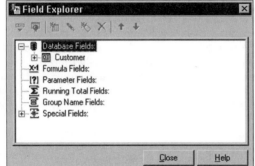

**Figure 2-13:**
The Field
Explorer
dialog box.

8. **Double-click the Customer table name under Database Fields.**

   The list expands to reveal the individual fields in the Customer table.

   To insert the Customer Name field into the Report Design tab, follow these steps:

9. **Select the Customer Name field, as shown in Figure 2-14.**

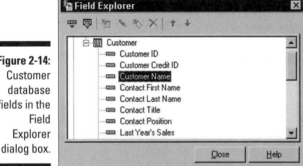

**Figure 2-14:**
Customer
database
fields in the
Field
Explorer
dialog box.

When you select a field, the Insert to Report and Browse buttons on the toolbar become active.

10. **Click the Insert button or press Enter.**

    A funny thing happens! The mouse pointer becomes the international sign for NO — a circle with a line drawn through it. No, you haven't violated any international treaty! Crystal Reports is simply telling you that a field is attached to the pointer, and it's ready for insertion — but not in the section where the mouse is currently positioned.

**11. Drag the pointer out of the Field Explorer dialog box.**

When the pointer is positioned in the layout area (the white area of the screen) of the Design tab, the pointer transforms into a long rectangle, which means that the field can be properly inserted.

**12. Position the rectangle in the layout area of the Details section, as shown in Figure 2-15, and click your mouse to place the field in position.**

You may notice that the field can be dropped into any section but remember that whatever is in the Details section will show for every record selected from the database. In this example, you want to see every customer's name so put the Customer Name field in the Details section.

Figure 2-16 shows the result of the insertion. Notice also that Crystal Reports automatically inserted another field, which is the name of the field that appears in the Page Header section.

After you insert a field, the length of the rectangle represents the maximum size of the data you can get from your database. The length of the field comes from the database field, not from Crystal Reports. So a single field can cross all the way from left to right. (I show you how to shorten a long field in the "Changing Field Length in the Design Tab" and "Changing Field Length in the Preview Tab" sections later in this chapter.)

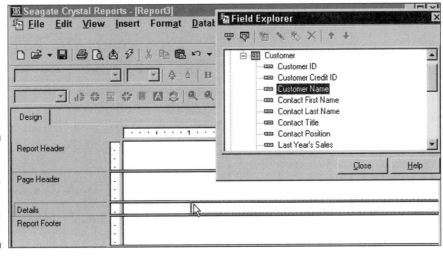

**Figure 2-15:**
The Field
Explorer
rectangle in
the Details
Section.

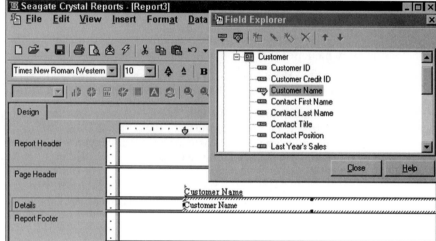

**Figure 2-16:**
The
Customer
Name field
inserted in
the Details
section.

# Previewing a Report

Crystal Reports has a very powerful Preview feature, which enables you to preview a report. When used in conjunction with the Design tab, Preview lets you see the result of placing a field into the report's design. (If you previously used the Report Expert to create a report, you saw the Preview feature.) You can make virtually any kind of change in your report in the Preview tab or the Design tab, including inserting fields, adding formatting or formulas, and so on. You can see immediately the effect of the change by going to the Preview tab.

To Preview a change in a report, complete the following steps:

1. **Click the Print Preview button on the Standard toolbar.**

   After following the steps to insert the Customer Name field in the Design tab in "Creating a Report from Scratch" earlier in this chapter, you can see the result in the Print Preview feature, as shown in Figure 2-17. Crystal Reports opens the Preview tab and inserts the actual data from the Customer Name field into the report, adding the name of the field as a column heading at the top of the list of customer names.

   When you begin creating a new report, the Preview tab isn't displayed; only the Design tab appears. To display the Preview tab, you must first generate a report by using the Print Preview button.

2. **After you preview the report, click the Design tab.**

   Voilà! You immediately switch back to the Design tab.

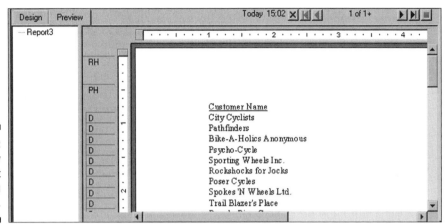

**Figure 2-17:**
A preview
of the first
field you
inserted.

You need to understand this concept: In the Design tab, you work with place-holders for the data. In the Preview tab, you work with the actual data itself.

This two-window view of a report — the Design tab and the Preview tab — sets Crystal Reports apart from many other report writers. Switching back and forth between the two helps you build a report exactly as you want it, because you can see the changes as quickly as you make them.

When you work in Preview, your computer's response time may slow because the changes you make have to be made to all the records on the report.

# Inserting an Additional Field

To add a second or subsequent field to a report, you follow the procedure for inserting an initial field, as described in the "Creating a Report from Scratch" section, except that you position the second or subsequent field in a different location in the Details section of the Design window. Crystal Reports assumes that you want to continue to add fields to the report, so the Insert Fields dialog box remains open.

 If you accidentally close the dialog box, click the Insert Fields button to open it.

Because you want the example report to include the customer name and the city in which the customer is located, you want to insert the City field next. To do so, follow these steps:

1. **In the Field Explorer dialog box, click and hold the mouse button on the City field name and drag it to the right of the placeholder for the Customer Name in the Details section of the report.**

2. **Release the mouse button.**

   The second field is inserted into the report.

3. **Click the Preview tab to see the newly inserted field.**

   The report preview appears, as shown in Figure 2-18.

Everything you place in a report — field, text, or graphics — is referred to as an *object* in the Crystal Reports lexicon. If you're following along in creating the example report, you've inserted four objects: the Customer Name and City data fields and their associated title fields in the Page Header.

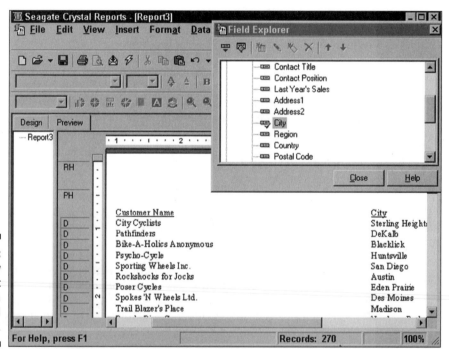

**Figure 2-18:**
The preview of a report with a second field inserted.

# *Browsing Data*

Many databases have multiple tables and multiple fields, so you can't be expected to remember exactly which table has the field you need to complete a report.

Before inserting a field into a report, you can look at a sampling of the data in the field to see whether that data is correct The Browse button is also available when you use the Report Expert to insert fields.

When you use the Browse feature, you get a sampling of data. You see the first 500 unique values for the field you're browsing. In this situation, unique means that if you browse the City field, for example, you see Vancouver only once, even if it has 100 records. Crystal Reports doesn't show you all the data, just a sampling. Would you really want to see the Order Number for a million records?

To Browse field data, follow these steps:

1. **In the Field Explorer dialog box, click the field name that you want to view.**

   In the example report, I use the Customer Name field.

2. **Click the Browse button.**

   Crystal Reports opens a dialog box, listing the actual data from the field and showing the type of data field that it is. An example appears in Figure 2-19.

   At the top of the dialog box, Crystal Reports indicates that the Type is String and the Length is 40. Of course, this information means nothing to you if you haven't previously worked with data types. If that's the case, see the "Type" and "Length" sections that follow in this chapter.

The Browse button is also accessible on the Fields tab of the Report Expert dialog box.

**Figure 2-19:**
The data
dialog box
that appears
after you
click the
Browse
button.

## Type

The first piece of information that the Browse process yields is the *type* of the field. A *string* data type indicates a character field. A character field has nothing to do with personal values. Rather, it's a field where you can enter letters or numbers. So a valid entry for a character field can be 12345 or ABCDE. This property is important because you cannot calculate a total for a character field (you can summarize a string, but you can't sum it up). You may be thinking, "If the field can have numbers, why can't I get a total?" The answer goes back to the type, which allows you to *mix* numbers and letters. The database designer, not Crystal Reports, decided that this field could include either numbers or letters. If the designer had designated the field as Numbers, rather than String, you could perform calculations because the field wouldn't include letters.

## Length

The second piece of information that the Browse process yields is the *length* of the field. You only see this if you're browsing a String-type field. (The database designer, not Crystal Reports, determined the length.) In the example, the field length is 40 characters, which means that 40 letters, numbers, or a mixture of the two can be entered into the field. So when you insert the Customer Name field into the Details section of the report, Crystal Reports draws a rectangle long enough to hold 40 characters. This allocation doesn't mean the data in the field is that long — it only means the database designer designated that much space. As you construct reports, you may find that a field's designated length is too long for the report. If so, you can shorten the space allowed.

# Changing Field Length in the Design Tab

The length of a field in the database is a waste of space if the data isn't long enough to warrant the space allowed.

Here's how to change the length of a field after it's selected:

1. **In the Design tab, position the mouse pointer in the object that you want to resize and then click.**

   The sizing handles appear on the selected object.

2. **Position the mouse pointer over the sizing handle on the right edge of the rectangle.**

The mouse pointer changes to a small (tiny, even) two-headed arrow that points left and right. This transformed pointer indicates that you can horizontally adjust the size of the rectangle. Plus, Crystal Reports adds vertical lines at the beginning and end of the field to give you a visual reference as you move or resize the object. Note that the ruler line at the top of the window changes.

3. **Hold down the mouse button and drag the mouse to the left.**

   The right end of the rectangle moves with your mouse pointer. (If the entire rectangle moves, you haven't made sure to get the two-headed arrow. If the pointer switches to a four-headed arrow, you've got the object-moving arrow and you'll end up moving the entire field. Drag the mouse back to where you started and try again.)

4. **After you resize the field to your liking, release the mouse button.**

   In Figure 2-20, the Customer Name field has been resized to a much shorter length.

5. **Perform the same resizing steps on the Customer Name field in the Page Header, directly above the Customer Name data field in the Details section.**

6. **Click the Print Preview button on the Standard toolbar or the Preview tab to see the resizing.**

In the example report, the City field is still a long way to the right of the now-shortened Customer Name field. To make the report easier to read and to have room in case you want to add more fields to the report, put the two fields closer together.

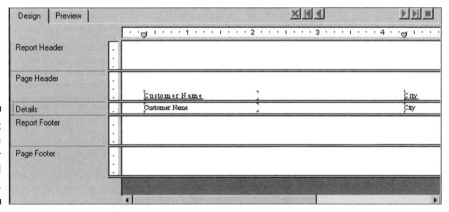

**Figure 2-20:** The Customer Name field resized.

If you had too much coffee this morning to hold the mouse still or you can't get that darned two-headed sizing arrow, do this to resize the field when you're in the Design tab:

1. **Select the field you want to resize.**

2. **Hold down the Shift key while pressing the left or right arrow keys.**

   Notice the right end of the field moving left or right, changing the size of the field.

Now go get some decaf.

When you resize a data field, hold down the Ctrl key and click the data field and the title field to resize them both in one step.

# Changing Field Length in the Preview Tab

If you've resized a field in the Design tab, you may be asking "But how do I know what size to make the field?" The beauty of being able to resize in the Preview tab is that you can see the actual data.

Look at the report in the Preview tab. The method for changing the length of a field may not be as readily apparent as it is in the Design tab, but you can do it — you only have to click the field you want to resize.

To change a field length in the Preview tab, follow these steps:

1. **Click the field you want to resize.**

   The outline of the field appears, as shown in Figure 2-21.

2. **Move the mouse pointer to the right side of the field outline so that the pointer becomes a two-headed arrow pointing left and right.**

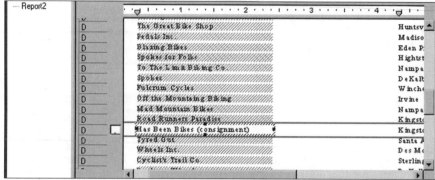

**Figure 2-21:**
You can see Design tab parameters in the Preview mode, as well.

3. **Drag the pointer to the left, until the field is reduced to the desired length.**

   The right end of the rectangle moves with your mouse pointer. (If the entire rectangle moves, you haven't been careful to get the two-headed sizing arrow. If the pointer switches to a four-headed arrow, you have the object-moving arrow and you end up moving the entire field. Drag the mouse back to where it was and try again.)

4. **Release the mouse button.**

   From the Preview tab, check out the Customer Name field at a reduced size, as shown in Figure 2-22.

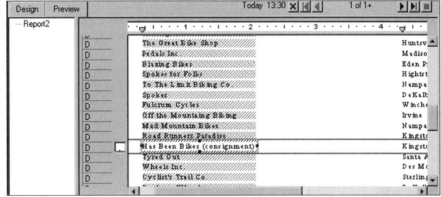

**Figure 2-22:**
The reduced
Customer
Name field
in the
Preview tab.

# Moving a Field

After you reduce the size of a field, you gain more distance between that field and the next. In the example, this means that you can move the City field to the left, leaving more room for fields you may want to add. Crystal Reports enables you to move fields in either the Design tab or the Preview tab.

My preference is to move fields in the Design tab where I can more clearly see the different sections of the report. You already may have discovered that when you move a field in the Preview tab, you can unknowingly let it slip into the Page Header section so that you only see one customer name per page. OOPS! Thank goodness for the Undo button!

To show you what section you're in when viewing the report in the Preview tab, Crystal Reports puts an abbreviated section name on the left side of the report, such as RH for Report Header, PH for Page Header, and D for Details. You get the idea; but I still find it easier to move fields around in the Design tab. Try moving a field from the Report Header to the Report Footer in Preview, and you'll see what I mean.

The Preview tab accurately reflects what you will see on paper after you print the report. Besides reducing the length of individual fields, you can also change the print orientation to *landscape,* if you have many fields in the report. Doing so means that the report prints along the 11-inch edge of a piece of paper rather than along the standard 8½-inch edge. As you work with a report, you may also want to change the page size. You can do this at any point by selecting File➪Printer Setup and changing the paper size, page orientation, or even the printer.

To move a field in the Design or the Preview tab, complete the following steps:

**1. Click the field you want to move.**

When you place the cursor over the field, Crystal Reports displays the formatting outline, as shown in Figure 2-23. The cursor is a four-headed arrow, indicating that you can drag the field in any direction.

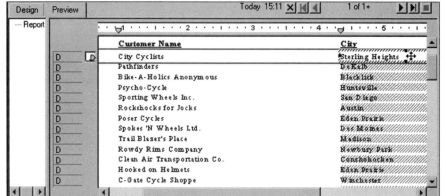

**Figure 2-23:**
The field
formatting
outline.

**2. Hold down the mouse button, drag the field to the left (as shown in Figure 2-24), and release the mouse pointer after the field is positioned correctly.**

Figures 2-23 and 2-24 show this operation being performed in the Preview tab. If you're in the Design tab (as I like to be), you can use the four arrow keys on the keyboard to move the selected field.

Well, the field moved all right, but the column title, City, did not. The reason is that the title field is a separate object from the data field. Even though Crystal Reports inserts the title with the data field when you insert a field into the Details section of a report (the program assumes that you want to use the field name as the column header), they are separate objects. Now you have to move the title field to line up with the new position of the data field. What a pain! Well, before you get upset, read the next section on guidelines.

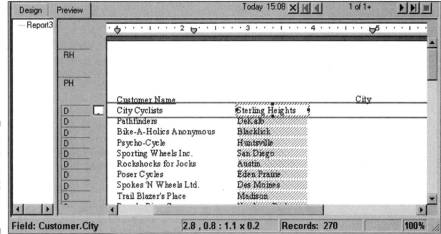

**Figure 2-24:**
The City
field moved
to the left
in the
Preview tab.

# Using a Guideline to Position Objects

Crystal Reports gives you a helpful tool (called guidelines) to keep the title field lined up with the data field or to keep any group of fields lined up with each other. You may not be able to see the guidelines (as shown in Figure 2-25) on your screen, so I suggest you do the following steps:

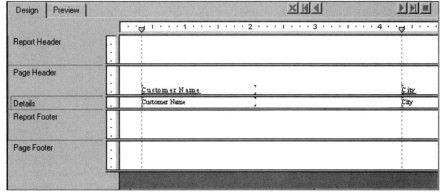

**Figure 2-25:**
The
Customer
Name and
City fields
and their
guidelines.

1. **Choose File⇨Options.**

   The Options dialog box appears.

2. **Click the Layout tab.**

   This tab offers a number of options, as shown in Figure 2-26.

3. **In View options, click the Show Guidelines in Design box to turn on this option.**

   By default, no check mark appears in front of this option, which indicates that it's turned off.

4. **Click OK.**

If you're in the Design tab, refer to Figure 2-25 to see what your screen should now look like. Notice the arrowhead in the ruler bar and the vertical line that borders the left edge of the Customer Name title field and data field? That line is a guideline. Crystal Reports automatically creates a guideline when a field is inserted into the Details section and attaches the title and data fields to it.

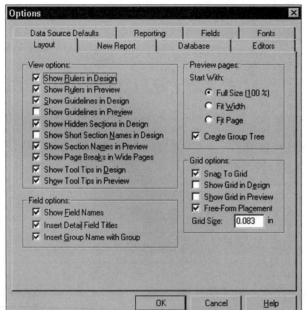

**Figure 2-26:**
The Layout tab of the Options dialog box.

Here's how to move fields that are attached to a vertical guideline:

1. **Click the guideline end in the ruler at the top of the window (it's the little upside-down triangle).**

   You can move fields in the Design or Preview tabs. If you're in the Preview tab, you have to select a field before the guidelines appear in the ruler bar at the top of the page.

2. **Hold down the left mouse button and drag the guideline to the desired position on the ruler.**

   For this example, drag the guideline to the 2-inch mark.

3. **Release the mouse button.**

A funny thing about a guideline is that objects *attached* to it line themselves up with it. In other words, you can use the guideline to arrange and align a series of objects in a report.

To attach an object to a guideline, follow these steps:

1. **In the Design tab, click the object you want to align.**

2. **Hold the mouse button down and drag the object so that its left edge is on the guideline.**

3. **Release the mouse button.**

In the Design tab only, you see little red marks on the edge of the field if the attachment is successful.

If you ever lose a guideline or need another one, simply click the ruler bar and a guideline will appear. You can even create horizontal guidelines by clicking the ruler to the left of the page.

You have to attach objects to the guideline by moving the objects to the guideline, NOT the guideline to the object.

# Aligning Fields without Using Guidelines

Guidelines are great if you know that an entire column or row of fields is going to get moved around a lot; but if you want to line up a group of fields once and be done with it, then try this new Crystal Reports feature:

1. **Select the group of fields you want to align by holding down the Ctrl key and clicking each of the fields.**

2. **With the mouse pointer on one of the selected fields, click the right mouse button.**

   A shortcut menu appears.

3. **Choose Align.**

   Another submenu appears, as shown in Figure 2-27.

4. **Select Lefts, Centers, Rights, or To Grid, depending on how you want the fields aligned.**

   The group of fields aligns to the field in which you clicked the right mouse button in Step 2.

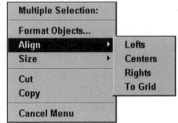

**Figure 2-27:**
The new
Align
function and
alignment
options
menu.

# Using a Grid to Place Objects

A *grid* is a pattern of equally spaced horizontal and vertical lines. (In fact, the term *gridiron* as a synonym for a football field comes from the fact that at one time the football field had vertical *and* horizontal lines.) Crystal Reports has a grid, too, which can aid in the placement of objects in a report. In fact, the grid has a property known as *Snap to Grid,* which means that when objects are placed, they snap into alignment vertically and horizontally. This feature is terrific for those reports that require many objects beyond simple text headers and fields. The switch for turning this property on or off is in the same Options dialog box mentioned in "Using a Guideline to Position Objects" earlier in this section.

To see the grid to line up objects, follow these steps:

1. **Choose File⇨Options.**

   The Options dialog box appears.

2. **Click the Layout tab and then under Grid options, click to put a check mark in the Show Grid in Design box.**

   You can also turn on the Show Grid in Preview option, but I find doing so makes the preview of the report too cluttered.

3. **Click OK.**

   The grid appears in the Design tab, as shown in Figure 2-28.

When you move objects around with Snap to Grid selected, the upper-left corner of the object always anchors to a grid dot.

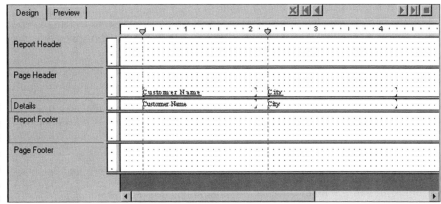

# Working More with the Report Expert

In the "Creating a Report with the Report Expert" section earlier in this chapter, you use the Standard Report Expert to create a report, up to the point in which you encounter the Group tab (refer to Figure 2-9). You stop there and preview the report, because the other aspects that you can add to a report from the remaining tabs require some discussion before they're useful. A brief description for each of the remaining tabs (and the chapters that provide the details for each) follows.

- **Group:** Provides a means of arranging the records in a report according to a common attribute, such as State, Zip Code, and so on, so that you can create a report that's grouped by State, for example, and see all the records that originate in that state. See Chapter 5 on creating groups for more details.

- **Total:** Crystal Reports assumes that you want to include some subtotals, summaries, and grand totals in your report. If you select a field such as Sales, you can create a subtotal for that field, provided you group the sales field by state or product. Adding subtotals is covered in Chapter 7.

- **TopN:** Provides a tool for determining which groups have, for example, the top five sales numbers, the top ten salespeople, or any other top number you need (you must have a group with a subtotal for this to work). If you were Casey Kasem, you'd want the top ten hit songs for the past week listed. You can bypass this tab if your report doesn't use the TopN feature. Chapter 5 deals with TopN Sorts and other types of sorting and grouping.

- **Chart:** Inserts a chart into your report. Crystal Reports has its own chart editor, so you can create virtually any type of chart, annotate it to fit your needs, and then insert it directly into your report, as described in Chapter 6. If you don't require a chart in the report, simply skip this tab.

✔ **Select:** This tab is an important feature of Crystal Reports. As you design your report, you may not want all the records in the source database to be part of the report; you may want only records of last month's sales or only the records of ski-boot sales. This tab lets you use only the records you want, as detailed in Chapter 4.

✔ **Style:** This tab offers a choice of layouts for formatting report data. After selecting a style, you can then proceed to Preview for a view of the report. I cover using a variety of formatting techniques in Chapters 8 and 10.

# Why you should use an Expert

Not all Experts arrive at the report in the same manner, but I still advise using them. The Expert leads you step-by-step through the report process, which eliminates any worry about forgetting a step. Not that you won't get a report without using an Expert, but on your own, you may not get the exact report you want.

# Chapter 3

# Crystal Reports: Basic Skills

. . . . . . . . . . . . . . . . . . . . . . . . . . . . . . . . . . . . . . . . . .

## In This Chapter

▶ Opening saved reports

▶ Inserting text objects

▶ Formatting text objects

▶ Moving among pages in a report

▶ Magnifying the report window

. . . . . . . . . . . . . . . . . . . . . . . . . . . . . . . . . . . . . . . . . .

*A*fter inserting fields, the next natural step is to add text to define and enhance your report. Text objects, as they're called in Crystal Reports, can be formatted in a number of ways, so I take a look at that, too. Also on my agenda for this chapter is a quick tour of how to move from page to page in a report.

## Opening a Saved Report

In Chapter 2, I create a report in which I insert two fields. I then save the report with the brilliant and unique name, Ch2. If you followed the steps in Chapter 2, you can continue using that report to follow along in this chapter. If not, you can use any of the example reports that Crystal Reports provides. Here's how to open a saved report, using the Ch2 report as an example:

1. **Start Crystal Reports.**

    Refer to Chapter 2 for information on ways to start Crystal Reports, depending on your operating system.

    The Welcome dialog box appears, as shown in Figure 3-1. (If you previously removed the check mark from the Show Welcome Dialog at Startup check box, the Welcome dialog box doesn't appear. In that case, choose File⇨Open. The Open dialog box appears, and you can skip to Step 3.)

**Figure 3-1:**
The
Welcome
dialog box in
Crystal
Reports.

**2. Select the Open an Existing Report radio button.**

Crystal Reports displays the most recently created reports. (You can see the saved report — Ch2 — in the dialog box in Figure 3-1.)

**3. Select (by clicking) the report that you want. Or to see more saved report files, click the More Files text to bring up the Open dialog box.**

I click Ch2, of course.

**4. Click OK.**

The Ch2 report appears, as shown in Figure 3-2.

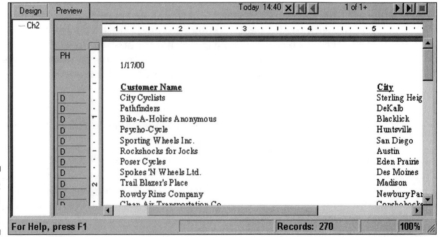

**Figure 3-2:**
The open
Ch2 report.

# Inserting Text Objects

A *text object* is a type of object that you can insert into a report to describe what is in the report, to highlight a particular record, or to add a description. The most common use of a text object is the title of the report. Text objects can be added in the report's Design or Preview tab. My advice is to add text objects in the Design tab for reasons that soon become obvious.

When you insert fields from a database table into the Details section, Crystal Reports automatically adds the field name as the header for the column. Because the header is a text object, you can modify the header by clicking it and typing a new name or changing the font style.

With Windows 98 or NT, you can add more text to the names of the reports that you create. Also, Crystal Reports provides a means to add descriptive text to a report, as described in Chapter 17.

## Adding a text object

Adding a text object from the Design tab is easier because of the available layout guides and the ability to see which section of the report the text object is being added to. All you need to do is click the Design tab (shown in Figure 3-3). Be aware, though, that in Preview the program slows considerably because you're working with live data.

The title for a typical report normally appears on the first page of the report. The Report Header section is where you put text objects that you want to appear on the title page of the report, because report headers are designed to print once, at the beginning of the report.

Everything that's part of a report is considered an object.

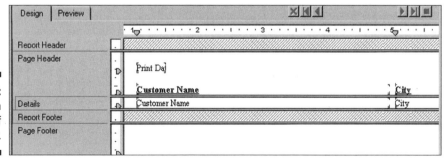

**Figure 3-3:**
The Design tab view of the report.

To insert a text object in the Report Header section of a report, follow these steps:

1. **Choose Insert⊃Text Object from the menu bar or click the Insert Text Object button on the Standard toolbar.**

2. **Move the mouse pointer into the layout area of the report.**

   A rectangular outline attaches to the mouse pointer, as shown in Figure 3-4.

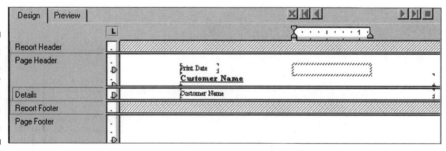

**Figure 3-4:**
A rectangle
attached to
the pointer.

3. **Position the rectangle where you want the left edge of the title object to begin and click the left mouse button.**

   For this example, place the text object in the Page Header section.

   As shown in Figure 3-5, Crystal Reports opens the text ruler above the rectangular text box. Don't worry about getting the size of the text box exactly right, because Crystal Reports resizes the text box for you as you type. You also see the insert-text cursor flashing in the text box.

**Figure 3-5:**
A text box,
ready for
text, with a
ruler line
above it.

If you decide not to insert a text object, click your left mouse button when the mouse pointer is not in the layout area of the report. The mouse pointer displays as a circle with a line through it.

4. **Type the text you want for your title.**

   For me, the title is Doug's Brilliant Report.

If you create the text object by following this example, you see the text box expand automatically to accommodate the length of the text you enter.

5. **To finish adding the text object, press the Escape (Esc) key or simply click another part of the report.**

   Do not press Enter. Doing so adds an unnecessary line inside the text object.

6. **Click the Preview tab.**

   The Preview tab gives you an accurate view of how any change looks before you print the report.

 The title, Doug's Brilliant Report, may be great, but its font size is too small for this or any report. Crystal Reports uses a 10-point font by default, so you need to increase the size of the title. Check Chapter 16 (on file options) for information about how to set the default sizes and styles of Crystal Reports objects.

## Editing a text object

You can make changes to a text object in either the Design tab or the Preview tab.

To modify a text object, follow these steps:

1. **Right-click the text object that you want to modify.**

   The format menu appears, as shown in Figure 3-6.

| Text: |
|---|
| **Edit Text Object** |
| Format Text... |
| Change Border... |
| Change Font... |
| Paragraph Formatting... |
| Move Backward |
| Move To Back |
| Object Size and Position... |
| Cut |
| Copy |
| Paste |
| Delete |
| Cancel Menu |

**Figure 3-6:** The Text Object format menu.

You can right-click to open a similar menu for other types of objects, too.

The top of the menu tells you which kind of object you have selected — in this case, text. Under Text is a list of options from which you can select. Edit Text Object puts the insertion point into the text field and reopens the ruler (refer to Figure 3-5).

2. **Select Format Text, Change Border, Change Font, or Paragraph Formatting.**

   The Format Editor dialog box appears, as shown in Figure 3-7. This dialog box has a myriad of options, which I touch on as needed. At the top of the dialog box are the tabs for different format options. Depending on which selection you make from the menu, that tab is the one displayed. In this example, you want to change the title's font.

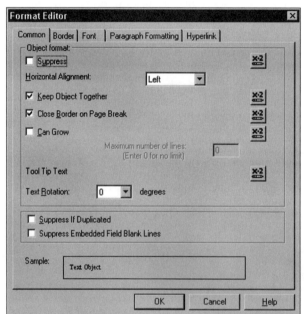

**Figure 3-7:**
The Format
Editor
dialog box.

3. **Click the Font tab.**

   The dialog box changes to display your selection, as shown in Figure 3-8.

   The various elements of the Font tab dialog box are

   - **Font:** Click the down-arrow and select the font style you want. The result of your selection appears in the Sample box. Your choice of fonts is determined by the fonts installed on your system.

   - **Style:** Click the down-arrow in the Style list box to select Bold, Italic, Bold Italic, or Regular.

- **Size:** Use this option to make the title bigger. You can either type the point size you desire or click the down-arrow and select a value from the list.

- **Color:** Click the down-arrow to select a color for the text.

- **Strikeout:** Check the box for strikethrough text.

- **Underline:** Check the box for underlined text.

- **Character Spacing Exactly:** This option specifies the value that each character in your selected font occupies. The value is defined as the distance in number of points measured from the start of one character to the start of the next. When you change the character spacing, you change only the spacing between adjacent characters, not the font size of the characters.

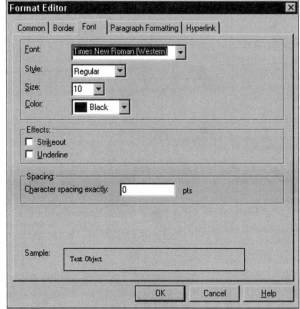

**Figure 3-8:**
The Font tab
selected in
the Format
Editor
dialog box.

4. **Select the option(s) you want to use to modify the text.**

5. **Click OK.**

In the example, simply change the font size to 14. You can see the change in the Design tab but click the Preview tab, as shown in Figure 3-9, for a better look. The size of the font you choose may be too big for the text object. To see the entire text, expand the text box by clicking the object and dragging the sizing handles to enlarge it.

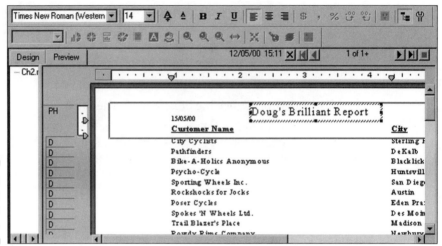

**Figure 3-9:**
The title size
changed to
14 points.

*Note:* In Figure 3-9, several outlines appear, one around the title and another across the top of the page. The outline around the title defines the area of the text object, and the outline across the top of the page defines the Page Header section.

## Adding a border and a drop shadow to the title

In addition to simply changing the size of the text, you can modify the look of the text object. In this example, you add a border and then a drop shadow to the title, giving it a neat 3-D effect. You can do this work in the Preview tab.

To add a border and/or drop shadow to a text object, follow these steps:

1. **Right-click the text object.**

   A shortcut format menu appears.

2. **Select Change Border.**

   The Format Editor dialog box appears with the Border tab selected, as shown in Figure 3-10.

   Most of the time, you want a border to go completely around the text object, but not always. So Crystal Reports gives you the option of picking which sides of the rectangle to include in the border. If you really get fanciful, you can combine different fonts and type sizes with one or more borders to create a variety of effects.

**Figure 3-10:**
The Format
Editor dialog
box with the
Border tab
selected —
ready to add
a border
of your
choosing.

In Chapter 8, you discover how to use another option in this dialog box. The small X+2 icon is a *conditional formatting tool,* meaning that you can have Crystal Reports execute a formula that determines whether the border is visible. The practical aspect of this tool is that a report's title can be easily identified by formatting that appears when printed. For example, if the report shows a net loss in the number of products sold, the border can be printed in a special color (red comes to mind) and with double-lined borders.

3. **Click the pull-down arrow next to the rectangle side(s) that you want to be visible (Left, Right, Top, or Bottom) and select the type of border you want.**

   I put a single line around the entire box.

   A preview of the border change appears in the Sample box.

4. **To get a drop shadow, with or without any border, click the Drop Shadow check box to select it.**

5. **Click OK.**

   The border and drop-shadow results appear, as shown in Figure 3-11.

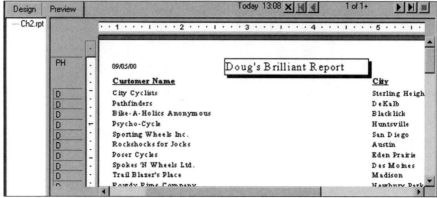

**Figure 3-11:**
A single-
lined border
with a drop
shadow
added to the
title text
object.

# Adding other fields

The database fields inserted into the report are data objects. (They become objects after being inserted into the report.)

Say that you decide you need more information about the customers on this report, specifically where they live (the Region) and how much they sold (their Last Year's Sales). Both of these fields are in the Customer Table; Region is a String field and Last Year's Sales is a Currency (or Numeric) field. The way you add these fields to the report is no different, but numeric fields can be formatted in a number of ways that string fields cannot.

To add a field to a report, follow these steps:

1. **Click the Design tab.**

2. **Choose Insert⇨Database Field from the menu bar or click the Insert Fields button on the Standard toolbar.**

   The Field Explorer dialog box appears.

3. **Click the field name you want to insert. You may have to double-click the name of the table so that you can see all the fields.**

   For this example, select the Region field.

4. **Click the Insert to Report button on the toolbar in the Field Explorer dialog box.**

   The field attaches to the mouse pointer.

5. **Position the mouse pointer so that the field outline is in the Details section, to the right of the City field, and click the mouse button.**

6. **Repeat Steps 3 to 5 with the Last Year's Sales field.**

   The results appear, as shown in Figure 3-12.

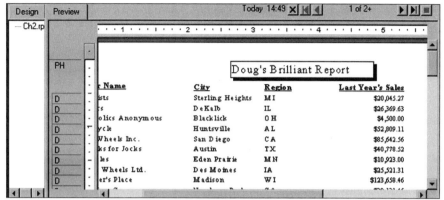

**Figure 3-12:**
A preview
of the report
with new
fields
added.

# Formatting the Numbers

With the text in good shape, you can move to the newly inserted number field (it's actually a CURRENCY field). Because the field is numeric, the formatting choices are different than with text, as you may expect. This procedure is easier to execute in the Preview tab because you're using live data so you see the results immediately.

To format a number field, follow these steps:

1. **Click the Preview tab.**

2. **Click a record in the number column that you want to format.**

   In this example, that's Last Year's Sales.

3. **Right-click the field.**

   The shortcut menu appears, as shown in Figure 3-13.

4. **Select the Format Field option.**

   The Format Editor dialog box appears, as shown in Figure 3-14. As you see in Figure 3-14, you need only concern yourself with the number of decimals printed for this example. Currently, the column of numbers includes two decimal places — an unnecessary clutter. Making a change, however, is easy.

5. **Click the number format that you want and then click OK.**

   Figure 3-15 shows the reformatted numbers.

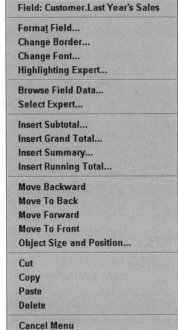

**Figure 3-13:**
With a right-click, you have the shortcut menu for numbers.

| |
|---|
| Field: Customer.Last Year's Sales |
| Format Field... |
| Change Border... |
| Change Font... |
| Highlighting Expert... |
| Browse Field Data... |
| Select Expert... |
| Insert Subtotal... |
| Insert Grand Total... |
| Insert Summary... |
| Insert Running Total... |
| Move Backward |
| Move To Back |
| Move Forward |
| Move To Front |
| Object Size and Position... |
| Cut |
| Copy |
| Paste |
| Delete |
| Cancel Menu |

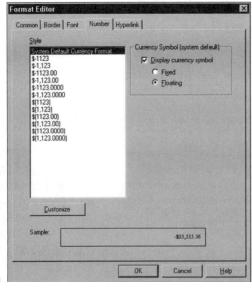

**Figure 3-14:**
The Format Editor dialog box for number fields.

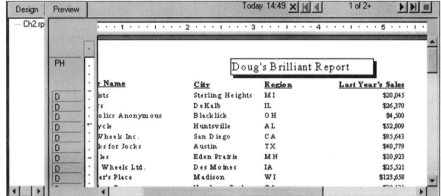

**Figure 3-15:**
The number column with zero decimals displayed.

# Using the Highlighting Expert

Sometimes, you may want to display numbers that exceed a set amount or are below a predetermined amount in a unique color (and, if you have a color printer, subsequently print them that way). Because you had to create a formula to do so in earlier versions of Crystal Reports, many novice users decided it was easier to print the report and use a highlighting pen. All that changed in Version 7 and remains true in Version 8, thanks to the Highlighting Expert feature that appears on the shortcut menu for numbers (refer to Figure 3-13). To display the shortcut menu for numbers, right-click while the mouse is positioned on a number field (such as the Last Year's Sales field in the sample report).

By selecting Highlighting Expert, you get the Highlighting Expert dialog box, which provides a simple way to automatically apply a specific font color based on the value of a number.

First, though, you must decide what values you want to highlight. In the example, values that are greater than 49,500 are shown in white on a black background. To create this formatting, follow these steps:

1. **In the Highlighting Expert dialog box, click the down arrow to the right of the Value Is field to open the pull-down menu.**

2. **Select the type of condition you want.**

   Several conditional statements are available, as shown in Figure 3-16. Select the Greater Than condition. A sample of the condition appears at the left of the dialog box.

   To specify a number, you can open the drop-down list just below the Value Is field to see the numbers from the field in ascending order. Or you can enter the number you want directly in the box. A sample appears in a list on the left side of the dialog box.

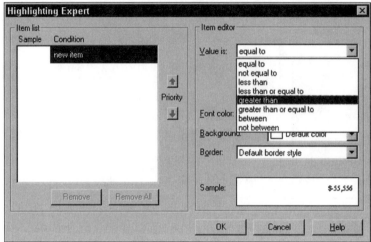

**3. Select the number you want from the list or type the number you want in the field.**

In this example, I type **49500** in the field, as shown in Figure 3-17.

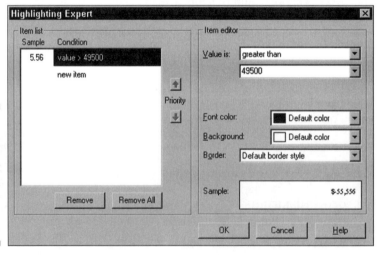

4. **In the Font Color drop-down list, select the color you want for numbers greater than 49500.**

   I select White.

5. **Select the background color in the Background drop-down list.**

   This time I select Black.

   A sample of the formatting you select appears so that you can adjust the settings before you apply them.

6. **Click OK.**

   Figure 3-18 displays the results.

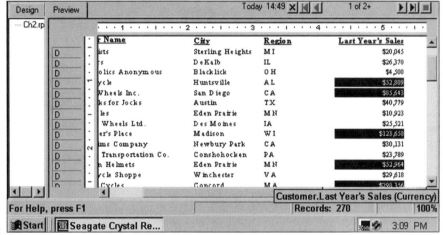

**Figure 3-18:**
A report with text color and border applied, based on the value of the number.

To add more sophistication to the report, you can add a second condition that highlights values that fall below a certain amount. By following the preceding steps, select the condition Less Than or Equal To and type the number **12000**. Figure 3-19 shows the dialog box with both conditions ready to apply. Click OK to apply the conditions and to highlight numbers that meet these conditions. Figure 3-20 shows the report with both ranges of numbers highlighted in their own unique way.

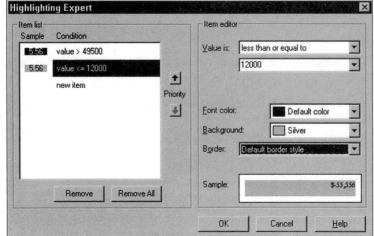

**Figure 3-19:**
A second
condition
added in the
Highlighting
Expert
dialog box.

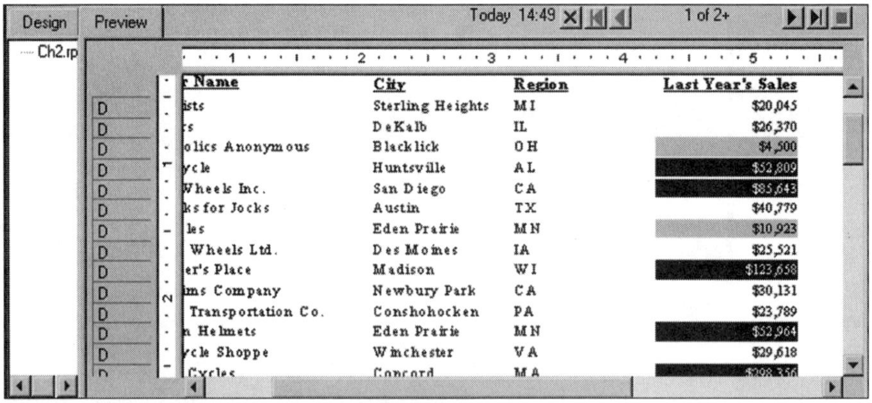

**Figure 3-20:**
A report
with two
conditions
highlighting
affected
numbers in
the records.

# *Moving from Page to Page in a Report*

Frequently, your reports run longer than a single printed page. However,
when you create your reports, you can view only one page at a time. So you
need to know how to move from the current page to a previous or following
page, which is quite easy. At the top-right corner of the Preview tab is a series
of three boxes, followed by numbers, and then three more boxes (refer
to Figure 3-20). These buttons are commonly referred to as *VCR buttons*
(because to some extent they imitate the buttons on your VCR) but their real
name is Page Control Buttons. (By the way, my VCR clock shows the correct
time. Look for my next book, *VCR Clocks For Dummies*.)

Table 3-1 explains how these Page Control buttons work.

| Table 3-1 | Page Control Buttons in the Preview Tab |
|-----------|------------------------------------------|
| *Button* | *Function* |
| Close Preview | Closes the Preview tab, which you may want to do if your system resources (computer memory) are running low and Crystal Reports starts to slow down. |
| First Page | Displays the first page of the report. |
| Previous Page | Displays the page preceding the current page. |
| Next Page | Displays the page following the current page. |
| Last Page | Displays the final page in the report. |
| Stop Transfer | Operates only when getting or refreshing database records. If you open the Preview tab and find that the report is taking a long time to appear, click this button to stop any records from transferring to the report. |

# Magnifying the Page

As you add more and more objects to a page, the clutter can overwhelm even the sharpest eye. Sometimes, you may add a combination of objects that you need to see close up before you print your report. For just such situations, you can *zoom* in or out on an area of your report for a better look.

To zoom in or out on your report, follow these steps:

1. **Choose View⇨Zoom from the menu bar or click the arrow in the Zoom Control drop-down list box on the right side of the Standard toolbar.**

   From the drop-down list, you can select a percentage that zooms in on the report (if greater than 100 percent) or zooms out (if less than 100 percent).

   The Magnification Factor dialog box appears, as shown in Figure 3-21.

**Figure 3-21:**
The
Magnification
Factor dialog
box for
zooooooming.

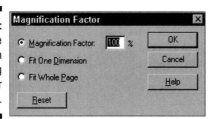

**2. Set the Magnification Factor to enlarge or shrink:**

- To enlarge, type a larger value in the field provided.

   The default value is 100 percent. If you increase the value, you zoom in on the report. You can enter a number as large as 400. When you do, the report looks like the one in Figure 3-22, which gives you an idea of the ease with which you can see detail by using this method.

- To shrink, decrease the number in the field provided.

   You may want to do so to see the entire page at one time. Figure 3-23 shows a 40-percent magnification factor.

The reasons for viewing the entire page are more apparent after you add headers and footers and summary data, which I cover in Chapter 9. Looking at the entire page may save you the chore of printing the report to check the formatting.

If you want, save this newly formatted report under a new name, such as Ch3. Although I do refer to Ch3 in Chapter 4, you don't need this particular report to follow the example.

To save your report under a new name, simply choose File⊅Save As from the menu bar, type **Ch3** as the new filename, and then click OK.

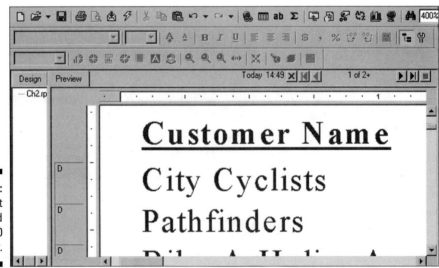

**Figure 3-22:**
A report
zooooomed
to 400
percent.

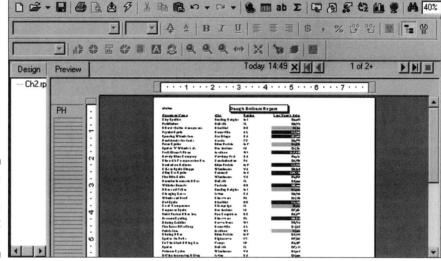

**Figure 3-23:**
Page
magnification
set at
40 percent.

# Undoing or redoing a format change

If you make a mistake applying a format by using the Highlighting Expert, you can click the Undo button to remove the last formatting change. The Undo button looks like a curved arrow, pointing left. If you click the button immediately after applying the new format, the original format returns. After you click the Undo button, the Redo button (with a curved arrow pointing right) becomes active, allowing you to reapply the undone format. These two buttons give you an opportunity to toggle between formats to decide which one you want to keep.

In addition, you can always right-click the field and select the Highlighting Expert to remove any conditional formatting you have applied.

# Part II
# Manipulating Records

The 5th Wave                    By Rich Tennant

"GENTLEMEN, I SAY RATHER THAN FIX THE 'BUGS', WE CHANGE THE
DOCUMENTATION AND CALL THEM 'FEATURES'."

## In this part . . .

Stage two, and the whole department is on pins and needles wondering whether your next report is going to show that the entire West Coast sales division is a bunch of slackers who talk a good game but don't sell anything. Everyone knows, of course, that everything loose rolls west, but who would have thought all those salaries were going to pay for hot tubs and Moet & Chandon! Outrageous! Well, this part of the book gives you the power to ferret out the wheat from the chaff, the men from the boys, and the quick from the, er, not so quick.

# Chapter 4

# Selecting Records

• • • • • • • • • • • • • • • • • • • • • • • • • • • • • • • • • • • • • • • •

## In This Chapter

▶ Understanding records selection

▶ Using Select Expert

▶ Handling data requests

▶ Working with saved or refreshed data

▶ Using Parameter fields

• • • • • • • • • • • • • • • • • • • • • • • • • • • • • • • • • • • • • • • •

*W*hen you create a report, you may or may not want to include in it every record in the database. You can limit the number of records and specify which records to include. This chapter gives you the lowdown on selecting records.

## What Is Selecting Records?

When you generate a report, you have to access an existing table to create the report. A problem arises when the table consists of thousands of records. You may want a report that consists of records from a specific geographic area, a certain sales division, or of only products that interest you — such situations are the primary reason to use record selection. The folks at Seagate Software anticipated your needs and built in a way for you to select only the records that fit the report criteria or only a few records to design the report.

## Using Select Expert

Select Expert is a tool that walks you through the process of selecting the records you want to include in the report. Think of the process as filtering the data in the field. If the data is a certain size, it passes through the filter and is included in the report; otherwise, it isn't included.

Open Select Expert by clicking the Select Expert button on the Standard tool-bar. You can also open Select Expert by choosing <u>R</u>eport⇨<u>S</u>elect Expert. The Choose Field dialog box appears, as shown in Figure 4-1.

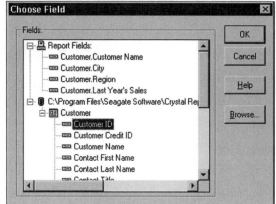

**Figure 4-1:**
The Choose
Field dialog
box awaits
your wise
choice.

*Note:* If you select a database field prior to clicking Select Expert, you bypass the Choose Field database and go directly to Select Expert.

Notice two things in the Choose Field dialog box. First, if you have a report open on the screen, the fields that are part of the report are listed as possible candidates for record selection. Second, field names from the source data-base table are displayed, with good reason. The record selection process isn't restricted to the fields in the report. You can use *any* field from the table as the filter. So even though your report may include the fields you want, you can use an entirely different field to restrict the records that are included.

To understand how this process works, use the Ch3 sample report. (Keep in mind that you can use any previously created report and modify the steps to pertain to that report.) Just follow these steps:

1. **Open the report.**

   For this example, use the report named Ch3 and view the report in the Preview tab.

2. **Click the Select Expert button on the Standard toolbar.**

   The Choose Field dialog box appears.

3. **Click the Last Year's Sales field and then click OK.**

   The Select Expert dialog box opens, as shown in Figure 4-2.

4. **(Optional) To make sure that the field includes the data you want to filter, click Browse (see Figure 4-3), and then click Done.**

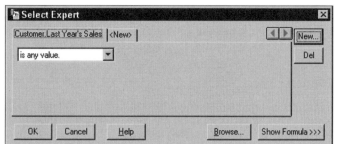

**Figure 4-2:**
The Select
Expert
dialog box.

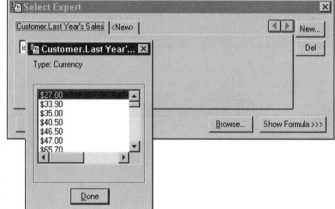

**Figure 4-3:**
Browsing
Last Year's
Sales data.

Browsing the data lets you double-check that this is the field on which you want to base your record selection; clicking Done returns you to the Select Expert dialog box.

5. **Click the drop-down arrow to open the Operator list, as shown in Figure 4-4.**

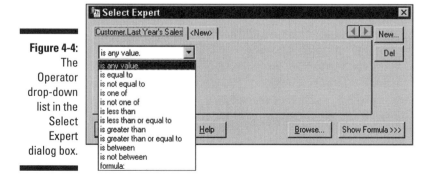

**Figure 4-4:**
The
Operator
drop-down
list in the
Select
Expert
dialog box.

6. **Select the operator you want.**

   For this example, you want the records with sales greater than $50,000, so you select the Is Greater Than operator, which is then inserted into the field.

   The criteria reads LAST YEAR'S SALES IS GREATER THAN.

   So far so good. When you enter the Is Greater Than operator, another box opens to the right. This box is for entering a number that completes the criteria. Again take a look at the data, as shown in Figure 4-5, by clicking the down arrow on the right side of the edit box.

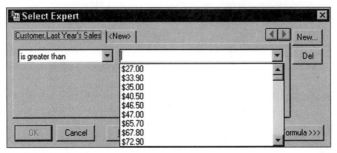

**Figure 4-5:** The Field data revealed so you can select your criteria.

7. **Type the number you want in the text box or select a number in the drop-down list.**

   In this example, type **50000** in the text box, as shown in Figure 4-6. *Note:* You do *not* include a comma as a separator, because the comma is not interpreted as part of a number.

   The criteria reads LAST YEAR'S SALES IS GREATER THAN 50000. Although the subject-verb agreement may be suspect, the criteria syntax is correct.

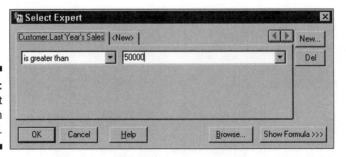

**Figure 4-6:** A value that you type in the text box.

8. **Click OK.**

   The Change In Record Selection Formula Detected dialog box (shown in Figure 4-7) appears, asking you an important question — should the report use the current set of saved records or refresh the data. (For more information, see "Using saved or refreshed data" later in this chapter.)

Change In Record Selection Formula Detect...
Use saved data from: Today 14:49 ?
Use Saved Data
Refresh Data

**Figure 4-7:** The dialog box for choosing saved or refreshed data.

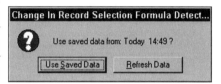

9. **Click Refresh Data.**

   If you're in the Preview tab, you can simply click Refresh. If you're in the Design tab, however, Crystal Reports doesn't ask you whether you want to save or refresh data until you decide to move to the Preview tab. Data is shown only in Preview, so you must be in Preview to see the change.

   Figure 4-8 shows the new, highly filtered report.

Design
Preview
Today 15:30
1 of 1
Ch3.rp
Doug's Brilliant Report
Customer Name
City
Region
Last Ye
Psycho-Cycle Huntsville AL
Sporting Wheels Inc. San Diego CA
Trail Blazer's Place Madison WI
Hooked on Helmets Eden Prairie MN
Alley Cat Cycles Concord MA
Whistler Rentals Tualatin OR
Uni-Cycle Blacklick OH
Extreme Cycling Clearwater FL
Tek Bikes Philadelphia PA
SAB Mountain Bern Cantons
Platou Sport Stavanger Rogaland
Piccolo Salzburg Salzkammergut

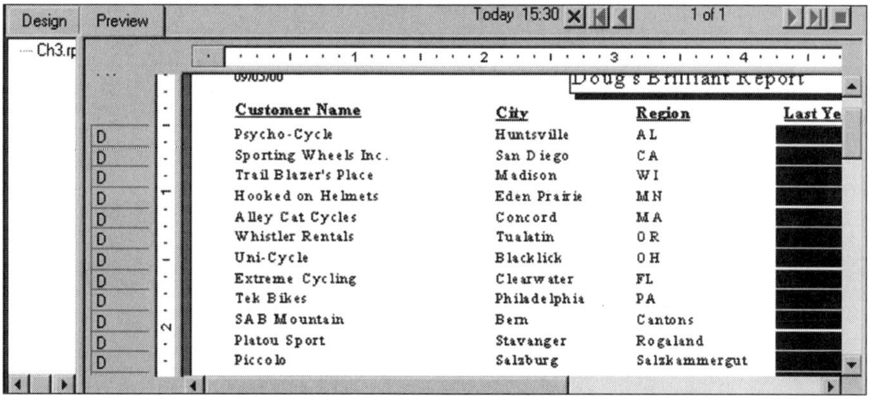

**Figure 4-8:** A report with filtered records in the Preview tab.

## Using saved or refreshed data

Crystal Reports reads the data from the tables you include in your report only when necessary, so that your computer system isn't burdened and the creation of your report is speeded up. On your home computer, you may not think this feature is a big deal, and it probably isn't. However, in a setting in which you're creating reports from a shared database, such as a network with SQL servers, having Crystal Reports read the shared database at every turn can really slow down your report-building process.

So why are you sometimes asked the immortal question: Use saved data? Crystal Reports has some built-in smarts and won't bug you for an answer to this question when it knows that it's necessary to get more data for the report by going back to the database. Crystal Reports only asks you to decide when it isn't sure whether rereading the database is necessary. So how do you determine the answer to the question?

If you're narrowing your record selection, click Use Saved Data. For example, perhaps when you first build your record selection, you include all records with sales greater than 0. If you change the record selection to sales greater than 50,000, you then select Use Saved Data because you're narrowing the record selection.

If you're not positive whether you're narrowing your record selection, click Refresh Data just to be safe.

## Refreshing the report on demand

Because Crystal Reports saves the records with the report, and because time may pass between when you create the report and when you plan to use it again, Crystal Reports gives you several options for asking it to reread the report's records. To refresh report data, do one of the following:

- ✔ Click the Refresh button on the Standard toolbar.
- ✔ Choose Report⇨Refresh Report Data.
- ✔ Press F5.

Crystal Reports displays an indicator, as shown in Figure 4-9, that lets you know exactly when you last refreshed your report data. If the report was refreshed several weeks ago, for example, the exact date and time of the last refresh are displayed.

Record selection can be *case sensitive,* depending on the database in which the records are stored. This means that if the abbreviation for California is entered as CA, ca, or Ca in your database, the report will only include those records where the Region is exactly CA and not ca, Ca, or cA — which is one reason to use the Browse Field Data button in Select Expert to find out how the data is stored.

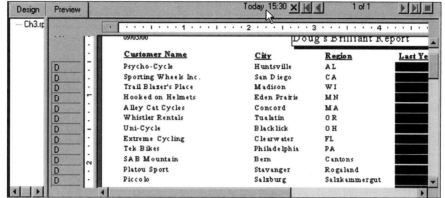

**Figure 4-9:**
The pointer
shows you
the report
date/time
indicator.

When working with SQL/ODBC data, you have the ability to select whether you want record selection to be case sensitive or insensitive. By default, the option is not selected and your SQL/ODBC record selection will be case sensitive. The Case-Insensitive SQL Data option (available under File⇨Options⇨Database or from File⇨Report Options) is where you set whether you want a case-sensitive or case-*in*sensitive record selection. This option is only available if your database server supports case insensitivity.

## *Specifying Select Expert options*

After you understand how the filtering process works, take a look at Table 4-1 for other ways in which you can filter records (using the preceding CA example) by using the drop-down list in the Select Expert dialog box. Remember, you don't have to use a field that's in the current report; any field in the database table works. Also, all the filtering options aren't available for every field. For example, if you're filtering on a text field, the date options aren't available.

| Table 4-1 | Filtering Options |
|---|---|
| *Operator* | *What It Does* |
| Is Any Value | Means you have no record selection for the field. This option is the same as saying, "Give me all the records on the report; I don't care about the sales amount." |
| Is Equal To | Filters records so that only an exact match passes through. For example, if you want to see only records from California, the field data is equal to CA (assuming the name for California is entered as an abbreviation). Figure 4-10 shows this operator in use. |

*(continued)*

### Table 4-1 *(continued)*

| Operator | What It Does |
|---|---|
| Is Not Equal To | Gives you every record that does NOT match with the value you enter. Use this option when you want to include all records except those where the region is CA. |
| Is One Of/Is Not One Of | Allows you to specify records that match or do not match values from a series so you can enter one of CA, MN, or BC. This filter only allows records that are from CA, MN, or BC to pass through to the report. |
| Is Less Than Or Equal To or Greater Than Or Equal To | Cuts off records at the specified value. |
| Is Between/Is Not Between | Selects those records that do or do not fall into the range you want. For example, enter between 20,000 and 75,000 to get only those records. |
| Starts With/ Does Not Start With | Selects records by using a text field. If you want all records with a field entry beginning with the letter S, use this filter. If you want to find records beginning with SON, enter these three characters. If you want to find records that do not start with a certain value or values, use the Does Not Start With option and enter the offending characters. |
| Is Like/Is Not Like | Although the world now sees computers through Windows, tricks from the DOS era still linger in the background. For example, the entry D*G (an asterisk) filters records with any entries in the field beginning with D and ending with G. So the words DOG, DOUG, DARING, and DECIDING all pass (or don't pass) through this filter. The asterisk, called a *wildcard* character because it matches any character(s), works with text data only. The question mark (?), also a wildcard, matches any character, but only one at a time. So the D?G filter retrieves/excludes records such as DOG and DIG but not DOING, because more than one letter appears between the D and G. |
| Formula | Creates complex filters or filters that don't fit the format of the other filter tools. Chapter 7 is devoted to formula language and the concepts of using formulas. You can use the information there to select records here. You open the Formula Editor portion of the dialog box by clicking Show Formula (which then changes to Hide Formula). To access Formula Editor, click the button. Even if you haven't specified a formula, Crystal Reports creates a formula for every type of record selection that you create. |

| Operator | What It Does |
|---|---|
| Is In The Period/<br>Is Not In The Period | Conducts date-range searches. Suppose you're trying to create a report for a recurring date range. This selects records in which the value in the date field falls within the date range specified. When you select this condition, the dialog box displays a scroll list of all Crystal Reports date ranges. Select the range you want from the list and include all records in which the date falls within the calendar first quarter of the year. Crystal Reports includes only dates from January 1 to April 30, inclusive — no other dates. *Note:* The Is In The Period option always evaluates the record selection relative to your computer's current date. For example, the LastFullMonth option gives you the preceding calendar month. If you preview your report on April 1, 2000, you see all data for March 2000. |

**Figure 4-10:** Is Equal To — a filter for CA data, displayed in the Select Expert dialog box.

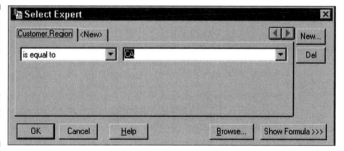

# *Selecting records on more than one field*

After working with the record-selection process on a single field, you need to know how to create a compound-record selection by using two or more fields. An example of a compound-record selection is a report that includes only records from a certain region with sales over a certain amount. You can approach this type of selection in two ways. You can create the first filter, execute it, reopen Select Record Expert, and then add the second filter. Or you can create both filters in one step. The advantage of the two-step process is that you can check your work step-by-step, previewing the records at each step to make certain they're what you want.

*Note:* This is a different way of getting to the Select Expert with the field you want to work with. If a database field is selected on your report when you go to Select Expert, Crystal Reports assumes that's the field you want to work with.

If you add a record selection as described in the first section of this chapter, remove the selection by following the steps in the "Removing Record Selection" section later in this chapter and remove all the tabs in the Select Expert dialog box.

Using the example report, filter the records so that the report includes only CA (California) with sales from last year that are greater than 10,000. Just follow these steps:

1. **In the Design tab, click the Region field.**

2. **Click the Select Expert button on the Standard toolbar.**

   The Select Expert dialog box appears.

3. **Select the Is Equal To operator in the first drop-down list box and CA in the second drop-down list box.**

4. **Click New (either the button or the tab).**

   The Choose Field dialog box appears, from which you can select a field that's already in the report or any field from the table.

5. **Select Last Year's Sales, select the Is Greater Than operator, and type** 10000 **as a value.**

   Two tabs exist now in the Select Expert dialog box, as shown in Figure 4-11. Each tab has the filter criteria for one field. The filter criteria for the report is the union of them all; the filter criteria in each tab is joined to the others with the word "AND".

   In the Select Expert dialog box, click the Show Formula button to see the entire record selection formula. Crystal Reports does most of the work. I simply clicked a few buttons, and Crystal Reports created this formula that your database can understand.

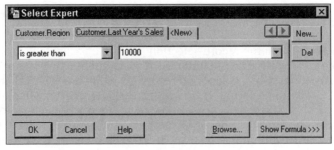

**Figure 4-11:**
Two filters
set and
ready to go.

6. **Click OK.**

   Crystal Reports filters the records and, in the Preview tab, displays those records that meet the criteria, as shown in Figure 4-12.

This tool is powerful and can be used in many ways to fine-tune the reports you create, so that only the records you want are included. Adding a third or fourth filter follows the same procedure as adding a second.

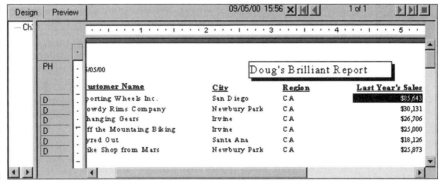

**Figure 4-12:**
Filtering
produces a
report that
displays
California
records'
land sales
greater than
$10,000.

# Removing Record Selection

After selecting records for a specific report, you can save the report and then print it. If you want to use the same table to create a different report but need to access all the records, you can remove the filter. To remove a Select Expert filter, follow these steps:

1. **Click the Select Expert button on the Standard toolbar.**

    The Select Expert dialog box appears.

2. **Select the tab that has the filter for the field you want to remove.**

3. **Click the Del (delete) button.**

4. **Continue deleting filter tabs until the records you want can be part of the report.**

5. **Click OK.**

    If you're in the Preview tab, Crystal Reports prompts you with a dialog box asking whether you want to use saved data or refresh the data.

6. **Click Refresh Data.**

    Crystal Reports executes the query to the database with the new filter in place.

Select Expert is meant to make your life simpler. Just point and click to create your record selection. Although doing this is probably sufficient for most reports, you can get more sophisticated if you need to. See Chapter 7 for more info.

# Using a Parameter Field

A Crystal Reports feature that ties in to the Select Expert is the capability to ask the report user a question every time a report is refreshed. *Parameter fields* automate the process of selecting which records you want to include in a report. In the example about using Select Expert earlier in this chapter, you discover how to manually add record-selection criteria. When adding a parameter field, the person running the report is prompted for the selection criteria. In other words, when you refresh data, a dialog box appears and asks which records you want to include or exclude — so that you (or someone else) doesn't have to use Select Expert to enter a set of record-selection criteria. This tool is terrific for helping an inexperienced user correctly run reports.

Imagine that you run the same report, which includes records for a specific region, several times a day. Rather than using the Select Expert to change what region you want, you can add a parameter that asks for the region every time you run the report.

## Parameter field details

By adding a parameter field to a report, you get an added benefit. If you have coworkers who also need to run the report, you don't have to teach them anything about the Select Expert or about changing the record-selection criteria. Imagine all the free time you'll have because they're not phoning you to say "I forget how to get the New York customers on this report!"

This section takes a detailed look at adding a parameter field to show you how easy it is to do so. Use the report that includes the Customer Name, City, and Last Year's Sales fields from the Xtreme database.

1. **Open the report.**

   For this example, use the report named Ch3 and view the report in the Preview tab.

2. **Click the Insert Fields button on the Standard toolbar to open the Field Explorer dialog box.**

3. **Select Parameter Fields.**

4. **Click the New button on the toolbar in the Field Explorer dialog box.**

   The Create Parameter Field dialog box appears, as shown in Figure 4-13, offering the following options:

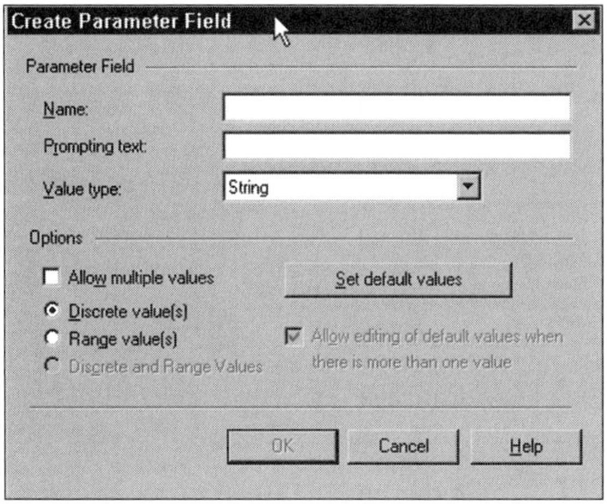

**Figure 4-13:**
The Create
Parameter
Field dialog
box.

- **Name:** (This one's easy.) Type a name for the parameter field. For the example, use Region as a reminder that the region is what the selection is based on.

- **Prompting Text:** This text contains the question you want to ask the report user. It appears in the Parameter dialog box when the report is refreshed. For the example, the text reads `Select the region you want included in the report`.

- **Value Type:** Crystal Reports needs to know what kind of data will be used in this parameter. To use this parameter in a record selection, the data must be the same type as the field data in the database you're using as your filter. The standard data types are, for example, String, Number, Date, and DateTime. The program also helps to make the entry of value as foolproof as possible by forcing you to enter a date, text, or whatever you specify in a designated format. The online Help explains each option in detail.

- **Allow Multiple Values:** This option lets the report creator enter multiple values as selection criteria. For example, if Region is the field, more than one region's records can be part of the report.

- **Discrete Value(s)/Range Value(s):** A discrete value setting means that each entry in the Value field is considered individually. If you want a range, such as a pair of dates or numbers from 1 to 50 or letters from T to W, select Range Value(s). You cannot choose Discrete and Range Values unless you also select Allow Multiple Values. (But that's getting way too advanced for what you want to do here.)

- **Allow Editing of Default Values When There Is More Than One Value:** This option is grayed out unless you click the Set default values and actually build a default value list (see Step 5). The check box is selected by default. When checked, this option enables you to either choose from the list you create or enter your own value.

5. **Set the defaults for the parameter by clicking the Set Default Values button.**

   This step is optional but REALLY useful if you want to avoid more phone calls from coworkers. The Set Default Values dialog box (shown in Figure 4-14) appears with the following options:

- **Browse Table:** Select the table used for developing the report. If the report draws information from several tables, you can select the table that has the field you need to create record selection.

- **Browse Field:** After selecting the table to browse, select the field you want to include from that table.

- **Select or Enter Value to Add:** After you select the table and the field, a list of values from that field is generated. You can then select all or some of the values as defaults. Click the value(s) you want and then click the > button to add them to the list.

- **Length Limit:** If you enter your own values, you can check this box to specify a minimum and a maximum number of characters. For example, if you set the maximum limit to 2, the word CAT is not allowed.

- **Edit Mask:** An edit mask is a way to force the value being entered to conform to a certain style, such as XXX-XXX-XXXX. With this mask, only a value such as 555-555-1212 is accepted as a valid entry. You can create general or very specific masks by mixing numbers and letters.

- **Import/Export Pick List:** If you create a list in another report, you can export the list from that report and then import it into the current report, relieving you of the burden of recreating it.

- **Define Description:** You may add a description for each value, which may help if the values from the database are a code, such as CA for California.

- **Display:** If you add descriptions to your Default value list, you have the option of displaying the value and the description, or just the description.

- **Order:** Select a manner of sorting the Default values. This option does not affect the report, only the default displays.

- **Order Based On:** If you select a sort order, the defaults can be sorted by the values themselves or by their description.

6. **Select Customer in the Browse Table box and then select Region in the Browse Field box.**

7. **Click the > button to add all the values from the database to the Default Values list.**

8. **Click OK to close the Set Default Values dialog box.**

9. **Leave the Allow Multiple Values option unchecked and select Discrete Value(s) in the Edit Parameter Field dialog box.**

10. **Click OK and then click Close to close the Field Explorer dialog box.**

## Adding a parameter field to a report

After you complete the parameter field, the next step is to add it to the example report. To do so, follow these steps:

1. **Click the Select Expert button on the Standard toolbar.**

    If you've been following along for a while, the report you're using may already have a record selection. In that case, remove any filters you may have (see "Removing Record Selection" earlier in this chapter) and click the New button or the New tab.

    The Choose Field dialog box appears.

2. **Select the field that matches the one you used to create the parameter field.**

    In this example, Region.

3. **Click OK.**

    The Select Expert dialog box appears, as shown in Figure 4-15. You want the records on the report to be equal to the parameter chosen by the report user (you or that coworker down the hall).

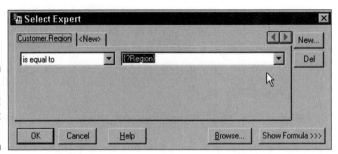

**Figure 4-15:**
The Select
Expert
dialog box.

4. **Open the drop-down list and select the Is Equal To operator.**

5. **Open the drop-down list that now appears to the right and select the Parameter Fields entry.**

   For this example, select the {?Region} entry. All the parameters you created that match the field data type used in the filter appear at the top of this list.

6. **Click OK.**

   Because you're in the Preview tab for this example, the Crystal Reports's intruder alarm goes off, and you see the Change In Record Selection Formula Detected dialog box.

7. **Click Refresh Data.**

To see the parameter field in action, follow these steps:

1. **Click the Refresh button on the Standard toolbar.**

   The Refresh Report Data dialog box appears, as shown in Figure 4-16.

2. **Select the Prompt for New Parameter Values option and click OK.**

   The Enter Parameter Values dialog box appears, as shown in Figure 4-17.

   The pull-down list in the middle gives you the default values list from which you can choose the Region you want to filter the records for the report.

**Figure 4-16:**
The Refresh
Report Data
dialog box.

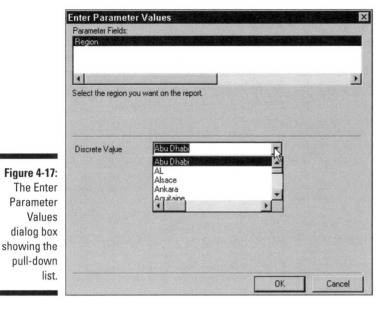

**Figure 4-17:**
The Enter
Parameter
Values
dialog box
showing the
pull-down
list.

In this example, select the second suggested value, AL.

**3. Click the Add button and then click OK.**

The report appears, as shown in Figure 4-18.

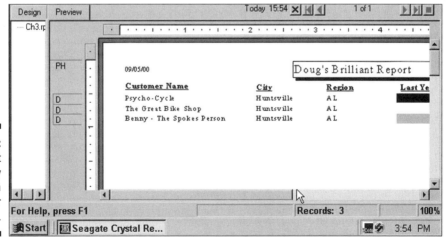

**Figure 4-18:**
A report
created by
using a
parameter
field.

This feature is powerful for making it easier for you and your coworkers to run reports. In this example, I use a single parameter field. However, you can create several more parameter fields. By having a tool that asks report users questions every time a report is refreshed, you can build in a user-specified restriction that filters the records to be included in a report. Then you can design a report and hand it off to less-experienced users, confident that they can easily get the correct records for the report they need.

# Chapter 5

# Sorting and Grouping Records

. . . . . . . . . . . . . . . . . . . . . . . . . . . . . . . . . . . . . . . . . . . . . .

## In This Chapter

▶ Sorting records

▶ Inserting groups

▶ Working with summaries or subtotals

▶ Inserting a grand total

▶ Modifying a group

▶ Doing a Top N Sort

. . . . . . . . . . . . . . . . . . . . . . . . . . . . . . . . . . . . . . . . . . . . . .

*W*ith an existing report, you may want to sort the records by one or several fields, such as by state or by salesperson. Or you may want to group the records. Suppose you're creating a sales report and want to group the records by sales region. Within that region, you also want to sort by the amount of sales and to calculate subtotals for each region. In this chapter, you discover the steps to sort and group.

## Sorting versus Grouping

When you sort records in a report, you are restricted to alphabetical or numerical conditions. That means the report records can be sorted, for example, in ascending order by state. Grouping, however, is more powerful because it can arrange records to create summaries that sorting cannot. Read on to see how this feature works.

If you've been following along and in Chapter 4 added a Record Selection Formula to the Chapter 3 report, you must now delete it to make all records available. To delete an existing Record Selection Formula, follow these steps:

1. **Open the Chapter 4 report and click the Select Expert button on the Standard toolbar.**

2. **In the Select Expert dialog box that appears, click any tabs that display and then click the Delete (Del) button.**

3. **Click OK.**

   The Change In Record Selection Detected dialog box appears.

4. **Click Refresh Data.**

5. **Save the report as Ch5.**

The process of sorting and grouping is best accomplished in the Preview tab, as shown in Figure 5-1. If you don't have a Preview tab, you haven't read the database yet. To get a Preview tab, click the Print Preview button or the Refresh button on the Standard toolbar, or press F5.

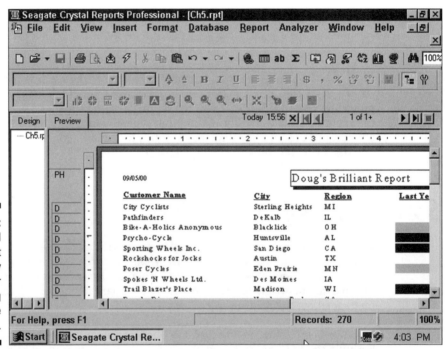

**Figure 5-1:**
A typical report without any sorting or grouping in the Preview tab.

# *Sorting Records*

With any set of records, you may want to add a sort order. In any report, the steps to change the sort order are as follows:

1. **With the Ch5 report open, choose <u>R</u>eport⇨Sort <u>R</u>ecords (or click the Sort Order button on the Standard toolbar).**

   The Record Sort Order dialog box appears, as shown in Figure 5-2.

   A list of the fields that can be used to perform a sort appears in the Report Fields box on the left. Your report may have more or fewer fields available for sorting.

**Figure 5-2:**
The Record
Sort Order
dialog box.

2. **Select a field to use for the sort and then click Add.**

   The field name appears in the Sort Fields box on the right.

   For this example, select the Customer.City field.

3. **In the Sort Direction box, click the Ascending or Descending radio button to select it.**

4. **Click OK.**

Only the fields on the report are available to sort in the Record Sort Order dialog box.

The number of sorts you can perform is limited only by the number of fields and the sense it makes to do so. If you sort too much, you become, well, out of sorts.

If you perform a sort but then want to return to the previous sort order, click the Undo button on the toolbar — right after performing the sort.

# Breaking Ties

If several records have identical values in your sorted field, you can add a second sort field to break the tie. For instance, if a set of records is sorted primarily by the City field, the possibility exists that several records are from the same city. In the sample report, Ch5, several records have Blacklick listed as their city. So adding a second sort, such as Last Year's Sales in ascending order, shows the records sorted first by the name of the city and then by the sales volume.

To add a second sort value to the Ch5 report, follow these steps:

1. **Choose Report⇨Sort Records from the menu bar (or click the Sort Order button on the Standard toolbar).**

   The Record Sort Order dialog box appears.

2. **Select the field name you want as the second sort value, click Add, and then select Ascending or Descending as the sort order.**

   In the example, click the Last Year's Sales field and Ascending.

3. **Click OK.**

   The records are sorted at two levels, as shown in Figure 5-3. The Blacklick records are sorted from the smallest sales amount to the largest.

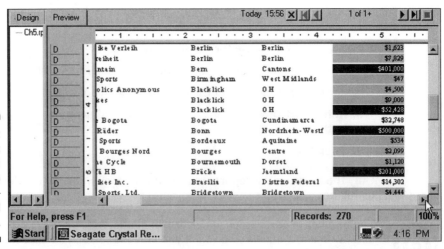

**Figure 5-3:**
Records sorted on two levels — city and sales.

# Inserting Groups

Grouping the records on a report is the same as sorting the records, but it gives you the power to do more in each group. Say, for example, you have a box of business cards that you want to put into a card file. Sorting puts the cards in order by name, and grouping arranges them according to the state they're from. By grouping the cards, you can count the number of cards from each state and calculate the sales for each state. In fact, you can do a myriad of things with each state, including the order in which you want the states to be filed. That's the power of grouping in Crystal Reports.

If you change your mind after creating (inserting) a group, you can easily delete it (covered later in this chapter). If you decide to use another grouping method, you can easily change the group and replace it with another.

To insert a group into any report, follow these steps:

1. **Choose Insert⇨Group from the menu bar.**

   The Insert Group dialog box appears, as shown in Figure 5-4.

2. **In the first drop-down list box, select the field by which you want the records grouped.**

   In this example, group the records "by" Region.

3. **In the second drop-down list box, select the order (ascending or descending) that you want the groups to appear on the report.**

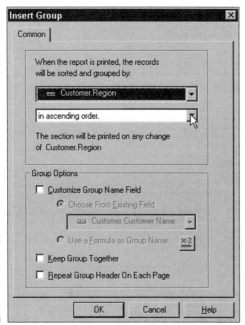

**Figure 5-4:**
The Insert Group dialog box.

Crystal Reports offers you several Group Options (two of them deal with how the groups print on paper), which are

- ✓ **Customize Group Name Field:** After you create a group, the name of the group that displays or prints is based on the name of the field that's used to create the group. By selecting this option, you can create a customized group name from an existing database field. For example, although your report is grouped on Customer ID, you may want to display the Customer Name.

- ✓ **Choose From Existing Field:** Select a field that's in the report as the name of the group from the pull-down list.

- ✓ **Use a Formula as Group Name:** Select this option to create a customized group name by using a formula. Click the formula button, X+2, to open the Group Name Formula Editor. See Chapter 7 for more information on formula creation.

- ✓ **Keep Group Together:** Keeps grouped records contiguous on the same printed page. Crystal Reports calculates whether the next group can fit on what remains of the current page and, if not, begins printing the group on the page following. Selecting this option (by inserting an X in the box) turns on this feature. This could use up a lot of paper, though.

- ✓ **Repeat Group Header On Each Page:** If the group of records is longer than a single printed page, you can print the Group Header at the top of each new page by turning on this option. This sure helps when each group carries on for several pages. The name of the group is always right there on the top of each page so that you know what group you're looking at.

The best way to use these options is by clicking OK to see the results of the grouping. If the records cover more than one page, decide how to best divide the groups.

If you're not happy with the results of a grouping and decide to remove the group for whatever reason, you cannot undo your action. You must recreate the group. But at least Crystal Reports warns you!

## Setting a Group Name

When you insert a group into a report, Crystal Reports puts the group name into a space called the Group Header, which comes before each group of records. A specific setting that is turned on by default when you install Crystal Reports determines whether this name should be inserted automatically.

To check the Group Name setting or change any of the default report options, follow these steps:

1. **Choose File⇨Options from the menu bar.**

   The Options dialog box appears, as shown in Figure 5-5. This dialog box offers a plethora of choices, but the one you're interested in is Insert Group Name with Group in the Field Options area of the Layout tab.

2. **If it isn't already check marked, click the Insert Group Name with Group box to select it.**

3. **Click OK.**

   Whenever you insert a group, the group name appears in the space between the groups.

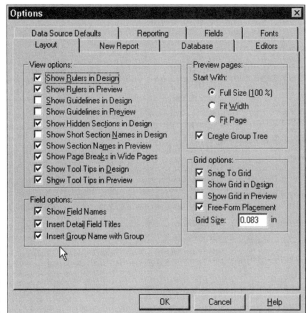

**Figure 5-5:**
The Options
dialog box.

Here's another example of how grouping is more powerful than sorting. You can use the Customer Country field as the grouping field despite the fact that it is not on the report. (Remember that the field has to be on the report to use it in the Sort Order.)

To add a group by using a field that's not on the report, follow these steps:

1. **Choose Insert⇨Group from the menu bar.**

   The Insert Group dialog box appears.

2. **Click the down arrow in the top box to open a list of fields in the tables. Scroll down the list to see first the fields already on the report**

**and then the fields in all the tables that you've selected for this report. Select from this list the field by which you want to group your records.**

For the example, select the Customer Country field.

3. **Select the sort order from the drop-down list in the second box.**

For this example, select In Descending Order, as shown in Figure 5-6.

4. **Click OK.**

Figure 5-7 shows the result. As you can see, the grouping effect is to arrange the records by country. So for this example the first group has Zimbabwe as its header followed by Wales, Vietnam, and so on.

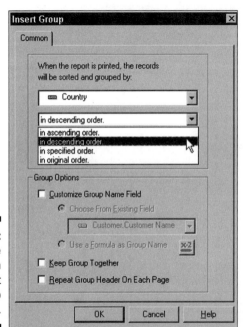

**Figure 5-6:**
Select the sort order in the Insert Group dialog box.

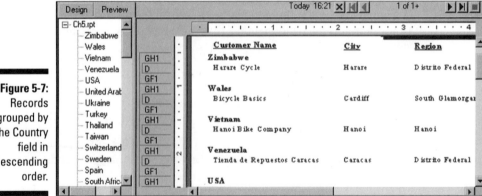

**Figure 5-7:**
Records grouped by the Country field in descending order.

# Using Group Tree Options

On the far left side of the Preview tab, you see the list of groups that have been created. This list is called the Group Tree, and it makes moving to the group that's associated with the records easy. For example, to see the detail records that are associated with a particular Country, you simply click the group name, and the Preview window shows the page that contains those records.

In addition, the Group Tree can be used to create a Drill-Down Preview window. A *drill down* is a subset of the report's detail records and has its own tab at the top of the Preview window. Click a group name in the Group Tree and then right-click to open the shortcut menu. The Hide and Drill Down choices appear. Click Drill Down, and the report preview includes a tab with the group name; only the records associated with this group are displayed. You may drill down as many groups as you want. When you print the report, only the main report in Preview prints. To print a drill down, you must click the Drill Down tab and then click the Printer icon.

The other option that's available in Group Tree — the Hide option — closes the Group Tree. To get the Hide option, right-click Group Tree. You may want to do this if you need more space in the Preview window to see your report columns. To restore a closed Group Tree, choose <u>V</u>iew⇨<u>G</u>roup Tree on the menu bar or click the Group Tree button on the Formatting toolbar.

# Viewing Groups on the Design Tab

If you add a group to the report, switch to the Design tab and take a look at the way adding a group changes the underlying report structure.

Note that on the Design tab, the Group section surrounds the Details section of the report. This arrangement makes sense because the groups are created by arranging the individual records in the Details section of the report.

# Undoing versus Deleting a Group

If the results of a grouping are not what you want, you can undo or delete the group. In the case of undoing, you *toggle* — that is, you can undo the group and then turn the group back on without going through the steps to create the group. Here's how to use these options:

✔ To undo a group, choose <u>E</u>dit⇨<u>U</u>ndo. You can also press Ctrl+Z.

✔ To redo a group, choose <u>E</u>dit⇨Redo Group. You can also press Ctrl+Y.

If you use any formatting or formula commands after using undo on a group, the toggle is no longer available because Crystal Reports assumes you want to undo only the most recent action.

Unlike undoing a group, deleting a group permanently removes it and should only be used if the grouping is entirely unsatisfactory. Just follow these steps:

1. **Choose Edit⇨Delete Group from the menu bar.**

   After you select this option, an Alert box pops open to warn you that deleting a group cannot be undone.

2. **Click OK to proceed.**

3. **Click Yes to accept the warning and delete the group.**

# Inserting a Total

With the records grouped by country, or whatever grouping you choose, you can add calculations for each group in the form of a subtotal and a summary. The difference is the type of data you choose. Numbers can be calculated; text, such as names, can't be added together but can be counted. Crystal Reports distinguishes between a subtotal and a summary this way: A subtotal works only on number or currency fields. A summary works on all data types.

A total can be inserted on the Design or Preview tabs. To understand how this process works, use the Ch5 example report. (Keep in mind that you can use any previously created report and modify the steps to pertain to that report.) In the example, add a total to Last Year's Sales to see the total amount of sales by Country. Just follow these steps:

1. **Click the field on the Details tab that has the numbers you want to calculate.**

   For this example, select Last Year's Sales.

 2. **Choose Insert⇨Summary (or click the Insert Summary button).**

   The Insert Summary dialog box appears, as shown in Figure 5-8.

3. **Click the down arrow in the drop-down list box to see the types of calculations available and then select Sum.**

   The list changes based on the type of field you previously selected.

   In the third drop-down list box, any grouping you previously performed is automatically inserted as the sorting and grouping to be used. You can make a change to this sort/group by clicking the down arrow and selecting a new field on which to group.

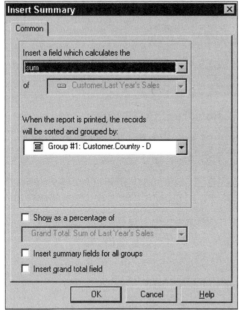

**Figure 5-8:**
The Insert
Summary
dialog box.

4. **Make sure that Group #1: Customer.Country - D appears in the middle text box.**

5. **Click OK.**

   Figure 5-9 shows the result of adding the summary to the Ch5 report.

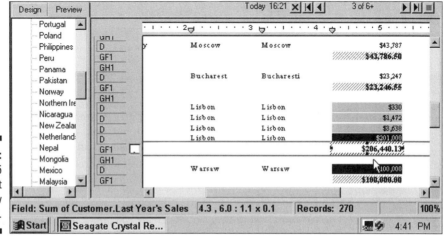

**Figure 5-9:**
The Ch5
report
with new
summary.

In this example, the total is calculated on a *number* field. Another way to use summary totals is to count the number of records in a particular group. Doing so requires that you use a different type of calculation, called *count*.

To count the number of records in a report or by group, follow these steps:

1. **Click a field that you haven't already used for a summary.**

   In the Ch5 example report, select the City field.

2. **Choose Insert⇨Summary (or click the Insert Summary button).**

   The Insert Summary dialog box appears.

   You can also open the Insert Summary dialog box by right-clicking the field to open the shortcut menu and then selecting Insert Summary.

3. **Select the calculation you want in the first drop-down list box.**

   For this example, select the Count calculation.

4. **Click OK.**

   The results are shown in Figure 5-10.

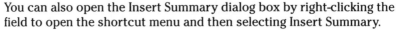

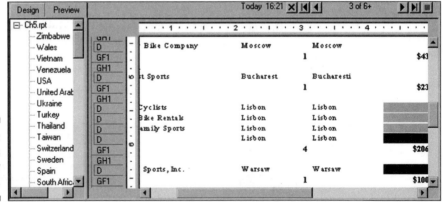

**Figure 5-10:**
Records counted by group.

In this example, the number of records per group is calculated, and the result is inserted in the Group Footer section, between the groups. For the Australian group, you see seven records. With a small group such as this, you can count the records yourself. But as your report grows in length, the number of records can become overwhelming; after all, this work is what *computers* are supposed to do, not people.

In the two previous examples, you see how to total a series of numbers and how to generate a count of records by group. You can also calculate the total of Last Year's Sales for the entire report and a total count of all records in the report.

# Inserting a grand total

You can insert the grand total from any page in a report, but you must move to the last page to see that grand total. You don't have to have any other totals, by groups for example, for this to process properly, but you must be in the Preview tab to see the result.

To insert a grand total, follow these steps:

1. **On the Details tab, click the field for which you want to create a grand total.**

   Do not select a field for which you previously created a grand total (although inserting the results of a grand total in more than one place in a report is possible).

   For the example report, select Last Year's Sales.

2. **Right-click the field you select in Step 1 and from the shortcut menu, click Insert Grand Total or choose Insert⇨Grand Total from the menu bar.**

   The Insert Grand Total dialog box appears.

3. **Select a type of calculation.**

   For the example, select Sum, as shown in Figure 5-11.

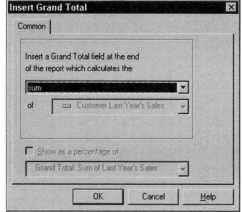

**Figure 5-11:**
The Insert
Grand Total
dialog box.

4. **Click OK.**

 5. **Click the Last Page control button to go to the last page of the report and see the result.**

   You may have to scroll down the page by using the vertical scroll bar on the right side of the window.

   Figure 5-12 shows the result.

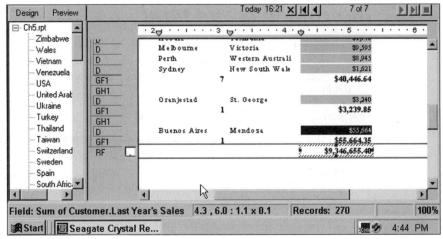

**Figure 5-12:**
A grand
total added
at the end of
the report.

To see whether the number is correct — that is, whether the field you chose
is calculated — move the mouse pointer onto the number. A pop-up window
displays the definition, as shown in Figure 5-13.

**Figure 5-13:**
The mouse
pointer
reveals the
type of
calculation
in use.

By moving the mouse pointer onto the value for any summing operation, you
can verify that the calculation is what you want. If you right-click the value,
the shortcut menu allows you to change the summary operation if desired.

## Inserting a grand total for text

Another total that is useful for any report is a grand total of the number of
records in the report. Crystal Reports indicates the number of records in a

report on the Preview tab at the bottom right of the window — but it doesn't automatically print the number of records in a report. The grand total usually prints at the end of the report, but you can manually insert it into the Report Header. You must be in Preview mode to see the result.

To insert the grand total of the number of records in a report, follow these steps:

1. **Click a field in the report that you haven't already used to tally a grand total.**

   (Do not presume that you can't grand total a field twice. However, for this set of steps, use a field without a grand total because it's easier to see the result.)

2. **Right-click and from the menu that appears, select Insert Grand Total.**

   The Insert Grand Total dialog box appears.

3. **Select Count as the type of calculation you want.**

4. **Click OK.**

 5. **Click the Last Page control button to go to the last page of the report and see the result.**

   You may have to scroll through the report by using the vertical scroll bar at the right of the window. Figure 5-14 shows the results of grand totaling the number of records in a report, which in this example is 270 records.

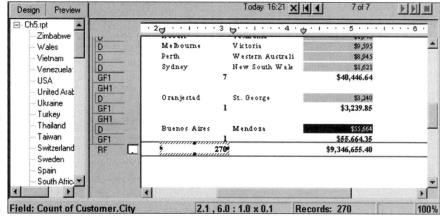

**Figure 5-14:** The grand total of all records in the report.

# *Defining other calculations*

The kind of summary operation you can perform depends on the type of data in the field you select. Table 5-1 shows the types of calculations you can perform and their respective uses. Some of the summaries are more for the statisticians in your company.

| Table 5-1 | Calculations You Can Perform on Fields |
| --- | --- |
| **Calculation** | **What It Does** |
| Maximum | Works on text or numbers and prints the largest value in the field. |
| Minimum | Works on text or numbers and prints the minimum value in the field. |
| Count | Works on text or numbers and prints the number of entries in the field. |
| Distinct Count | Works on text or numbers and prints the number of unique records in the field. For example, if you have three records that are from Doug's Cycle Shop, they're counted as a single entry. |
| Sum | Works only on numeric and currency fields and prints the total of the values in the field. |
| Average | Works only on numeric and currency fields and prints the average of the values in the field. |
| Sample Variance | Works only on numeric and currency fields and prints the sample variance of a series of values. |
| Sample Standard Deviation | Works only on numeric and currency fields and prints the standard deviation of the values in the field. If you have grouped data, then the standard deviation is printed by group. |
| Population Variance | Works only on numeric and currency fields and prints the population variance of the data. |
| Population Standard Deviation | Works only on numeric and currency fields and prints the population standard deviation. |
| Correlation | Compares the values in two fields. If you previously created a report that has the fields Advertising amount and Last Year's Sales, you can see the correlation between Last Year's Sales and the amount spent on advertising. The formula returns a value of -1 to 1, with zero returned if there's no correlation. |

| Calculation | What It Does |
|---|---|
| Covariance | Measures the linear relation between paired variables (the tendency of two fields to vary together). Fields are covariant if they vary according to a specific mathematical relation-ship. The circumference of a circle and the radius of a circle are covariant. |
| Weighted Average | Enables you to calculate the weighted average of the specified fields. When you calculate a weighted average, you actually calculate the average of one field and then use the values in another field to "weigh" the contribution of each value in the first field to the average. In a normal average, all the weights are equal to 1. |
| Median | Calculates the median of the given numeric fields. The median is the middle value in a sequence of numeric values (or the average of the two middle values in an even-numbered sequence of values). |
| Pth Percentile | Determines which value represents the percent-age you seek. If you want the 20th percentile, Crystal Reports returns $2,302 as the value at the 20th percentile (if 20% of {Customer.LAST YEAR'S SALES are less than $2,302). |
| Nth Largest Value | Calculates the Nth largest value in a given field, either for the entire report or for each group. |
| Nth Smallest Value | Calculates the Nth smallest value in a given field, either for the entire report or for each instance of the (condFld) group. |
| Mode | Identifies the most frequently occurring value in the field. If the number 500 appears in the field six times and occurs the most frequently of any number, the number displayed will be 500. |
| Nth Most Frequent Value | Calculates the Nth-most-frequent value in a given field, either for the entire report or for each instance of the (condFld) group. If no values in the field appear more than once, the function returns the minimum value by default. |

I must admit that several of the summary operations listed in Table 5-1 are out of my scope of knowledge. Consult your statistics textbook for explanations.

# Changing a Group

If you previously created a group, you can delete the group if you want or you can modify it. A modification is best made in the Design tab, although you can do so in Preview mode. To modify an existing group, follow these steps:

1. **Click the Design tab.**

2. **At the left edge of the Design tab, locate the group you want to modify, and then right-click the Group Header band.**

3. **From the menu that appears, select the Change Group option.**

   The Change Group Options dialog box appears, as shown in Figure 5-15.

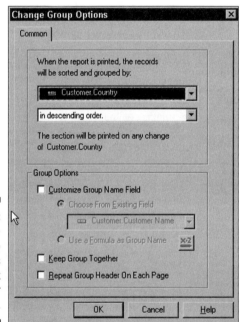

**Figure 5-15:**
The Change
Group
Options
dialog box
awaits your
command.

You can change the group by selecting a different field on which to group and/or by changing the sort order. Two other options that control the way the report prints appear, as follows:

✓ **Keep Group Together:** Prints all the records in a group on the same page of the report. If the group starts printing at the middle of the page and the page isn't long enough for all the records, a blank space ends the current page and the records begin printing on a new page. If a group of records is longer than a single page, you can change the font size to reduce the amount of space used. See Chapter 3 for more information on text formatting.

↙ **Repeat Group Header on Each Page:** In a case where the group covers more than a single page or if you want to use the least number of pages for the report but want to be able to easily identify the groups, you can print the heading for the group at the beginning of each new page.

# Doing a Top N Sort

A Top N Sort is a way to group the records based on the value of a summary field in the group. For example, if you want to determine which states are the top 5 for product sales, you first group the records by state, create a subtotal of sales by state, and then add the Top N Sort. The *N* refers to any number. You can sort the top 5, the top 10, the top 100, or whatever value you want to use. In the examples earlier in this chapter, the records are sorted in ascending or descending order as an entire report or within groups. This sort is a different kind, but one that is very useful.

To create a Top N Sort, you must have a group section with a summary field in it, then, follow these steps:

1. **Choose <u>R</u>eport⇨<u>T</u>opN/Sort Group Expert from the menu bar.**

   The Top N/Sort Group Expert dialog box appears.

2. **Select the type of sort you want by clicking the down arrow.**

   In this example, you want to sort the top 5. In the dialog box (shown in Figure 5-16), you have the following three sorting options:

   • **Top N:** Groups the top 5 (or whatever number you designate) and throws the remaining records into another Group labeled *Others.* Notice that each of the top 5 groups has its total printed by group; if you scroll down, the Others group has a single total.

   • **Sort All:** Rearranges all the groups in ascending or descending order.

   • **Bottom N:** Allows you to arrange the number of groups by using the smallest N records as the sort (such as the sales regions with the lowest 5 sales amounts).

3. **Select the field on which you want the sort to occur. (It must be a summary field.)**

   In Figure 5-16, you're asking to show the Top 5 Country groups, ranging (descending) from the countries with the greatest Sum of Last Year's Sales to the fifth greatest. All the other countries will appear in one large group, called Others, at the end of the report.

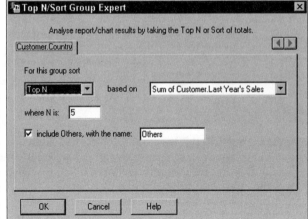

Figure 5-16:
The Top
N/Sort
Group
Expert
dialog box
filled with
sort values.

### 4. Click OK.

The report is sorted, as shown in Figure 5-17.

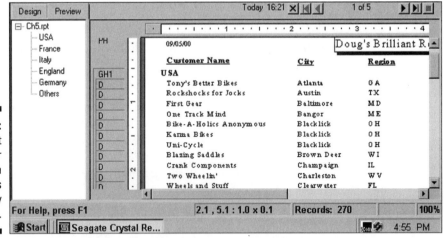

Figure 5-17:
A report
sorted for
the Top 5 in
each of its
Country
groups.

# Part III
# Formatting and Formulas for Success

The 5th Wave    By Rich Tennant

LARRY MAKES HIS LAST BIG BUSINESS DECISION.

@RICHTENNANT

LARRY'S HOUSE OF SOFTWARE

MAGNETS 'R US

Yeah, I'm gonna buy out the guy next door and combine the two operations.

HOME AND INDUSTRIAL USE

POWERFUL! PORT

## In this part . . .

Time to add the dazzle and sizzle. Add a couple of charts so the boss looks good — and you look even better. Add the company logo and a picture of the president of the company doing a rumba on the table at the company picnic, and you'll really hit the big time! And why not — you can link all kinds of graphics to a report by using the techniques in this part. Every department will covet you as the person needed to get its reports just right. No, I am *not* going to repeat that tired cliché about a picture being worth a thousand words. I refuse to stoop so low.

# Chapter 6

# Charting and Mapping Data

● ● ● ● ● ● ● ● ● ● ● ● ● ● ● ● ● ● ● ● ● ● ● ● ● ● ● ● ● ● ● ● ● ● ● ● ● ● ● ● ● ● ● ● ● ● ●

## In This Chapter

▶ Creating a chart

▶ Modifying a chart

▶ Drilling down on a chart

▶ Changing the chart type

▶ Applying chart templates

▶ Creating a map

● ● ● ● ● ● ● ● ● ● ● ● ● ● ● ● ● ● ● ● ● ● ● ● ● ● ● ● ● ● ● ● ● ● ● ● ● ● ● ● ● ● ● ● ● ● ●

*O*ne of the outstanding features of Crystal Reports is its charting and mapping capability. I can think of a dozen ways for a company to use charts and maps in conjunction with reports. A chart can add clarity to sales trends. A decision about where to locate a new distribution hub for a company's products may be based on a report that plots where its orders originate. In this chapter, I cover both the charting and mapping aspects of Crystal Reports.

## Creating a Chart from a Report

I believe in clichés, because a cliché almost always has a strong element of truth. So the cliché that a picture is worth a thousand words is, to me, quite true. People can more easily understand relationships among numbers if the numbers are displayed in a chart. With this fact in mind, Seagate Crystal Reports includes a charting function. Charts can be drawn for any summary or subtotal field, detail or formula, running total fields, OLAP data, or cross-tab data. As is true with other aspects of a report, a chart is considered an *object* in the report and is amenable to being moved around.

The chart is dependent on the section of the report in which it's placed. For instance, placing the chart in the Report Header or Footer section means that the data for the entire report is represented. If the chart is in a Group Header or Footer, the data in that group is represented in the chart.

After you decide what to chart, your next decision is which kind of chart to use. Different chart types are better at displaying different kinds of information. For example, a pie chart is the best choice when you want to identify portions of a whole. Column charts are preferable for representing data over a period of time, as in the amount of sales for a product, month by month over the course of a year.

By trying out different chart types on your data, you can discern which chart best conveys the information. Fortunately, Crystal Reports makes creating a chart easy as pie.

# Creating and Inserting a Chart

Crystal Reports includes a Chart Expert to walk you through the process of creating or editing a chart. Here are the basic steps for inserting a chart into your report:

1. **Open the report into which you want to add a chart.**

 2. **Choose Insert➪Chart from the menu bar or click the Insert Chart button on the Standard toolbar.**

   The Chart Expert dialog box appears.

3. **On the Type tab, select the Chart type you want.**

4. **Click the Data tab and select the data you want charted, the number of times you want the chart to appear, and where you want it to appear (the Header or Footer).**

   With a report containing only one level of grouping, your choice is Once Per Report, by default. (For details about groups, see Chapter 5.)

5. **In the Show box, select the summary or subtotal information to be charted.**

6. **Click the Axes tab to set the gridlines, data values, and the number of data divisions.**

   The Axes tab doesn't appear if you're adding a pie or a doughnut chart.

7. **Click the Options tab to display the chart in color or not, to display data points, to determine the marker type, or to show a legend.**

8. **Click the Text tab to determine the text that accompanies the chart.**

   You can have a title, subtitle, footnote, group title, and data title. At minimum, you need to include a title.

9. **Click OK.**

   Crystal Reports inserts the chart into the section you selected in Step 3 (the Header or Footer).

# Crystal Reports charts

You can chart four types of data with Crystal Reports: Advanced, Group, Cross-Tab, and OLAP.

**Advanced:** Displays database or formula-field data from the Detail section of the report. For example, in your sales report you may want to show a bar chart of individual sales within each region. This option can also display two or more summaries or subtotals in one chart. Because creating this type of chart isn't covered in this chapter, refer to the the Crystal Reports online Help for more information.

**Group:** Displays one summary or subtotal in a chart. For example, when creating a Sales by

Region report, you may want to create a Group chart that shows the sales subtotals for each Region and then place the chart at the beginning of your report. (You find out about creating a Group chart later in this chapter.)

**Cross-Tab:** Shows cross-tab data in a chart. This option is available only if you select an existing cross-tab object on your report before choosing Insert⟹Chart on the menu bar.

**OLAP:** Charts an OLAP grid. OLAP data can be used as a basis for this chart, and groups or summary fields are not required. This type of chart requires an OLAP object or what Seagate calls Cubes.

Whew! Those steps are numerous and offer many choices, but the number of choices makes it easier to highly customize your chart.

To modify a report for Group chart creation, open the Ch5 report (saved in the last chapter). For simplicity's sake, use the Select Expert to modify the Ch5 report so that it includes records from four regions.

The Group chart is the chart you most often create because it charts data from summary fields. (Keep in mind that you can use any previously created report that has groups and summary fields and modify the steps for creating a Group chart accordingly.)

To modify the Ch5 report, follow these steps:

1. **Open the Ch5 report and then choose Edit⟹Delete Group on the menu bar.**

2. **In the Delete Group dialog box that appears, select the Customer.Country group and then click OK. When prompted, confirm the deletion.**

3. **Open the Select Expert dialog box by clicking the Select Expert button on the Standard toolbar or choose Report⟹Select Expert from the menu bar.**

   The Choose Field dialog box appears.

4. **In the list of Customer Table fields, select Region and click OK.**

5. **In the Select Expert dialog box that appears, click the drop-down arrow in the first list box and select the Is One Of option and then click the next drop-down arrow and choose the AL, AR, AZ, and MN regions.**

6. **Click OK to complete the selection.**

7. **To add a group, choose Insert⇨Group from the menu bar to open the Insert Group dialog box.**

8. **Select the Customer.Region field and then click OK.**

9. **To add a subtotal, click the Last Year's Sales field, right-click to open the shortcut menu, and then select Insert Subtotal.**

10. **Save the modified report as Ch6.**

# Creating a Group Chart

With the Ch5 report reconstructed as Ch6, you're ready to add a Group chart.

1. **Choose Insert⇨Chart from the menu bar or click the Insert Chart button on the Standard toolbar.**

The Chart Expert dialog box appears, as shown in Figure 6-1.

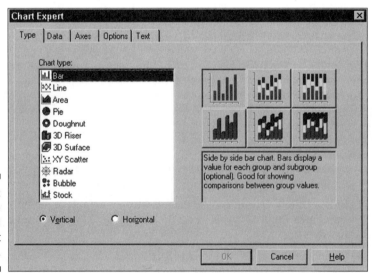

**Figure 6-1:**
The Type
tab selected
in Chart
Expert.

Chart Expert

Type | Data | Axes | Options | Text

Chart type:
- Bar
- Line
- Area
- Pie
- Doughnut
- 3D Riser
- 3D Surface
- XY Scatter
- Radar
- Bubble
- Stock

Side by side bar chart. Bars display a value for each group and subgroup (optional). Good for showing comparisons between group values.

○ Vertical    ○ Horizontal

OK    Cancel    Help

2. **In the Chart Type field on the Type tab, select the type of chart you want.**

   For this example, select Pie.

   The single, flat, default Pie Chart type is selected for you from the choices on the right.

3. **Click the Data tab to select the chart placement and the data to be charted.**

   Crystal Reports inserts what it thinks you're trying to chart and guesses correctly.

4. **Click the Options tab and accept the options as presented.**

5. **Click the Text tab and accept the Auto Text options.**

6. **Click OK to accept the settings for the chart.**

7. **Select the Region field, click Add, and then select the Is One Of option and the four regions.**

   Your report should resemble the one shown in Figure 6-2.

Crystal Reports inserts the chart in the top-left edge of the specified section. You can move or resize the chart after it's been placed in the report. To make the chart easier to see, reduce the magnification to 75 percent. You can do so by choosing View⇨Zoom and typing 75% in the Percent box in the Zoom dialog box that appears.

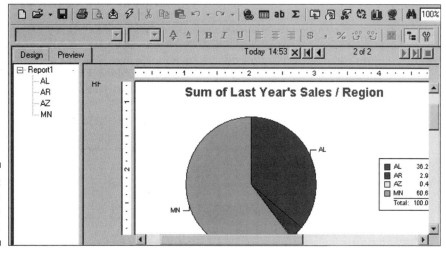

**Figure 6-2:**
The finished
example
chart.

# Modifying a Chart

If you decide to make adjustments to your chart, you can do so. Crystal Reports gives you full formatting control of every chart element.

Because each chart becomes an object in a report, each chart can be moved, resized, and reformatted just like any other object.

## Moving the chart to the footer

The easiest way to move a chart is to let the Chart Expert move it for you. First, check out your chart and where it displays in the report. In either the Design or the Preview tab, you can use the Chart Expert's Data tab to have Crystal Reports move a chart to the header or footer for you. Here's how:

1. **In the Ch6 report, click the chart.**

2. **Choose Format⇨Chart Expert from the menu bar or right-click the chart and select Chart Expert from the shortcut menu that appears.**

   The Chart Expert dialog box appears.

3. **Click the Data tab and then select the Footer radio button.**

   Doing so tells Crystal Reports to move the chart to the Report Footer.

4. **Click OK.**

   Crystal Reports places the chart in the Report Footer and returns you to the Design or Preview tab.

You can even fine-tune a chart's position. Where you place the chart determines where the chart prints in the report and what data is included in the chart. Use Table 6-1 to determine the best location for your chart.

| Table 6-1 | Choosing a Location for a Chart | |
|---|---|---|
| *Chart Location* | *Prints* | *Includes Data* |
| Report Header | At the beginning of the report | For the entire report |
| Group Header | At the beginning of the group | For each group |
| Group Footer | At the end of the group | For each group |
| Report Footer | At the end of the report | For the entire report |

# *Moving the chart*

If you want to move a chart that you previously placed in any report, be assured that you can move it as you would any other object. Because the chart is an object, clicking the chart displays the gray border with handles, which shows you the outline of the object. The handles are the square boxes in the corners and in the middle of the lines.

To move a chart, folllow these steps:

1. **On the Preview tab, click in the chart to display the handles.**

   After you position the pointer on the object border, the pointer turns into a magnifying glass, which indicates that you can either move the object or drill-down on the selected portion of the chart (see "Drilling down on a chart" later in this chapter).

2. **Hold down the left mouse button and drag the chart to where you want it.**

3. **Release the mouse button.**

   The chart appears in the new location.

# *Resizing a chart*

If you decide you want to resize a chart, you can do so easily. Just follow these steps:

1. **Click in the chart to display the handles.**

2. **Move the pointer over a handle so that a two-headed arrow appears.**

3. **Click and drag the two-headed arrow until the chart is the size you want.**

   If you do this in a corner of the object, you change the shape of the object in a diagonal direction, reducing the overall size of the chart. If you do this on a side of an object, you move that side in or out, changing one dimension of the chart.

Resizing and moving an object by using the handles and the two-headed arrows works the same way with every object.

# *Resizing the chart another way*

Clicking and dragging is the fast way to resize a chart, but if you need added precision, you can specify the exact dimensions of the chart by using the Object Size and Position dialog box. To do so, follow these steps:

1. **Right-click the chart to open the shortcut menu.**

2. **Select Object Size and Position.**

   The Object Size and Position dialog box appears, as shown in Figure 6-3.

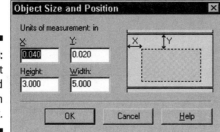

**Figure 6-3:**
The Object
Size and
Position
dialog box.

3. **Enter the dimensions you need to make the chart the size you need.**

   In addition to the size, you can change the position of the chart relative to the page margins. The X value is the distance from the left margin and the Y value is the distance from the top (or the bottom in a footer) margin.

4. **Click OK to finish.**

   You can click the Undo button if the resizing isn't what you want.

## Adding a border

A chart, like any object, can be formatted. You may want to add a border to enhance a chart by following these basic steps:

1. **In the Preview tab, right-click the chart to open the shortcut menu.**

2. **Click Change Border.**

   The Format Editor dialog box appears, with the Border tab displayed, as shown in Figure 6-4.

3. **Click the drop-down arrows to choose single borders for the Left, Right, Top, and Bottom of the chart.**

4. **Select the Drop Shadow check box.**

   If a check mark already appears in the check box, skip to Step 5.

5. **Click the drop-down arrow in the Color Border box and select Navy.**

6. **Click OK.**

   The chart appears with a navy, single-line border with a drop shadow, as shown in Figure 6-5.

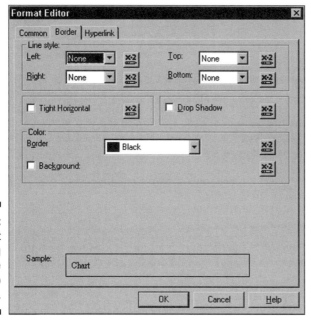

**Figure 6-4:**
The Format
Editor dialog
box with the
Border tab
displayed.

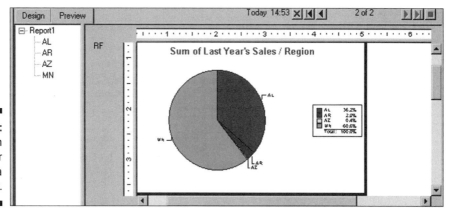

**Figure 6-5:**
A chart with
a border
added for a
nice effect.

# Customizing your chart

In Crystal Reports, you can customize a chart in different ways by using the following two options:

- ✔ **Chart Expert:** Enables you to select the type of chart, the data to be charted, several display options, and the text titles.

- ✔ **Format Chart menu:** Enables you to change chart templates, chart options, and titles.

Changing the type of chart you use or exploding the wedges of a pie chart are just a couple of examples of customizing your chart.

### Changing the chart type

Some types of data work better with different types of charts. Earlier in this chapter, in "Creating and Inserting a Chart," you see how effective a pie chart is for showing four sales regions. If you're plotting percentages of a whole, pie charts show the proportion of each section to the whole very well. If you want to show monthly sales over the past year, a line chart is effective in showing the highs and lows.

To see how the Chart Expert enables you to change from one chart type to another, just follow these steps:

1. **Click the chart.**

2. **Choose Format⇨Chart Expert from the menu bar or right-click the chart and select Chart Expert from the shortcut menu that appears.**

   The Chart Expert dialog box appears.

3. **In the Chart Type field on the Type tab, select Bar and then click the bar chart style from the display on the right side of the dialog box.**

4. **Click OK.**

   Figure 6-6 shows the chart in bar chart format.

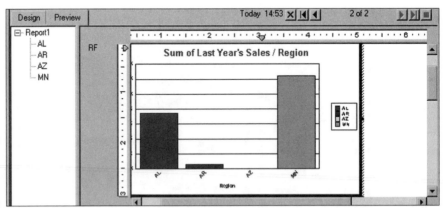

**Figure 6-6:**
The chart in bar format.

### Exploding the pie pieces

While the Chart Expert enables you to change the type of chart that's displayed, the Format Chart enables you to modify the chart details.

To see how the Format Chart works, follow these steps:

1. **Right-click the Pie chart to open the shortcut menu.**

2. **Select Format Chart and then select General from the submenu that appears.**

   The Chart Options dialog box appears, as shown in Figure 6-7.

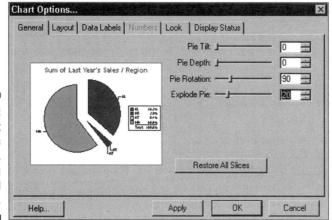

**Figure 6-7:**
The Chart
Options
dialog box,
displaying
the General
tab.

You can try some cool adjustments in this dialog box! On the right side of the General tab, click any of the slider bars and move them to the right. The pie chart shows you the adjustments you make to any of the settings. In Figure 6-7, I moved the Explode Pie slider bar to the 20 value to make the pie appear as it does in Figure 6-8.

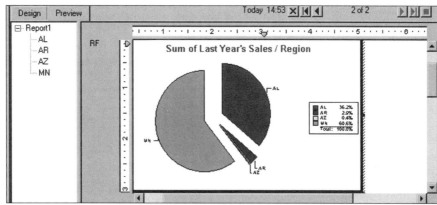

**Figure 6-8:**
The pie
chart
exploded
to 20.

What's elegant about this dialog box is that you need not make an adjustment and then close the dialog box to see the results on the real chart — it's visible as you make the change. To reset the chart to the default values, click the Restore All Slices button. After closing this dialog box, you can still revert to the default setting by using the Undo button.

### Other Format Chart options

The Chart Options dialog box includes several other tabs, which are

- ✔ **Layout:** When you right-click a chart, the variety of changes you can make depends on the type of chart you're using. For example, you can display the pie chart as a Ring pie chart. If you start with a bar chart, you can change the way the bars are displayed.

- ✔ **Data Labels:** These are the small text elements that describe the individual pie pieces or the bars. You can display the actual underlying data, the data as a percentage, and where in the chart the labels are displayed.

- ✔ **Numbers:** If numbers are part of the chart, you can choose how the numbers are formatted, such as general, currency, date, time, and so on. The Show Data labels must be selected for this tab to appear.

- ✔ **Data2:** Only available for charts with two numeric axes, this option enables you to format the second axis.

- ✔ **Look:** This tab is for formatting the legend for charts.

- ✔ **Display Status:** This tab contains the settings for other labels you want to appear, such as the name of the chart or a legend.

## Undoing changes

Oops! You make a big mistake, and you have spheres floating in your chart — but you don't want them. If you do something you don't want to do, you can undo the changes; but you must do so immediately after you make the mistake. Repeatedly clicking the Undo button moves you back a step at a time, allowing you to undo changes in the same sequence that you added them. To undo a change in a chart that you don't like, choose Edit⇨Undo from the menu bar or click the Undo button on the Standard toolbar. This action undoes your last action.

## Deleting a chart

In Crystal Reports Versions 7 and 8, you can undo deleting a chart — but not in previous versions of the software. Use caution when deleting a chart.

To delete a chart, follow these steps:

1. **In either the Design tab or the Preview tab, click in the chart to display the gray border and handles.**

2. **Press Delete on the keyboard, or right-click the chart and select Delete from the shortcut menu that appears.**

## Drilling down on a chart

*Drill-down* is a process that enables you to see the details of summary information in a report. The example pie chart in this chapter shows the summary information of top sales by region. As you view the chart, you can see the summary-information details that *gave* you the charted results.

To drill-down on a chart to see more detailed information, follow these steps:

1. **Click the Preview tab and position the pointer over a segment of the chart.**

   The pointer becomes a magnifying glass.

2. **Double-click a section of the chart.**

   A drill-down tab appears at the top of the Report window, displaying the details of the summary information. Figure 6-9 shows a drill-down tab for the Alabama Region.

3. **To create a drill-down tab for each section, double-click each pie section in turn. In a bar chart, you click each bar in turn for the same effect.**

4. **Close a drill-down tab by clicking the Close Tab button (the red X to the right of the date and time display on the Preview tab).**

   Closing the drill-down tab does not close the report.

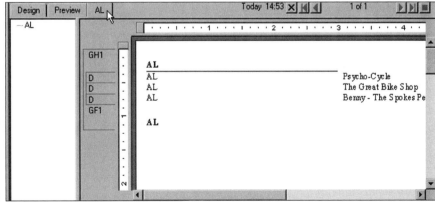

**Figure 6-9:**
Drill-down
into
Alabama.

## Underlaying a chart on a report

A chart is more useful if it's visible at the same time as the data it represents. So Crystal Reports Versions 7 and 8 enable you to underlay a chart next to or underneath the details in a report. The feature isn't what I would call automatic — that is, you have to tweak the results you get.

By using the report that's the example in this chapter in the following steps, take a look at what happens when I try to underlay the chart:

1. **Place the chart in either the Report Header or a Group Header section of the report.**

2. **Choose Format➪Section from the menu bar or click the Section Expert button on the Standard toolbar.**

   The Section Expert dialog box appears.

3. **On the left side of the dialog box under Sections, select Report Header.**

4. **At the bottom right, select the Underlay Following Sections check box.**

5. **Click OK.**

   Figure 6-10 shows the result of underlaying the chart.

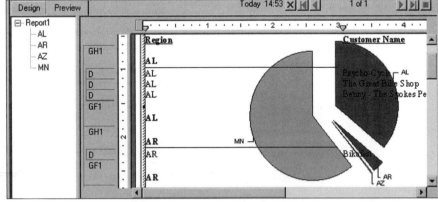

**Figure 6-10:**
The chart underlaying the Details section of the report.

As you can see, this action makes it difficult to make out anything very clearly. One remedy is to move the entire chart to the right. To do so, follow these steps:

1. **Click the Design tab.**

   The remedy is easier to apply in this tab.

2. **Click in the chart and hold down the left mouse button, drag the chart to the right, and then release the mouse button.**

   The chart is moved to the right.

 3. **Click the Print Preview button on the Standard toolbar.**

## Analyzing a chart

The Chart Analyzer opens a new tab that enables you to manipulate the components of a chart.

To open the Analyzer on a chart, follow these steps:

1. **Right-click the chart to open the shortcut menu.**

2. **Select Chart Analyzer.**

   A new tab that holds only the chart and is called Analyzer appears.

   With the Analyzer tab open, right-click the chart and select Format Chart to accomplish the following:

   - Zoom in and out on bar and line charts

   - Save the current template to a file

   - Apply a new template to the chart

   - Change the template specifications of the chart

   - Change the chart titles

   - Change the numeric axis grids and scales of the chart

   - Perform any additional formatting operations specific to the chart type

   - Auto-arrange the appearance of the chart

The choices that appear are consistent with the chart component that was selected before right-clicking the chart.

# Mapping a Report

Crystal Reports includes the capability to insert a map that creates a visual representation of different parts of a report. You can create a map that details groups, fields, cross-tab summaries, and OLAP data. The procedure to produce a map of your data is similar to creating a chart. When you add a map, you can add it as you do a chart, in the header or footer or in a group header or footer. The distinction is whether the map depicts the entire report or only the data in the specific group.

Brief descriptions of each type of map are outlined in Table 6-2.

| Table 6-2 | Mapping Options |
|---|---|
| *Map Type* | *Description* |
| Ranged | A ranged map has nothing to do with cowboys. Rather, it depicts data by first selecting a range (for example, 1 to 10) and then assigning a color to each range. The ranges can be modified if you want. You can make a range an equal-count range, strictly equal ranges, a natural-break range, or a standard deviation. For more on how ranges work, check the online Help. By default, Crystal Reports uses this style of map and equal count as the range type. |
| Dot Density | Have you ever looked at a photochart of the United States from space? If so, then you have a good idea of what this map illustrates. This map gives impressions rather than hard-data analysis. For example, if you are uncertain where to locate a new distribution warehouse, you can use this map to illustrate the location of your dealer network, and then you have some idea of where your business is generated. |
| Graduated | Use this type of map to generate a pictorial representation of the relative size of a value. If your report is of total sales by store, the marker increases with the larger number of sales. |
| Pie Chart | This map displays a pie chart over each area of the map associated with data. So this type of map is a chart inside a map. The pie chart is generated by the individual values in the map region. |

## Inserting a map

After you create a report, you can insert a map. In this example, the Ch6 report is the source of the map. To insert a map, follow these steps:

1. **Choose Insert⇨Map from the menu bar or click the Insert Map button on the Standard toolbar.**

   The Map Expert dialog box appears.

2. **Select the Header or Footer for the location of the map.**

3. **Click OK.**

   The map appears in the designated section, as shown in Figure 6-11.

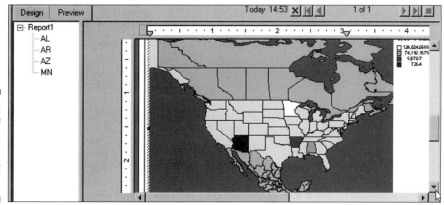

**Figure 6-11:**
A map of
the United
States in
the Report
Footer.

# Changing the type of map

You can easily try a different type of map and see whether the data is better served. To do so, follow these steps:

1. **Right-click the map to open the shortcut menu.**

2. **Select Map Expert.**

   The Map Expert dialog box appears.

3. **Click the Type tab and then select another Map type from the list.**

4. **Click OK.**

   The map is redrawn in the new format.

# Analyzing a map

Sometimes the report user wants to get a closer look at the map on the report and perhaps analyze some of the data. The Map Analyzer allows a report user to enlarge the map, zoom in on particular areas, and even change the type of map shown.

To use the Map Analyzer, just follow these steps:

1. **In Preview, right-click the map to open the shortcut menu and then select Map Analyzer.**

   An Analyzer tab appears, showing the map. The Analyzer toolbar, which contains the buttons useful for analyzing the map, appears below the Formatting toolbar.

   You can easily zoom in or out or pan the map.

2. **Right-click and from the shortcut menu that appears, select Zoom In or click the magnifying lens with the + sign on the Analyzer toolbar.**

   The mouse pointer changes to the shape of a magnifying glass with a plus sign (+).

   From this point, every time you click the left mouse button, the view of the map zooms in, showing greater detail. (Be patient, too, as this takes lots of horsepower to draw.) Conversely, you can right-click and select Zoom Out from the shortcut menu. When you do, the magnifying glass shows a minus sign (-). Each click reveals more of the big picture. Selecting Pan from the shortcut menu enables you to easily scroll the map in several directions.

3. **To close the Map Analyzer tab, click the red X next to the report date and time stamp located above the map.**

## Underlaying a map on a report

As with a chart, a map can underlay the sections of a report. To underlay a map, move the map to a Report Header or Group Header and use the Section Expert as discussed in the "Underlaying a chart on a report" section earlier in this chapter.

The capability to add a map to your reports is truly remarkable. It enables you to see reports in a context that's easy to comprehend.

# Chapter 7

# Using the Crystal Formula Language

● ● ● ● ● ● ● ● ● ● ● ● ● ● ● ● ● ● ● ● ● ● ● ● ● ● ● ● ● ● ● ● ● ● ● ● ● ● ● ● ● ● ● ● ● ● ● ● ●

## In This Chapter

▶ Inserting formulas in a report

▶ Discovering basic calculations and summary operations

▶ Manipulating strings

▶ Creating date calculations

▶ Constructing if-then-else calculations

▶ Developing Boolean formulas

▶ Accessing ready-to-use formulas

● ● ● ● ● ● ● ● ● ● ● ● ● ● ● ● ● ● ● ● ● ● ● ● ● ● ● ● ● ● ● ● ● ● ● ● ● ● ● ● ● ● ● ● ● ● ● ● ●

*I*f you hated algebra and dreaded calculus, don't skip this chapter because you think that math is what Seagate Crystal Reports formulas are about. You can do many easy calculations without being a Hawking or a Newton.

In this chapter you acquaint yourself with the several distinct parts of a formula: database fields on which the calculations are performed, operators that perform calculations, and functions that are hybrid operators — meaning they perform an operation beyond simple addition and subtraction calculations.

## What Is a Formula?

A formula is simply a symbolic statement that manipulates the data in your report — that's all it is. The tricky part is getting the formula to work with your data the way you want. But that tricky part is why you bought this book, isn't it, so you can get these things to work? Go ahead . . . give it a whirl!

Chapter 5 helps you understand how to insert predefined summary calculations into a report by using built-in subtotal and summary operations. You don't need to type the particulars to make that happen; you only need to indicate where and what field you want totaled. In this chapter, you see how to create mathematical and other calculations to suit your specifications.

An example of a basic formula is one that calculates the gross profit of products sold by your company. To figure the gross profit, you subtract the cost of the product from the sale price. A more complicated formula is one that calculates the time elapsed between two dates; you use this type of formula to determine whether a client is past due on a bill, for instance. Or suppose that the database stores numbers as string values. In other words, the entries in the field look like numbers, but the database designates the field entries as characters. Crystal Reports cannot perform a numeric calculation until you convert the characters to numbers — something you can do with a formula.

A really cool formula is a branching, or conditional, formula also known as an *if-then-else formula.* For example, a conditional calculation says that *if* the total amount owed is more than $1,000, *then* call your lawyer or *else* call the client yourself. So the formula branches in two directions, depending on the result of the condition. You make this kind of calculation every time you shop; however, computers aren't as smart as you, so you have to create a precise formula for them to calculate what you do intuitively.

# Getting to Know the Formula Editor

You can insert a formula into a report whenever you want to perform a calculation beyond a simple sum in a database field. Follow these general steps to insert a formula:

1. **Open the report in which you want to insert a formula.**

2. **Choose Insert⇨Formula Field from the menu bar.**

   The Field Explorer dialog box appears, displaying any formulas that already exist in the report, as shown in Figure 7-1.

3. **Click the New button on the toolbar in the Field Explorer dialog box.**

   The Formula Name dialog box appears, as shown in Figure 7-2.

**Figure 7-1:**
The Field Explorer dialog box with Formula Fields highlighted.

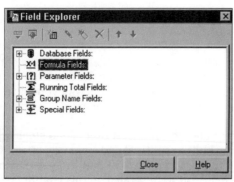

**Figure 7-2:**
The Formula
Name
dialog box.

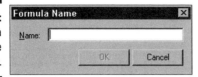

**4. Type a name for the formula.**

This step is important because Crystal Reports uses the formula name as the field header in the report. The field header can contain spaces and special characters — and can contain as much text as you can fit in the text box. The name needs to be descriptive enough so that you can interpret what the formula does. In this example, I name the formula Test.

**5. Click OK.**

The Formula Editor dialog box appears.

To see more details in the Formula Editor dialog box, grab the border with your mouse pointer and expand the dialog box. You can also expand the size of each list box by positioning the pointer on the frames between the lists and dragging left or right.

The Formula Editor dialog box may be a little intimidating, but it's very approachable. On the left is the Report Fields list that is the list of fields already part of the report. In the middle is the list of Functions and on the right is the list of Operators. The formula process consists of picking from each list, just like a menu, except that you have no limits! That means you can select six Fields, two Functions, and ten Operators — if you want.

## *The Report Fields window*

All the fields in the table(s) that are used in the report are listed in the Report Fields window. If you previously inserted fields into the report, those fields are listed at the top of the list under the heading Report Fields. Fields are listed with the table name preceding them, followed by a period and then followed by the field name, so that you can always tell where the fields originated. As a result, if you have a report with fields from unique tables, you can identify the source of each field. Any formulas that are inserted into the report have an @ sign preceding them; parameter fields have a ? sign.

At the bottom of the list of Report Fields is the path to the tables from which the report is constructed. You can get fields for your formula here, even if they haven't been inserted on the report. If you double-click the pathname or click the + sign to the left of the field, a list opens to reveal the tables that have been added to the report. Under the tables, the fields in each table are listed.

If you have a group on your report, all the information regarding the group (the Group Name field and any subtotals or summaries for the group) is also listed under Report Fields.

## The Functions window

*Functions* are those exotic creatures that are *prebuilt* formulas of a sort. Functions are usually applied to a field or a group of fields to perform operations that would be difficult for the average person to build, such as calculating the remainder of one number that's divided by another or to change a string of letters to uppercase. In other words, these tools exist so that you don't have to build them yourself.

Notice that if you scroll through the Functions window, you find a ton of information. How do you find what you're looking for? The functions are organized to make your life easier. Math is the first category of functions; double-click it to see the functions for working with numbers. The next category is Summary, where you find the functions you use in Group Sections or Grand Totals. The remainder of the functions list is organized in the same manner.

***Note:*** In the top-middle section of the Formula Editor dialog box is a drop-down list with two syntax options: Crystal or Basic. Because the functions and operators differ from syntax to syntax, changing the syntax from Crystal to Basic or vice versa changes the Functions list, as well as the Operators list. Crystal syntax is the formula language included in all prior versions of Seagate Crystal Reports; Basic syntax is new to Crystal Reports Version 8.

If you're familiar with Microsoft Visual Basic, or other versions of Basic, then Basic syntax may be more familiar to you. In general, Basic syntax is modeled on Visual Basic but has specific extensions to handle reporting. If you're already comfortable with Crystal syntax, you can continue to use it and benefit from the new functions, operators, and control structures inspired by Visual Basic. For more information on Visual Basic, check out *Visual Basic 6 For Dummies* by Wallace Wang, published by IDG Books Worldwide, Inc.

## The Operators window

*Operators* in a formula are the actions that take place between variables. Some of the Math operators may be more familiar to you because the symbols are mathematical symbols, such as addition, subtraction, and so on. You can also use other categories of operators with other data types or in other situations. Double-click to see individual formulas, and note that Crystal Reports shows you the correct way to use the operator by including both an X and a Y as substitutes for the values.

# The Formula text window

This window is where you do the work and create a formula. When you double-click on a Field, Function, or Operator, Crystal Reports inserts your selection into the Formula text window. That way, you can see exactly what you're building as you go. You can also type parts of your formula in the Formula text window.

# Buttons available in Formula Editor

The following buttons are available as tools to use in creating your brilliant formulas.

 ✔ **Check:** You can have Crystal Reports check a formula for any syntax problems simply by clicking this button. No, *syntax* is not a form of taxation on liquor or cigarettes (that is a *sin tax, of which politicians are so fond*), but rather it is the proper placement of the parts of the formula. If a mistake is found, Crystal Reports moves the cursor to the area of the formula that it thinks is incorrect and prompts you with a message in a dialog box.

 As you work on a long or complicated formula, you can check it at any time. Simply click the Check button, and Crystal Reports verifies that it can understand what you've done to that point in the formula. Then you can continue with the rest of the formula, confident that it's correct.

 ✔ **Save:** After you create a formula and check that it's correct, click this button. By the way, if you forget to execute a check before clicking Save, Crystal Reports does it anyway. If a mistake is found, you're given the option to correct the formula.

 ✔ **Save and Close:** Click this button after you complete your work and are ready to return to the report.

 ✔ **Undo/Redo:** As you create complex formulas, use these buttons if you make mistakes that need to be undone or if you mistakenly undo something that should be left as is.

 ✔ **Find/Replace:** In long formulas, you may need to make a series of replacements to refresh a formula. Locating every instance of a particular value or field name by the eyeball method works for short formulas but not for lengthy ones. Use this button to ensure you don't miss any values you're intending to edit or replace.

 ✔ **Browse Field Data:** This button will only be active if you have selected a field in the Fields window. Click on it to get a quick sample of the data from the database or to find out the data type of any field.

## *Syntax 101*

Table 7-1 lists the most common symbols used by Crystal Reports in its formula syntax. Pay close attention to these to make formula creation fast and easy and to get fewer slaps on the wrist (error messages) from the syntax checker.

| Table 7-1 | Tools for Creating a Formula |
|---|---|
| *Tool* | *What It Does* |
| // | Forward slashes add a comment to the formula. Use comments to document the formulas and what they do, which makes modifying reports in the future much easier. So in any formula in which you type //, the text after // isn't treated as part of the formula and doesn't print. |
| () | Parentheses denote the arguments following a function. When you use a function in a formula, the function must have arguments inside the parentheses to work. For example, if you insert the Trim (str) function in a formula, the function has to have something inside the parentheses to act on. |
| {} | French braces (Oo La La! . . . but don't get excited) simply indicate that the enclosed information is a Database field, formula, parameter field, running total fields, SQL expressions, or special field. You see them a lot. |
| [ ] | Square brackets surround a range or an array of numbers or fields. If you want every character in a string from the fourth to the eighth, you use [4 to 8]. |
| " " | Any character enclosed in quotation marks is called a *literal.* In a formula, a literal is text that you want to print at a certain point in the report. For example, if the formula calculates how long it's been since a customer paid your company, you can instruct Crystal Reports to print PAST DUE by inserting "PASTDUE" into the formula as a literal. |

Crystal Reports ignores upper- or lowercase characters in the formula (except when looking at database values), as well as carriage returns (pressing Enter, for you post-typewriter types). Line breaks are okay, too, as are spaces. Crystal reads the formula left to right and then top to bottom, regardless.

# Creating a Formula

The best way to understand formulas is to work with examples using real data. In the remainder of this chapter, you add formulas to the example Formula report (instructions follow on how to create this report). To do so, you can create the example formula report and follow along exactly or you can try adding individual formulas to reports that you have previously created with your own data.

If you want to work through the example, please take a moment to create the report. If you need a bit of help, refer to previous sections of the book as indicated. (This is good practice if you're new to creating reports.)

To create the sample report, follow these steps:

1. **Choose File⇨New Report from the menu bar.**

   The Seagate Crystal Report Gallery dialog box appears.

2. **Click Using the Report Expert button to select it, then select Standard from the Choose an Expert list, and then click OK.**

3. **Click the Database button.**

   The Data Explorer dialog box appears.

4. **Double-click Database Files and find the Xtreme database.**

   If the Xtreme database file isn't listed under Database Files, double-click Find Database File to find it. This database is located in the C:\Program Files\Seagate Software\Crystal Reports\samples\databases folder. When you click it, the database and all the tables appear in the Data Explorer dialog box.

5. **Add the following tables (Customers, Purchases, Orders, and Orders Detail) by clicking each name, then clicking the Add button, and then clicking Close.**

   Crystal Reports opens the Links tab, shown in Figure 7-3, to display a visual of how the fields in the tables are linked.

   For these tables to be used on the report, they must be linked. Crystal Reports makes an intelligent guess as to how they should be linked to save you the trouble. (For a detailed explanation of linking, page ahead to Chapter 14.)

6. **Click Next to go to the Fields tab and then add the following fields to the Fields To Display box on the right:**

   • Customer Name from the Customer table

   • Unit Price from the Orders Detail table

   • Quantity from the Orders Detail table

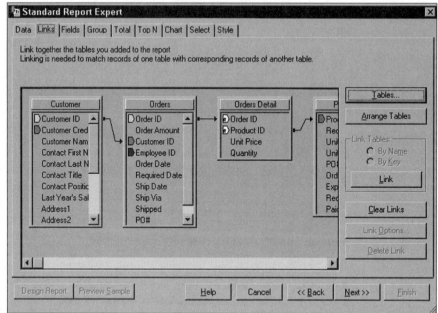

**Figure 7-3:**
The Links
tab with
visual links
between
tables.

7. **Click Next to bring up the Group tab.**

8. **Add the Region field from the Customer table to the Group By box on the right.**

9. **Click the Select tab.**

10. **Add the Customer.Region Field to the Select Fields box on the right.**

11. **Select the Is One Of condition from the drop-down list that appears below the Select Fields box.**

12. **From the drop-down list below the condition, select AL, AR, and CA.**

    Only records from Alabama, Arkansas, and California are included on the report.

13. **Click Finish.**

    Crystal Reports creates the report.

    I suggest reducing the length of the Group Name and the Customer Name fields and moving the other fields to the left to make more space at the right edge of the report.

14. **Save the report as Ch7, so you can use it to follow along with the example formulas in this chapter.**

    The finished example report appears, as shown in Figure 7-4.

With the report fields in place, you can use the example Ch7 report to create a formula that multiplies a quantity sold by the unit price (price each). Crystal Reports treats a formula as an object, and wherever you place the formula in the report is where the results of the formula appear.

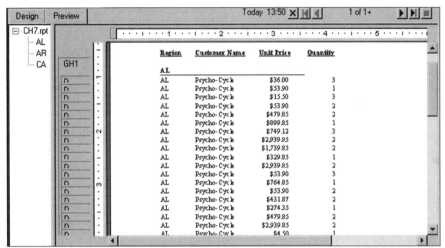

**Figure: 7-4:**
The finished
example
report.

To create a formula that multiplies two numeric fields together, follow these steps:

1. **Open any report that has two fields that can be multiplied.**

   To follow along exactly with this series of steps, choose File⇨Open to open the example Ch7 report previously created in this chapter.

2. **Click the Insert Fields button on the Standard toolbar.**

   The Field Explorer dialog box appears.

3. **Select the Formula Fields item and then click the New button.**

   The Formula Name dialog box appears.

4. **Type a name for the formula — use something original, such as Total (see Figure 7-5).**

**Figure 7-5:**
The Formula
Name dialog
box with
Total in the
Name field.

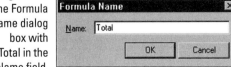

5. **Click OK.**

The Formula Editor dialog box appears.

You are on the brink of becoming a *Smarty*. Everything that you have done so far in this book has been pretty straightforward. Now, however, greatness is about to be thrust upon you — carpe diem!

Your goal is to multiply the unit price by the quantity. In the Report Fields list, you see a listing of the fields, formulas, and groups in the report. You want the Unit Price and the Quantity fields.

6. **Double-click the first field you plan to multiply.**

In the Report Fields list in this example report, double-click Orders Detail.Unit Price.

The field name pops into the Formula text box in the bottom half of the dialog box, as you see in Figure 7-6.

The name of the table in which the field is located is part of the field name — in this case, Orders Detail.Unit Price.

Next, you enter the mathematical operator that multiplies the numbers in this field by the numbers in the Quantity field. The Operators are located in the upper-right side of the Formula Editor dialog box. You want Arithmetic, which appears at the top of the Operator's list.

7. **Double-click Multiply (x*y).**

In the Formula text box, Crystal Reports inserts only the * symbol, which may be hard to see.

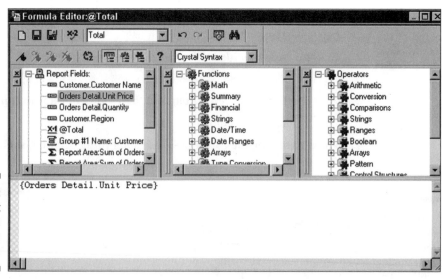

**Figure 7-6:** The Unit Price field in the Formula text box.

**8. In the Report Fields list, double-click the next field in the formula.**

In this example, double-click Orders Detail.Quantity. The second field is inserted into the Formula text box, which now looks like this:

```
{Orders Detail.Unit Price} * {Orders Detail.Quantity}
```

# *Check, please!*

Although Crystal Reports checks the formula automatically after you click the Save button or the Save and Close button, clicking Check is a good idea in order to confirm that your formula has the correct syntax.

To use the Check feature, follow these steps:

**1. Click the Check button on the toolbar in the Formula Editor dialog box.**

The No Errors alert box appears, as shown in Figure 7-7.

**2. Click OK to close the dialog box.**

If Crystal Reports finds a mistake, the cursor moves to the portion of the formula that is recognized as erroneous, and a message appears to assist you with the fix.

**Figure 7-7:**
Crystal
Reports tells
you that the
formula
checks out!

# *Saving the formula and placing it on the report*

So that you don't lose any of your hard work in the Formula Editor, save your formula as the final step. Then get out of the Formula Editor and place your formula on the report

Just because Crystal Reports examines the formula and determines that it is properly constructed, that doesn't necessarily mean the formula is correct. In a simple formula like the one in this chapter's example, you can feel confident that the results of the formula are correct. But if the formulas you create are highly intricate, they can give the wrong results — even if they're properly constructed. Be aware of this possibility and use a common-sense approach to the results you get when you check a formula.

When you're sure of your formula, save it by following these steps:

1. **Click the Save and Close button on the toolbar.**

   The Field Explorer dialog box remains open with the newly created formula listed.

2. **Select the formula name.**

   If you're following this chapter's example, select Total.

3. **Click the Insert to Report button.**

   The formula attaches to the mouse pointer.

4. **In the Design tab, insert the formula to the far right in the Details section of the report by clicking where you want the formula to go.**

   The inserted formula appears, similar to Figure 7-8.

5. **In the Field Explorer dialog box, click Close.**

6. **Hold on to your hat; this is the moment of truth. Click the Preview tab.**

   If everything goes according to plan, your new report looks similar to the one shown in Figure 7-9.

Pretty exciting stuff! The ability to calculate all kinds of results is limited only by your ingenuity. Later in this chapter, you can use the example report to work with other terrific formulas.

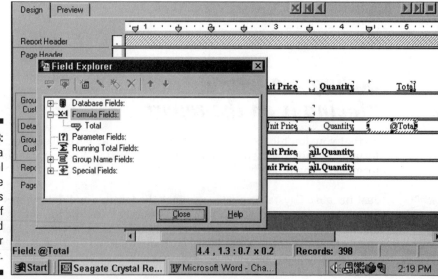

**Figure 7-8:** The formula name Total in the Details section of the Field Explorer dialog box.

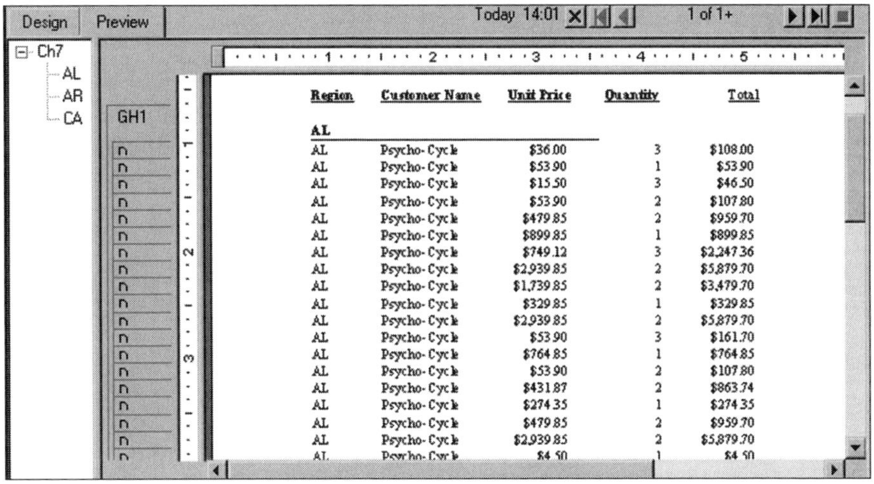

**Figure 7-9:**
A preview of
the report
with the
new formula
added.

## Editing an existing formula

You can easily edit a formula that's currently in a report. To understand how this works, use the Ch7 example report and add a calculation to compute the extended sales price *plus tax*. (Keep in mind that you can use any previously created report and modify the steps to pertain to that report.) Just complete the following steps:

1. **Open the Ch7 report and click the Design tab.**

2. **Under Formula Fields, select Total.**

3. **Right-click to open the short-cut menu and then select Edit Formula.**

   In the example, the top of the short-cut menu reads Field:@Total.

   The Formula Editor dialog box appears with the Total formula (or the formula you have selected to edit in your report) in the Formula text box. The text you see for the Total formula is currently

   ```
   {Orders Detail.Unit Price} * {Orders Detail.Quantity}
   ```

   For the purpose of this example, the sales tax rate is 7 percent. To add this percentage, you simply need to edit the formula.

4. **Click to the far right of the formula to insert the cursor.**

5. **In the Arithmetic field under Operators, double-click Multiply (x*y).**

   Crystal Reports inserts the multiplication symbol (*).

6. **Type** 1.07.

   Crystal Reports multiplies the results of the first portion of the formula by 1.07, which is equivalent to adding 7 percent. The formula text displays the following:

   ```
   {Orders Detail.Unit Price} * {Orders Detail.Quantity} * 1.07
   ```

7. **Click the Save and Close button.**

8. **Click OK.**

   The dialog box closes, and you return to the Design tab.

9. **Select the Preview tab to see the new Total column values, which include sales tax.**

# Adding a Formula that Totals by Group

With Crystal Reports, you can automatically insert Subtotals, Summaries, and Grand Totals into a report by using built-in summary operations (see Chapter 5). At times, you may also want to work with these summaries in the Formula Editor. Perhaps you want to calculate a percentage of a total, for example. In this section, I show you how to create these summaries within the formula language.

Remember, let Crystal Reports do the work for you if you simply want to place the summary on the report. You only need to create a summary as outlined in the following steps when you want to use it within a formula. The example report is grouped by Region and assumes that you have already created a total of the orders including sales tax. To understand how this works, use the Ch7 example report to create a formula that totals by the orders. (Keep in mind that you can use any previously created report and modify the steps to pertain to that report.) Just complete the following steps:

1. **Open the Ch7 report and click the Design tab.**

2. **Click the Insert Fields button on the Standard toolbar.**

   The Field Explorer dialog box appears.

3. **Select Formula Fields and then click the New button on the toolbar.**

   The Formula Name dialog box appears.

4. **Type a formula name, such as Group Sum.**

5. **Click OK to open the Formula Editor dialog box.**

6. **Start the formula by double-clicking the Sum (fld, condFld) function in the Summary list.**

   You can find Sum (fld, condFld) in the Functions list of the Formula Editor dialog box. Double-click the Summary header to see the formula you need. The function is inserted into the Formula text window.

7. **In the Report Fields list, double-click the formula name @Total, which is the first field to be summed and the formula that gives you the extended price plus the sales tax.**

   The first part of the formula is complete and looks like this:

```
Sum({@Total},)
```

*Note:* Crystal Reports automatically inserts a pair of French braces to enclose the formula name for you. In Crystal Reports Syntax, every field (database, formula, or parameter) is surrounded by the "curly" or French braces, {}. That way Crystal Reports can tell the fields from the rest of the words in the formula.

 8. **Still in the Formula text box, move your cursor to the right of the comma.**

You're ready to enter the group field to be subtotaled.

 9. **In the Report Fields list, double-click Customer.Region.**

The complete formula appears, as follows:

```
Sum ({@Total},({Customer.Region}))
```

 10. **Click the Save and Close button on the toolbar to close the Formula Editor dialog box.**

 11. **In the Field Explorer dialog box, double-click Group Sum.**

The formula attaches to the mouse pointer.

 12. **Click the mouse pointer in the Group Footer section to insert the formula there. (You probably want to insert the new formula below the Total formula.)**

This placement is important because you want the results to print after every group. Figure 7-10 shows the complete report on the Design tab. The mouse pointer indicates the location of the Group Sum formula.

 13. **Click Close in the Field Explorer dialog box.**

 14. **Click the Preview tab.**

Your report looks like the one shown in Figure 7-11. I formatted the field so that the results of the formula appear in bold print.

## Summing up

The two most-often-used summary functions are Sum (fld) and Sum (fld, condfld). You use Sum (fld) to sum up a field for an entire report. For example, if you want to create a total for Last Year's Sales for your entire report, you want your formula to be Sum ({Customer.Last Year's Sales}). Using this formula is equivalent to asking Crystal Reports to automatically create a grand total for you.

You use the Sum (fld, condFld) function when you want to create a total for each group. The fld is the actual field that you want to summarize, and the condFld is the group field for which you want a total.

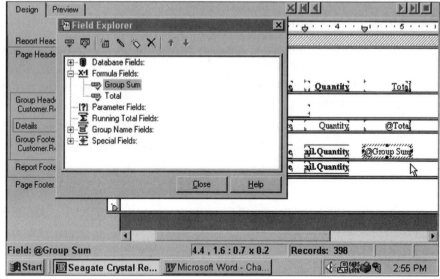

**Figure 7-10:** The Group Sum formula inserted in the Group Footer section of the report.

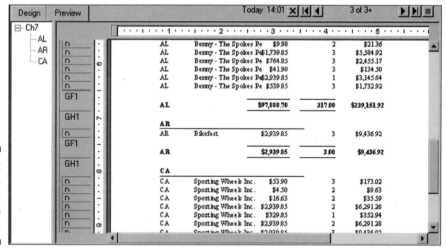

**Figure 7-11:** The Group Sum formula does its work!

# Inserting a Summary as a Percentage

Another new feature in Crystal Reports Version 8 is the ability to create a Summary field that's a percentage of another Summary field (the Grand Total, for example). In previous versions of Crystal Reports, you can create this formula but doing so isn't as easy as it is now. All that you basically need is a report with at least one Group. In this example, the Group is by Region. Here's how it's done:

1. **Click a numeric field in the Details section.**

   In this example, the field that's been generated by the Total formula (quantity times price) is the target.

2. **Choose Insert⇨Summary.**

   The Insert Summary dialog box appears.

3. **Select the Show As a Percentage Of box.**

   Notice that Crystal Reports automatically activates the Grand Total Sum of the @Total field and assumes that you want to create percentages from the column of numbers selected.

4. **Click OK.**

   Crystal Reports inserts the value at the bottom of the column, as shown in Figure 7-12.

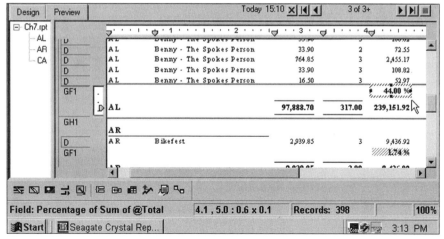

**Figure 7-12:** Percentage value inserted at the bottom of the column.

Scrolling up the report, you can see the other percentages inserted for each of the groups — in this case by region. So, each value represents the percentage that the subtotal is of the grand total.

# Entering a Running Total

In previous versions of Crystal Reports, you had to be facile with the Formula Editor to create a formula that would add the total of the previous record to the current record and then display that total. Because the need for this formula was so widespread and resulted in too many product-support calls, Crystal Reports built in the formula — sort of. (By the way, you can find knowledge-base articles, user forums, and a number of other helpful items for Crystal Reports at `support.seagatesoftware.com`.) You don't have to do a great deal of fancy footwork to get this type of formula to work the way you want. To understand how this process works, use the Ch7 example report. (Keep in mind that you can use any previously created report and modify the steps to pertain to that report.) Just follow these steps:

1. **Open the Ch7 report.**

2. **Click the Insert Fields button on the Standard toolbar.**

   The Field Explorer dialog box appears.

3. **Select the Running Total Fields option and click the New button on the toolbar.**

   The Create Running Total Field dialog box appears, as shown in Figure 7-13.

4. **In the Running Total Name field, type a name for the running total.**

   For this example, use RTotal.

   Okay, put on your thinking cap. You want a field that shows a cumulative total of each of the values by region, including the sales tax. So you want to use the value that's derived from the Total formula.

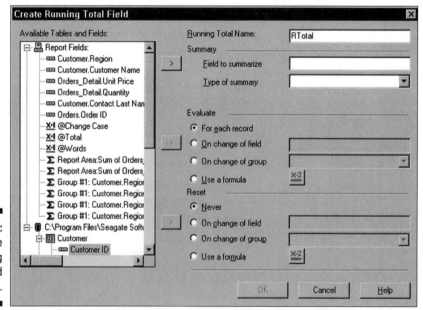

**Figure 7-13:** The Create Running Total Field dialog box.

5. **In the Available Tables and Fields box, click the @Total formula.**

6. **In the Summary section of the dialog box, click the right-pointing arrow that precedes the box labeled Field to Summarize.**

   Crystal Reports enters the @Total field name.

7. **In the Type of Summary list box, click the pull-down arrow to see the wide range of operations that can be performed.**

   For this example, select Sum.

8. **In the Evaluate section, determine at what interval the sum should be calculated.**

   In this case, you want every record included in the running total throughout the report. So select the For Each Record radio button.

9. **In the Reset section, determine at what intervals you want the total to reset itself.**

   For this example, you want the total to run without being reset, so select Never. You can really get creative and use a formula to determine when the reset should occur, such as when the value in the running total is greater than a predetermined amount. However, there's no need to get that out of hand here — leave that to the geeks who think they really need it. Figure 7-14 shows the completed Create Running Total Field dialog box.

10. **Click OK and insert the running total into the Details section of the report.**

    Figure 7-15 shows the running total at the far right of the report.

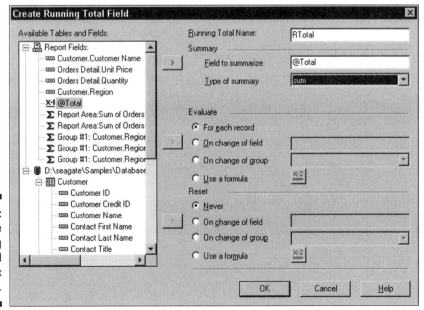

**Figure 7-14:**
The Create Running Total Field dialog box completed.

| Design | Preview | | | Today 15:19 ⊠ ⊩ ◀ | 1 of 1+ | ▶ ▶⊩ ■ |
|---|---|---|---|---|---|---|

| ⊟ Ch7.rpt | | | | | | | |
|---|---|---|---|---|---|---|---|
| — AL | | 1 · · · I · · · 2 · · · I · · · 3 · · · I · · · 4 · · · I · · · 5 · · · I · · | | | | | |
| — AR | | tomer Name | Unit Price | Quantity | Total | RTotal | |
| — CA | GH1 | | | | | | |
| | D | Great Bike Shop | 2,939.85 | 1 | 3,145.64 | 3,145.64 | |
| | D | Great Bike Shop | 33.90 | 2 | 72.55 | 3,218.19 | |
| | D | Great Bike Shop | 48.51 | 2 | 103.81 | 3,322.00 | |
| | D | Great Bike Shop | 53.90 | 2 | 115.35 | 3,437.34 | |
| | D | Great Bike Shop | 899.85 | 2 | 1,925.68 | 5,363.02 | |
| | D | Great Bike Shop | 539.85 | 2 | 1,155.28 | 6,518.30 | |
| | D | Great Bike Shop | 53.90 | 3 | 173.02 | 6,691.32 | |
| | D | Great Bike Shop | 15.50 | 1 | 16.59 | 6,707.90 | |
| | D | Great Bike Shop | 2,939.85 | 3 | 9,436.92 | 16,144.82 | |

**Figure 7-15:**
A running
total added
to the
report.

# Working with Text Strings

*Text strings* are characters that can be numbers or letters but are considered text *even if* they're numbers. Text strings can be manipulated to fit a variety of needs. A common need is that of combining a first and a last name in a report when the two pieces of information appear in two distinct fields in a table. For the combination of multiple fields, Text Objects is the easy and powerful way to go (see Chapter 11).

A database field that contains text is called a text string field. When a text string field is inserted in a report, Crystal Reports considers it to be a text object.

Even though you use text objects to combine fields, in certain situations you need the additional power of the Formula Editor feature to manipulate text. Perhaps you need to change the case of a name that appears in a field. To do so, you can create a formula that reverses the case from upper to lower or lower to upper.

In the Xtreme database, one table is the Customer table, which has a Contact Last Name field. You can use a formula to change the case of the letters in that field. To understand how this process works, use the Ch7 example report. (Keep in mind that you can use any previously created report and modify the steps to pertain to that report.) Just follow these steps:

1. **Open the Ch7 report and click the Design tab.**

2. **Click the Insert Fields button on the Standard toolbar.**

   The Field Explorer dialog box appears.

3. **Select the Formula Fields item and then click the New button on the toolbar.**

   The Formula Name dialog box appears.

4. **Type a name for the formula, such as Change Case, and then click OK.**

   The Formula Editor dialog box appears.

5. **Select Strings in the Functions window. Scroll through the list of string functions until you see Uppercase and then double-click it.**

   The Uppercase function is inserted into the Formula text window, and the flashing cursor is ready and waiting between the parentheses for your next insertion. The way that this function works is to read the characters in the field and convert them to uppercase — unless they're already uppercase, in which case they're ignored.

6. **Click the space between the two parentheses that follow the Uppercase function name to insert the cursor (if it isn't already there).**

7. **In the Report Fields window, scroll until you locate the Customer.Contact Last Name field.**

8. **Double-click the field name to insert it into the formula.**

   The formula reads

   ```
   UpperCase ({Customer.Contact Last Name})
   ```

9. **Click the Save and Close button.**

   The Formula Editor dialog box closes.

10. **In the Field Explorer dialog box, click the formula name Change Case, and then click Insert.**

11. **Insert the Change Case formula field in the Details section to the right of RTotal by clicking the mouse pointer there.**

    Figure 7-16 shows the results of the Change Case formula in the Preview tab.

A text object is the quickest and simplest way to combine multiple fields. You can use text objects to combine a first and last name, but you can also use them to combine formula fields with other fields or text, as described in Chapter 11.

| Design | Preview | | | | Today 13:23 ✕ |◀ ◀ | 1 of 2+ | ▶ ▶| ■ |

```
⊟ Ch7.rpt              · · · 2 · · · | · · 3 · · · | · · · 4 · · · | · · · 5 · · · | · · 6 · · ·
   ― AL
   ― AR
   ― CA
         GH1        e    Unit Price   Quantity        Total    RTotal   Change Case

         D          Shop      16.50        2           35.31     35.31   WITT
         D          Shop   2,939.85        1        3,145.64  3,180.95   WITT
         D          okes Person 33.90      3          108.82  3,289.77   JONES
         D          okes Person 23.50      1           25.15  3,314.91   JONES
         D          okes Person 539.85     3        1,732.92  5,047.83   JONES
         D          Shop      33.90        2           72.55  5,120.38   WITT
         D          Shop     539.85        2        1,155.28  6,275.66   WITT
         D          Shop      53.90        2          115.35  6,391.00   WITT
         D          Shop     899.85        2        1,925.68  8,316.68   WITT
         D                    36.00        3          115.56  8,432.24   MAST
         D                    53.90        1           57.67  8,489.92   MAST
         D                    15.50        3           49.76  8,539.67   MAST
         D          okes Person 764.85     2        1,636.78 10,176.45   JONES
```

**Figure 7-16:**
The Last
Name in all
uppercase
letters.

# Changing Numbers to Words

You may have a report that has numbers in a field that you prefer to display as words. To solve this problem, you can create a formula that converts the numbers to words. The most common use of this type of formula is for check writing. On most checks, you use both numbers and words to verify the amount of the check.

To understand how this process works, use the Ch7 example report to change the numbers in the Total Formula field to words. (Keep in mind that you can use any previously created report and modify the steps to pertain to that report.) Just follow these steps:

1. **Open the Ch7 report and click the Design tab.**

2. **Click the Insert Fields button on the Standard toolbar.**

   The Field Explorer dialog box appears.

3. **Select Formula Fields and then click the New button on the toolbar.**

   The Formula Name dialog box appears.

4. **Type a name for the formula, such as Words, and then click OK.**

   The Formula Editor dialog box opens.

5. **In the Functions window, scroll down and select ToWords, and then double-click the ToWords(x) function.**

   The insertion point appears inside the parentheses.

6. **In the Report Fields list, double-click @Total.**

7. **Click the Save and Close button.**

   The Formula Editor dialog box closes.

8. **In the Field Explorer dialog box, select Words.**

9. **Insert the Words formula into the Details section to the right of the Change Case formula field, as shown in Figure 7-17.**

   You may notice that you're running out of room across your report. You can move and resize fields to try to make enough room for the Words formula. But if you're part way through a report and realize that you need more room to work across, you can change the page layout.

10. **(Optional) Choose File➪Printer Setup on the menu bar.**

    In the Printer Setup dialog box that appears, change the print orientation from Portrait to Landscape. Crystal Reports immediately resizes the page, giving you more room to work. Be aware that changing the orientation also changes the way the report prints.

11. **Click the Preview tab to see the report, as shown in Figure 7-18.**

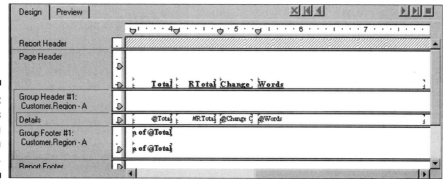

**Figure 7-17:**
The Words formula inserted in the report.

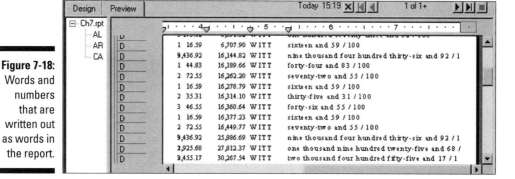

**Figure 7-18:**
Words and numbers that are written out as words in the report.

After you create the Words formula, you may notice that the Total formula is written out to two decimal places. If you prefer to control the number of decimal places displayed, you can use the second ToWords option, which is ToWords, x,#places. For example, if you want to convert the Total formula to words but display the results with zero decimal places, you can use the following formula:

```
ToWords((({@Total}),0)
```

Crystal Reports converts the Total formula to words and changes the display to zero decimal places.

# Going on a Date

Another popular type of formula determines the number of days that pass between two dates. For example, if your company records the date that a product is ordered and the date that it ships, you can determine how long your company takes to process the order. Using the Ch7 report, as an example, you can simply place on the report a formula that calculates the number of days. However, you may want to place on the report the Order.Ship Date and Order.Order Date fields, so you can check to see whether the formula is working correctly.

To understand how this process works, insert the date fields and create the formula in the Ch7 example report. (Keep in mind that you can use any previously created report and modify the steps to pertain to that report.) Just follow these steps:

1. **Open the Ch7 report and click the Design tab.**

   Before you can edit the Ch7 example report, you need to delete a few fields and/or field names to give you a little more room to work. To do so, click the Quantity field, hold down the Ctrl key, and then click the following fields: Total, Percent of Order, RTotal, Change Case, and Words. (Remember to click the column headers, too.) Then press the Delete key, and the fields and column headers disappear from the report.

 2. **Click the Insert Fields button on the Standard toolbar.**

   The Field Explorer dialog box appears.

3. **Scroll through the list until you see the Orders table and then double-click Orders.Order Date.**

4. **Click in the Details section of the report to insert the field to the right of the other fields.**

5. **Repeat Steps 3 and 4 with the Orders.Ship Date field.**

   Both fields appear with the date and time.

6. **To remove the time from both fields, select the Order Date field, press the Ctrl key, and then select the Ship Date field.**

7. **Right-click and select Format Objects from the shortcut menu.**

   The Format Editor dialog box appears.

8. **Click the Date/Time tab and then select a date option with no times displayed, for example, 03/01/1999, as shown in Figure 7-19.**

9. **Click OK at the bottom of the dialog box to close the Format Editor dialog box.**

10. **Select Formula fields and then click the New button on the toolbar in the Field Explorer dialog box.**

    The Formula Name dialog box appears.

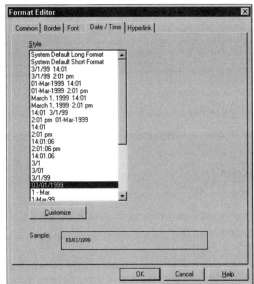

**Figure 7-19:**
The Format
Editor
dialog box.

11. **In the Name field in the Formula Name dialog box, type** Processing Days.

12. **Click OK.**

    The Formula Editor dialog box appears.

13. **In the Report Fields window, double-click Orders.Ship Date.**

    The field name is inserted into the Formula text window.

14. **In the Operators window, under Arithmetic, double-click Subtract (x-y), because the formula is a subtraction.**

## Undoing

Have you ever clicked a button and then regretted it? Perhaps you deleted a field you actually want on your report. Crystal Reports has an Undo feature that you need to remember in just such instances. If you ever want to back up one step, choose Edit⇨Undo from the menu bar.

Undo also lets you undo multiple steps. If you ever get into a jam, just keep choosing Undo

until you get back to where you want to be.

Some steps, however, can't be undone. When you see the Confirm command, Crystal Reports is reminding you to tread carefully — what you're about to do cannot be undone. If you don't want to proceed, simply click the No button.

**15. In the Report Fields window, double-click Orders.Order Date.**

The formula text should now read

```
{Orders.Ship Date} - {Orders.Order Date}
```

**16. Click the Save and Close button.**

The Formula Editor dialog box closes.

**17. In the Field Explorer dialog box, select the formula name, Processing Days.**

**18. Click the Insert button.**

The formula field attaches to the mouse pointer.

**19. To insert the field, click the pointer to the right of the date fields in the Details section of the report.**

**20. Click Close.**

The Field Explorer dialog box closes.

**21. Click the Preview tab.**

The results appear, as shown in Figure 7-20.

To format the results to 0 (zero) decimal places, right-click the Processing Days field, select the Format Field option from the shortcut menu, and then select the number of decimal places you want displayed.

When you want to change the number of decimal places in a number field, you can use the Increase or Decrease Decimals buttons from the Formatting toolbar (see the Cheat Sheet in the front of this book). In this case, simply click the Decrease Decimals button twice with the Processing Day formula selected to remove two decimal places.

| Design | Preview | | | Today 15:43 ✕ ◀◀ ◀ | 1 of 1+ | ▶ ▶▶ ■ |

| ...er Name | Unit Price | Order Date | Ship Date | Processing Day |
|---|---|---|---|---|
| Cycle | $36.00 | 02/04/1997 | 02/04/1997 | 0.00 |
| Cycle | $53.90 | 02/11/1997 | 02/13/1997 | 2.00 |
| Cycle | $15.50 | 02/11/1997 | 02/13/1997 | 2.00 |
| Cycle | $53.90 | 02/22/1996 | 03/04/1996 | 11.00 |
| Cycle | $479.85 | 02/22/1996 | 03/04/1996 | 11.00 |
| Cycle | $899.85 | 03/02/1997 | 03/03/1997 | 1.00 |
| Cycle | $749.12 | 03/02/1997 | 03/03/1997 | 1.00 |
| Cycle | $2,939.85 | 04/08/1997 | 04/10/1997 | 2.00 |
| Cycle | $1,739.85 | 04/08/1997 | 04/10/1997 | 2.00 |
| Cycle | $329.85 | 04/08/1997 | 04/10/1997 | 2.00 |
| Cycle | $2,939.85 | 04/15/1997 | 04/18/1997 | 3.00 |
| Cycle | $53.90 | 04/29/1997 | 04/29/1997 | 0.00 |
| Cycle | $764.85 | 04/29/1997 | 04/29/1997 | 0.00 |
| Cycle | $53.90 | 04/30/1997 | 05/01/1997 | 1.00 |
| Cycle | $431.87 | 06/01/1997 | 06/09/1997 | 8.00 |
| Cycle | $274.35 | 06/01/1997 | 06/09/1997 | 8.00 |
| Cycle | $479.85 | 06/08/1997 | 06/08/1997 | 0.00 |
| Cycle | $2,939.85 | 06/21/1997 | 06/21/1997 | 0.00 |

**Figure 7-20:** Two date fields and the results of subtracting the two.

# Using If-Then-Else Formulas

An *if-then-else formula* is a formula that you use to examine a value and then, depending on the value, execute one or more alternatives. A simple example is a case of someone owing your company money. This type of formula looks at the date and then either prints *30 Days Past Due* or *60 Days Past Due,* depending on how much time has passed since the last payment. The current date is the condition that determines the next action.

In Crystal Reports, the actions that take place after looking at the condition must be the same *type* of action. In other words, if the result is to print a text string (30 Days Past Due), the other option (60 Days Past Due) also must be a text string.

For those of you with a programming background, you don't have to include an *else* statement for these formulas to work. If the condition fails the if-then test, 0 is returned for numerics and "" (a blank text string) for text.

To understand how to use the if-then-else formula, use the Ch7 report with several fields that were added earlier. If you're using your own database, all you need is a report that has a numeric field. You can then adjust the conditional values to fit your data.

Before you can work with the Ch7 example report, you need to make a few modifications.

Make some room on the report by deleting the following fields: Order Date, Ship Date, and the Processing Day formula. In the Details section, insert the Orders Detail.Quantity field and the Total formula.

Your report should look similar to Figure 7-21 before continuing. If you need help creating this report, refer to Chapter 2.

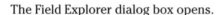

| | | Design | Preview | | | | | Today 15:49 | 1 of 1+ |
| | | | | | | | |

| Region | Customer Name | Unit Price | Quantity | Total |
| --- | --- | --- | --- | --- |
| AL | | | | |
| AL | Psycho-Cycle | $36.00 | 3 | $115.56 |
| AL | Psycho-Cycle | $53.90 | 1 | $57.67 |
| AL | Psycho-Cycle | $15.50 | 3 | $49.76 |
| AL | Psycho-Cycle | $53.90 | 2 | $115.35 |
| AL | Psycho-Cycle | $479.85 | 2 | $1,026.88 |
| AL | Psycho-Cycle | $899.85 | 1 | $962.84 |
| AL | Psycho-Cycle | $749.12 | 3 | $2,404.68 |
| AL | Psycho-Cycle | $2,939.85 | 2 | $6,291.28 |
| AL | Psycho-Cycle | $1,739.85 | 2 | $3,723.28 |
| AL | Psycho-Cycle | $329.85 | 1 | $352.94 |
| AL | Psycho-Cycle | $2,939.85 | 2 | $6,291.28 |
| AL | Psycho-Cycle | $53.90 | 3 | $173.02 |
| AL | Psycho-Cycle | $764.85 | 1 | $818.39 |
| AL | Psycho-Cycle | $53.90 | 2 | $115.35 |
| AL | Psycho-Cycle | $431.87 | 2 | $924.20 |
| AL | Psycho-Cycle | $274.35 | 1 | $293.55 |
| AL | Psycho-Cycle | $479.85 | 2 | $1,026.88 |
| AL | Psycho-Cycle | $2,939.85 | 2 | $6,291.28 |

**Figure 7-21:**
Does your report look like this?

The if-then-else formula you create in this example displays the word *Excellent* for any record that has a Total amount greater than 750. The formula looks at the value in the record and then prints the appropriate response based on that value. The formula is simple: If the value is less than or equal to a specific number, nothing is printed; if it's greater than a specified value, the word Excellent is printed. Here are the steps to create this formula:

1. **Open the Ch7 report and click the Design tab.**

2. **Click the Field Explorer button on the toolbar.**

   The Field Explorer dialog box opens.

3. **Select Formula Fields and then click the New button on the toolbar.**

   The Formula Name dialog box appears.

4. **Type** Great Sales.

5. **Click OK.**

   The Formula Editor dialog box opens.

6. **In the Operators list, under Control Structures, double-click If x Then y Else z.**

The If Then Else is inserted into the formula text window. You use this to start building a formula. Notice the cursor is positioned between If and Then because this is where you normally start building your formula.

7. **In the Report Fields list, double-click @Total.**

   The formula name is inserted at the cursor between If and Then.

   Your formula should appear as

   ```
   if {@Total} then else
   ```

8. **In the Operators list, under Comparisons, double-click Greater Than (x>y).**

   The operator is inserted into the formula.

9. **Add the test, Is Total Greater Than 750?, by typing > 750.**

   Your formula should now appear as

   ```
   if {@Total} > 750 then else
   ```

   Okay, 750 is now the condition (the If) in this formula. So if the result in the Total field is greater than 750 — then what? Well, you have to add the rest of the formula, that's what.

10. **Position the insertion point between the words Then and Else.**

11. **Type "Excellent".**

    You must have quotation marks on either side of the word. With this part of the formula inserted, Crystal Reports prints the word *Excellent* whenever the value in Total is greater than 750.

12. **Delete the word Else by double-clicking it and then pressing the Delete key.**

    You need to do this because the word *Excellent* is being printed when the condition is True (greater than 750). Nothing gets printed when the condition is False (less than 750) so the Else can be left out. You discover how to use the rest of this formula in the "Modifying an if-then-else formula" section later in this chapter

    With this formula in place, the condition is either met or not. If not, then a blank text string (which looks just like nothing) prints in the report. The finished formula looks like this:

    ```
    if {@Total} > 750 then "Excellent"
    ```

13. **Click the Save and Close button on the toolbar.**

    The Formula Editor dialog box closes.

14. **In the Field Explorer dialog box, select Great Sales.**

15. **Click the Insert to Report button.**

    The formula attaches to the mouse pointer.

16. **Position the pointer in the Details section of the report and click to insert the field to the right of the Total field.**

17. **Click Close.**

    The Field Explorer dialog box closes.

18. **Click the Preview tab.**

    The big moment is here. If it works for you, you pass into the higher ranks of Crystal Reports's users. Hopefully, your report looks like the one shown in Figure 7-22.

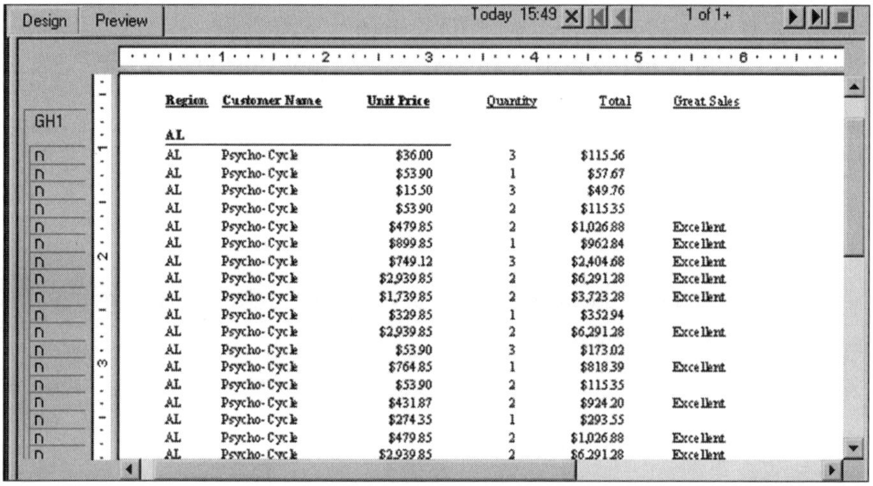

**Figure 7-22:**
An excellent report with a complex if-then-else formula.

Figure 7-22 demonstrates the work of this formula because only records with sales in excess of $750 have text printed in the Great Sales column. Although this formula works, the report would be better if every record had a notation of some sort. The section "Modifying an if-then-else formula" later in this chapter helps you modify the formula to include several more text options.

In this example, you use an if-then formula that tells the program what to do if the Total is over 750 and to do nothing if the total is not over 750.

But how do you create a formula if you want to display the word *Excellent* when sales are greater than 750 and *Poor* in all other situations? You use the following formula:

```
if {@Total} > 750 then "Excellent" else "Poor"
```

The `else "Poor"` part of the formula tells Crystal to display the word *Poor* if sales are less than or equal to 750.

# Modifying an if-then-else formula

Nothing is particularly tricky about modifying an if-then-else formula, but doing so may require some careful formula building. In the preceding example, you simply ask Crystal Reports to print *Excellent* if the Total is over 750. This time, you get a little more complicated. You still want to display *Excellent* for amounts over 750; but when the amount is over 500, you want to display *Good* and in all other situations — *Stinko*. When an if-then-else formula is used inside another if-then-else formula, it's called a *nested if*.

To modify an if-then-else formula and create a Nested If, follow these steps:

1. **Open the Ch7 report and click the Preview tab.**

2. **Right-click the Great Sales formula and choose Edit Formula from the shortcut menu that appears.**

   The Formula Editor dialog box appears, with the Great Sales formula in the formula text box.

3. **Position the insertion point after Excellent and type** else if.

   You can type the words needed to make the formula work; you aren't required to select them from the Operators list. If Crystal recognizes the functions and operators, the words turn blue. If they don't turn blue, you've misspelled them or you're using a term Crystal doesn't recognize.

4. **Double-click @Total to enter the formula name.**

5. **Type the rest of the formula:** > 500 then "Good" else "Stinko".

   The completed three-condition formula text should look like this:

   ```
   if {@Total} > 750 then "Excellent"
   else if {@Total} > 500 then "Good"
   else "Stinko"
   ```

   Notice that I break the formula over three lines. Crystal doesn't care where you insert line breaks, as long as they are not inside literals (text in quotes ""). Simply place the line breaks where they make sense to you.

   To get the three different comments, you use an *if-then-else-if* formula. The first line asks Crystal Reports to check if sales are greater than 750 and if they are, to display the word *Excellent*. The next line tells Crystal Reports that when sales are not greater than 750, continue to check to see if sales are greater than 500; and when they are, display the word *Good*. Think of the else "Stinko" as just saying: If it's not greater than 750 or greater than 500, then display the word *Stinko*.

6. **Click the Save and Close button to exit the Formula Editor dialog box.**

   The results of the newly modified formula appear on your report in the Preview tab, as shown in Figure 7-23.

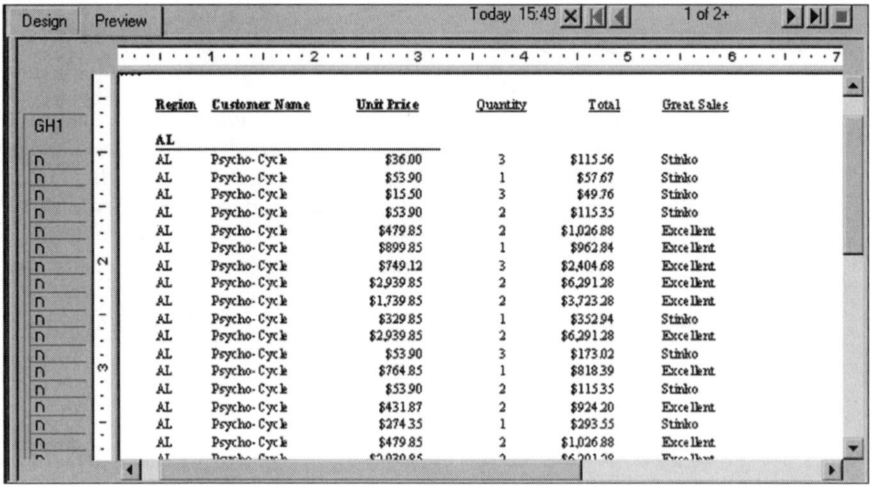

**Figure 7-23:**
A preview of
a report
after using a
Nested If
formula.

## Nested if-then-else formulas

Variations of the simple *if-then-else* formulas can get quite complicated. If you need to, you can create powerful multicondition formulas, known as *nested ifs*. A nested if-then-else formula can evaluate multiple conditions and then print a text string (as in the previous example) or whatever you designate.

The following nested formula looks at the country and the sales amount to determine a discount percentage:

```
if Country = USA
thenif Sales > 1000000
    then .25
    else .20
elseif Sales > 1000000
    then .15
    else .10
```

Try to work your way through what this formula shows. First of all, the formula checks to see which country the record deals with. If it's the USA, the formula continues to check the amount of that American sale. If the American sale is greater than 1 million, the formula sets the discount rate at 25 percent. If the American sale is not greater than 1 million, the formula sets the discount rate to 20 percent. However, if the country is *not* USA, the formula skips the test completely and assumes this is a foreign sale. The formula then checks the foreign sale to see if it is greater than 1 million. If it is, the discount rate gets set to 15 percent. Otherwise, it gets set to 10 percent.

# Adding a Summary without a Field

A new summary function in Crystal Reports Version 8 is the ability to add a summary field without the underlying field itself being in the report. In working with this new capability, one thing that seems to be required is the need to add a text field to identify the value generated by the summary operation. You can add a summary to the example Ch7 report used in this chapter by following these steps:

1. **In Preview mode, make certain that no object in the report is selected.**

2. **Choose Insert⇨Summary.**

   The Insert Summary dialog box appears, as shown in Figure 7-24.

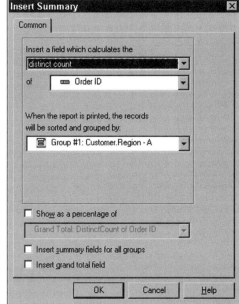

**Figure 7-24:**
The Insert Summary dialog box, with the Order ID field selected to be distinctly counted.

3. **Before you select the type of summary in the first drop-down list box, select the field you want in the second drop-down list box.**

   Crystal Reports responds by making available the allowable summing types. For this example, select Order ID, which is an Orders Detail field.

4. **In the drop-down list box above the field name, select Distinct Count as the calculation you want Crystal Reports to perform.**

**5. Click OK.**

Crystal Reports inserts the summary field where it thinks you want it. The total reflects the number of orders, by region. You can, of course, drag the summary field to wherever you want it, and I suggest you add a text object, as discussed in Chapter 10, describing the value. Figure 7-25 shows the summary field that's inserted.

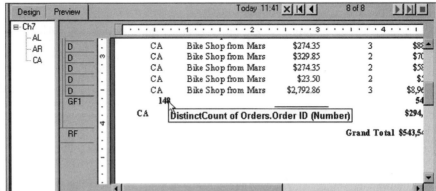

**Figure 7-25:** The Order ID Distinct Count summary field inserted for you.

# Record Selection Formulas

In this section, you see that the Select Expert helps you by building a formula that you can use to select the records for the report. Doing this is a lot easier than typing the formula yourself. One challenge of a real database is that it may include some data that's useless because it's only partially complete. In such a situation, you can modify your record selection formula to show you those records that are missing information. In the following situation, only the records that have a Quantity greater than zero are included.

To eliminate any records in which the quantity field is less than 1, follow these steps:

**1. Open the example Ch7 report and click the Select Expert button on the Standard toolbar.**

The Select Expert dialog box appears with a tab that contains the one condition of records from California, Alabama, and Arkansas only.

**2. Click either the New tab or the New button.**

The Choose Field dialog box opens.

3. **Double-click to select the Quantity field from the Report Fields list.**

   The Choose Field dialog box closes, and the Select Expert dialog box is again visible on-screen with the Orders Detail.Quantity tab displayed, as shown in Figure 7-26.

4. **In the drop-down list box, select the Is Greater Than condition.**

5. **In the second drop-down box that now appears to the right, type a zero (0).**

   By clicking the Show Formula button, you can view the formula created to extract only those records in California, Arkansas, and Alabama with a Quantity greater than 0.

6. **Click the Formula Editor button that appears.**

   You see the formula in the Record Selection Formula Editor dialog box.

   With the information you gain from this chapter, you can make further changes to this record-selection formula to create a criteria that the Select Expert couldn't do. That makes you smarter than the experts!

 7. **Click the Save and Close button on the toolbar.**

   The Formula Editor dialog box closes, and the Select Expert dialog box again appears on-screen.

8. **Click OK to exit the Select Expert and to complete the record selection process.**

   Crystal Reports asks whether you want to refresh or use saved data.

9. **Click the Saved Data button.**

   Any records with a zero quantity are eliminated.

**Figure 7-26:**
The Select Expert dialog box for selecting records with a quantity greater than zero.

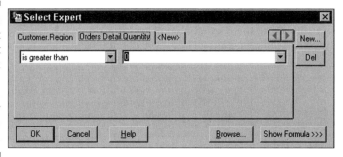

# Creating a Record Selection Formula

When you select a database and its table to be part of a report, you may want the entire set of records to be included in the report. But many times you don't, and Crystal Reports provides a way to select specific records for the report, as described in Chapter 4. Formulas that add precision to the selection process can be incorporated into it. As you create a report, you may want to add numeric ranges to capture records in certain sales volumes, transactions occurring in specific date ranges, or records that pertain to a certain area of the country. The simple selection criteria are handled easily via the Select Expert feature. But sometimes you need more advanced selections to create the report.

In the Ch7 example report, records are selected by using the Region field and CA, AR, and AL as the matches. But suppose that the records are entered into the underlying database in an inconsistent manner. Some records are entered with the region as *CA* and some with the region as *ca*. In Crystal Reports, record selection is dependent on the case sensitivity in the source database and must be precise. So any records that have *ca* in them when you indicate that you want records with *CA* are not included in a report. You can simulate this potential pitfall for yourself with the Ch7 report, by using Region as the selection field and replacing CA with ca in the Select Record dialog box.

To overcome this obstacle and make certain that all records are included in the selection, uppercase or not, you can use Boolean logic to create a Record Selection formula.

Use Select Expert as much as possible to get Crystal Reports to easily create your record selection formula. In Select Expert, you simply use the drop-down boxes to build record selection criteria. Behind the scenes, Crystal Reports creates a Boolean formula using what you have entered. Crystal Reports compares the Boolean formula against each record in the report, and when it returns True, the record is included. If it returns False, the record is not included in your report.

Keep this in mind when modifying the record selection formula. You need to ensure that you are creating a Boolean formula that returns True when you want to include the record in the report. To see how this works, assume that the Region field can be stored as ca, CA, Ca, or cA. You want to include all occurrences of ca in the report, regardless of which case they're in. To do this, convert the text in the Region field to uppercase and then search for an uppercase CA.

Use the Ch7 example to understand how to create a Boolean formula for record selection. (Keep in mind that you can simulate the following process with any appropriate database, preferably one that includes State as a field, and modify the steps accordingly.) Just follow these steps:

1. **Open the Ch7 report.**

2. **Click the Select Expert button on the Standard toolbar.**

   The Select Expert dialog box appears.

   In the example Ch7 report, the previous selection criteria, *Region equal to CA, AL, and AR* and *Quantity greater than 0,* are still in effect. If you're using your own database, the Choose Field dialog box opens first. Choose State as the field on which to make the selection (assuming that you have State as a field in your database). The Select Expert dialog box appears. Click the down arrow in the first box from the left and select the *equal to* setting. A second box opens to the right, and in that box enter the state from which you want records. Then follow the remaining steps.

3. **Click the Formula Editor button.**

   The Formula Editor dialog box opens.

   The underlying formula for record selection appears at the bottom of the dialog box, as shown in Figure 7-27.

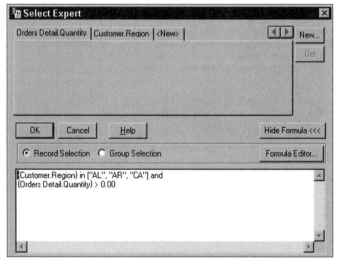

**Figure 7-27:** The Select Expert dialog box with the formula displayed.

4. **Place your cursor to the left of the {Customer.Region} field by clicking your mouse pointer in that location.**

   This is where you want to insert the Uppercase function.

5. **In the Functions window, under the String heading, double-click Uppercase ( ).**

   Headings listed in the Functions window designate what kind of function follows, which makes finding the function easier for you.

Crystal Reports inserts the function, but the close parenthesis (the one on the right) isn't enclosing the Customer.Region portion of the formula.

6. **Delete the close parenthesis from its current location and type it after Customer.Region and before the word** *in.*

 7. **Click the Save and Close button on the toolbar to close the Formula Editor dialog box.**

The completed formula appears in the Select Expert dialog box. The formula should look like this:

```
Uppercase ({Customer.Region}) in ["AL", "AR", "CA"] and

{Orders Detail.Quantity} > 0.00
```

8. **Click OK to close the Select Expert dialog box.**

To see the changes in the report, if any, click the Preview tab. Crystal Reports asks whether you want to use saved or refreshed data. Currently the saved records are only records that have CA, AL, and AR as regions, so click Refresh Data. Crystal Reports seeks out the database tables and finds any records that meet the new criteria. (See Chapter 4 for a full description of Saved versus Refreshed data.)

In this chapter, you only scratch the surface of what Crystal Reports can do with formulas. A complete listing of every function and operator is found in the *Seagate Crystal Reports User's Guide.*

 If you're trying to create a report from a database such as ACT!, you may encounter a problem when you try to access a field that in ACT! is supposed to be a currency or number field. To use Crystal Reports properly with ACT!, you need to have ACT! Version 3.08 or greater and updated registry files from Seagate Software. You can also get these from my Web site, www.howtosoftware.com.

# Trying More Formulas

Hopefully, this chapter gives you an idea of the range of formula possibilities that you can add to your reports. To exhaust them all would be an impossible feat. However, if you read this entire chapter, you'll have an idea about how to create your own formulas — and frankly, what's here only scratches the surface as to the number and types of formulas that you can create.

Seagate provides a bunch of tested formulas that fit most situations. These formulas are indexed and then explained in a step-by-step manner. Follow these steps to find out where this treasure trove is hiding:

1. **Choose Help⇨Seagate Crystal Reports Help.**

   The Seagate Crystal Reports Online Help dialog box opens.

2. **Click the Index tab.**

3. **Type the topic about which you want to see more information.**

   In this example, I typed Example Formulas.

4. **When you see the topic you want, double-click it to see the details.**

   Seventeen formulas are provided for you to look at and adapt to your particular needs.

   Figure 7-28 shows the Help window for Example Formulas (1).

I suggest that when you find a formula that's close to what you need, print the Help topic — it makes the information easier to follow. In addition, you can cut and paste the sample formula syntax from the Help window directly into the Formula Editor.

If all else fails, you can send an e-mail to the technical support folks at Seagate Software for an answer. Open the Help menu and select Seagate Software on the Web. From the submenu, select Online Support. Your Web browser cranks up and dials directly to the Seagate Software Web site.

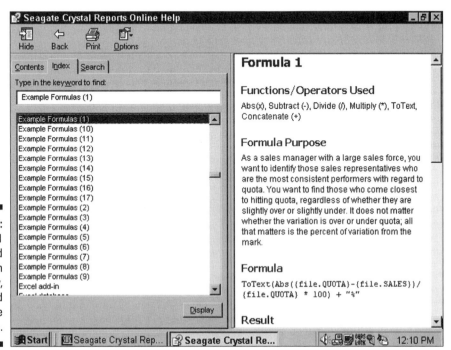

**Figure 7-28:**
The Formula 1 detailed explanation window, enlarged to the maximum.

# Chapter 8

# Using Conditional Formatting

*T*he idea behind *conditional formatting* is that objects (such as numbers of a certain value or page footers that indicate the end of the report) are displayed a certain way. So, depending on the data in a report, you can create formulas that determine a report's formatting. You can do the same for sections of a report. However, to better enhance your understanding of this chapter, you may first want to read Chapter 7 on formulas, if you haven't done so already.

## Absolute versus Conditional Formatting

After you format an object (whether a text object or a field of numbers), Crystal Reports displays that object and prints it per your formatting. (See Chapter 10 for more on formatting.) Formatting of this type is called *absolute* because it stays the same despite what numbers or values are being printed.

However, to add more sophistication to your report, you can have Crystal Reports evaluate the field and, based on the value, print the field in different formats. Formatting of this type is called *conditional.* A simple example is printing every negative number in red ink. Another example is having Crystal Reports look at a text string and effect a change for you, if that string matches a string that you designate. Yet another example is to have Crystal Reports add conditional formatting to your company invoices. For example, suppose you have customers who haven't paid their invoices for 90 days. Printing the amount owed in red makes identifying overdue invoices easier.

Be aware that conditional formatting overrides any fixed settings you create in the Format Editor.

In Chapter 3, the Highlighting Expert is used to provocatively display certain numbers. The Highlighting Expert is a faster and easier way to apply conditional formatting to a field but it is limited to only the font color, background color, and border of numeric fields. If you want to change any other format for a numeric field or any formatting of a string or date field, you must create the conditional formatting formula yourself.

# Using Attribute Properties

*Attribute properties* are identical in form to if-then-else formulas because several types of formatting can occur, depending on the result of the formula that you create. The Attribute property can print, for example, a number in red if the value is equal to or less than 1,000, in black if the value is greater than 100, or in blue if the value is greater than 500. See Chapter 7 on formulas for more information about this technique.

Crystal Reports tests each record and determines which format should be used, per your formula. A good start on finding out about conditional formatting is to print numbers in red if they are equal to or less than 100.

Figure 8-1 is a report that shows sales figures for a series of stores.

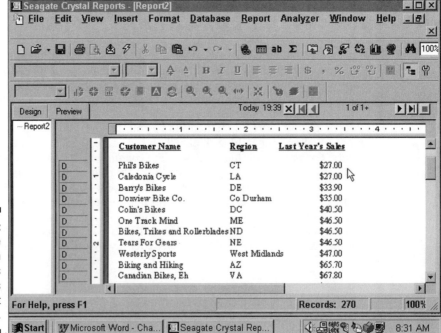

**Figure 8-1:**
A sample report with stores' sales records from last year.

This report includes several figures that are less than or equal to 100. Identifying these smaller numbers is much easier if they are more prominent in the report. Granted, you can easily identify small numbers if you simply sort the report by using the Last Year's Sales field in ascending order, as Figure 8-1 shows. But if you want any other type of grouping, the equal-to or less-than-100 values can get lost in the list.

To add conditional formatting to a report, follow these steps:

1. **Open a report in which you want to apply conditional formatting.**

   Because you may not have done the exercises in the previous chapters, I've created a report that simply shows the Customer Name, Region, and Last Year's Sales from the Xtreme Sample Data - Customer table to use in these examples.

2. **Right-click the field that you want to format.**

   You can pick any field on your report. The example used here changes the color of the number in the Last Year's Sales column to red if it is less than 100.

   A shortcut menu appears, as shown in Figure 8-2.

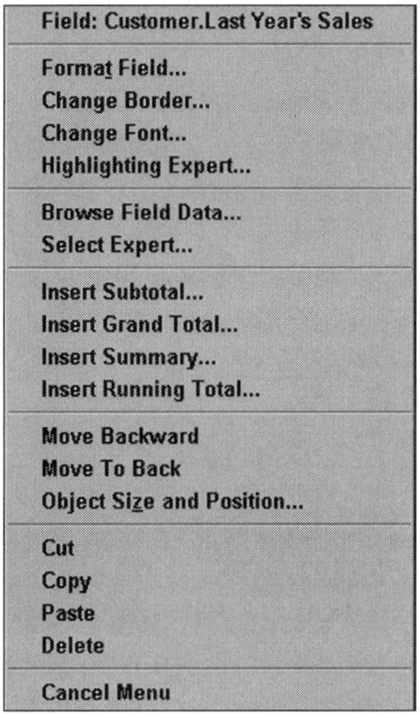

**Figure 8-2:**
The shortcut menu for a field.

| Field: Customer.Last Year's Sales |
| --- |
| Format Field... |
| Change Border... |
| Change Font... |
| Highlighting Expert... |
| Browse Field Data... |
| Select Expert... |
| Insert Subtotal... |
| Insert Grand Total... |
| Insert Summary... |
| Insert Running Total... |
| Move Backward |
| Move To Back |
| Object Size and Position... |
| Cut |
| Copy |
| Paste |
| Delete |
| Cancel Menu |

3. **Click Change Font.**

   The Format Editor dialog box appears, as shown in Figure 8-3.

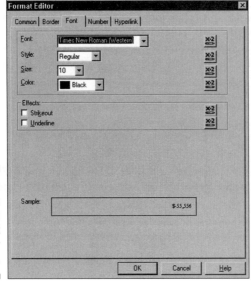

**Figure 8-3:**
The Font tab
displayed in
the Format
Editor
dialog box.

**4. Click the Formula button to the right of the Color drop-down list box.**

Wherever you see the Formula button, you have the opportunity to add conditions to that particular portion of the report.

The Format Formula Editor dialog box appears, as shown in Figure 8-4. This dialog box has four main components:

- **Report Fields:** Fields in the report, such as Groups, Formulas, and Report Source database tables

- **Functions:** Prebuilt procedures that perform specific calculations

- **Operators:** Actions and operations, such as Arithmetic

- **Formula text window:** The place where the actual formula is created

Because the font-color format has more than two choices, you need to use an if-then-else formula to say which color to use under what condition.

**5. Scroll through the Operators list to find the If x Then y Else z operator under the Control Structures heading and double-click it. (To see the entire list, click the plus sign in front of Control Structures.)**

The If-Then-Else operator is inserted into the Formula text box.

Note that the blinking insertion point is located inside the current formula, between if and then, right where it should be.

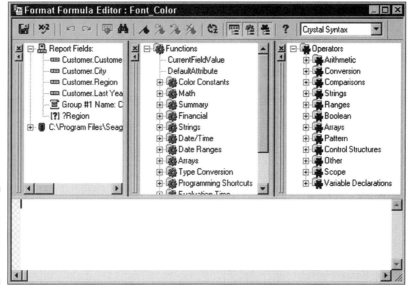

**Figure 8-4:**
The Format
Formula
Editor
dialog box.

6. **Double-click the field to which you want to apply conditional formatting.**

   The formula name is inserted into the formula text window. The formula for this example looks like this:

   ```
   if {Customer.Last Year's Sales} then else
   ```

   The insertion point moves to the end of the field name, outside the bracket. The next step is to indicate the condition that you want Crystal Reports to test. In this case, you want to format values that are less than or equal to 100 in a different color. So you need to insert the less than (<) and equal (=) signs.

7. **Scroll through the Operators list to find the Less or Equal (x < = y) operator under the Comparisons heading and double-click it.**

   The < = appears in the formula.

8. **Type** 100.

9. **Move the insertion point so that it comes after the word Then and type** Red.

   Other color choices are in the Functions window under the Color Constants heading. You can also double-click these to insert them in the formula text.

10. **Move the insertion point so that it comes after the word Else and type** Black.

    The completed example formula appears as follows:

    ```
    if {Customer.Last Year's Sales} < = 100 then Red else Black
    ```

 11. **Click the Save and Close button.**

    If the formula contains any errors, Crystal Reports doesn't accept it and displays a dialog box with a warning and the most likely cause of the error.

 Notice that the Formula button for any option that has a conditional format has the X+2 colored red and the pencil pointing up.

Because this is an exercise that uses color to define the output, I can't show you how it looks in this black-and-white book. You can see the effect of the red color after you enter the formula in your report, provided it contains numbers less than or equal to 100. If you have a color printer, you can share this wonderful format with your colleagues.

## *Another conditional format*

You may want a page number on every page except the first. To accomplish this task, you must add a conditional format after inserting the Page Number field into the Page Footer section, as follows:

1. **Open a report that when printed takes more than one page.**

2. **In the Design window, choose Insert⇨Special Fields.**

    The Field Explorer dialog box appears.

 3. **Select the special field that you want to insert and click the Insert to Report button.**

    In this case, the choice is Page Number. When you make the selection, the pointer changes to a grayed box, allowing you to insert the Page Number field anywhere in the report.

4. **Move the mouse pointer to the Page Footer section of the report.**

    Be careful that you position the field in the Page Footer section — it appears beneath the Report Footer, which can be confusing.

5. **Click the mouse button to insert the field.**

    Figure 8-5 shows the Page Number field correctly inserted into the Page Footer section.

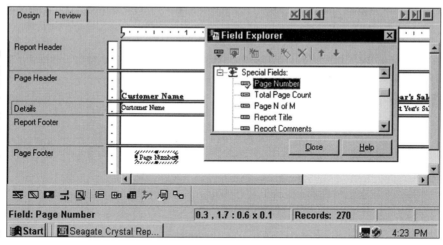

**Figure 8-5:**
The Field
Explorer
dialog box
with the
Page
Number
field
inserted in
the Page
Footer.

6. **Right-click the inserted field and choose Format Field.**

   The Format Editor dialog box appears with the Number tab showing.

7. **Click the Common tab.**

8. **Click the Formula button to the right of the Suppress option.**

   The Format Formula Editor dialog box appears.

9. **Scroll through the Function list to find the Print State heading, click the plus sign (+) to see the functions, and then double-click the PageNumber function.**

   Page Number appears in the Formula text box.

10. **After the function, type** = 1.

    The completed PageNumber formula appears in the Formula Text box as follows:

    ```
    PageNumber = 1
    ```

11. **Click the Save and Close button.**

12. **Click OK.**

This formula tells Crystal Reports to Suppress the Page Number only if the number is equal to one, which is the first page of the report. Because you have only two choices, Suppress or Don't Suppress, you don't have to build an if-then-else condition. You simply have to state the condition under which the page number is to be suppressed.

Looking at the Design window, you should see no discernible changes. The only way to see whether the formula works is to select the Preview tab and look at the bottom of the first page of the report (to see that the page number is not there) and then go to the next page (to see that the page number is there).

More information on this kind of formatting is covered in Chapter 10.

## Deleting a conditional format

The only way to delete a conditional format — unless you want to erase the field or object also — is to erase the text in the Formula Text box in the Format Formula Editor dialog box. The following steps show you how to delete a conditional format placed in any field:

1. **Right-click the field to which you have applied a conditional format.**

   A shortcut menu appears.

2. **Click Format Field.**

   The Format Editor dialog box appears.

3. **Click the tab that contains the conditional format.**

   For example, if you have conditionally formatted the font, click the Font tab.

 4. **Click the Formula button beside the format option you want to delete.**

   Notice that the Formula button for any option that has a conditional format has the X+2 colored red and the pencil pointing up.

   The Format Formula Editor dialog box appears.

5. **Click and drag the mouse across the formula you want to delete until it is completely highlighted.**

6. **Press the Delete key or right-click and choose Cut.**

 7. **Click the Save and Close button.**

Other conditional formats must be removed by selecting the object that's affected and opening the Format Editor dialog box to select the attribute to which you have applied a conditional format. Open the Format Formula Editor dialog box, delete the format, and then click the Save and Close button.

Conditional formatting is a tool that can be exploited throughout a report. Wherever you see the Formula button, you can tweak your report to get it just right. And if you're an obsessive-compulsive when it comes to perfecting reports, keep your Valium handy.

# Chapter 9

# Creating a Subreport

· · · · · · · · · · · · · · · · · · · · · · · · · · · · · · · · · · · · · · · · · · · · · · · · · · ·

· · · · · · · · · · · · · · · · · · · · · · · · · · · · · · · · · · · · · · · · · · · · · · · · · · ·

A subreport enables you to insert one report into another report. Suppose that you create two separate reports and for some reason you want to include one of the reports in the other report to illustrate something. You can use a subreport to do so. However, as with many features of Crystal Reports, subreports can be complicated — so pay attention!

Terminology helps here: The *container report* is the report into which you insert another report. The *subreport* is the report you insert into the container report. Although a subreport has many of the same characteristics as a regular report, a few subtle differences exist. First, a subreport is inserted as an object into a container report. Second, a subreport can be placed in any section of a container report. The entire subreport prints in the section in which you place it, not as a separate report. Third, a subreport can't be placed into a subreport. No double-dipping on subreports, folks! This chapter discusses when to add a subreport, how to add one, and how to view a linked subreport.

# Deciding When to Add a Subreport

At what point are you likely to want to add a subreport? Well, you can add a subreport any time you want to combine two unrelated reports into a single report. You can also add a subreport to connect data that can't be linked in another manner. You can add a subreport when you want to look at the same data two different ways in the same report.

# Creating a Scenario

To help demonstrate when you may want to use a subreport, I create a scenario in this section. Say that you're the head of marketing for Xtreme Mountain Bike, Inc. You have a fleet of sales representatives, but the vice president doesn't know all of them because they're dispersed around the globe. You plan to present a short report to the vice president using the quarterly sales report that you previously created. This report is called Employee Sales and is installed in the C:\Program Files\Seagate Software\Crystal Reports\ Samples\Reports\General Business folder. Note that you can use any of your own reports with appropriate substitutions to follow this example.

You intend to jog the memory of the vice president by adding each salesperson's employee profile to the report. The employee profile report is included with Crystal Reports, so you can conveniently add just that small bit of information to the quarterly sales report. You can find the employee profile report under Employee Profile in the C:\Program Files\Seagate Software\Crystal Reports\Samples\Reports\General Business folder.

Before you get started, notice that the Employee Sales report asks you a question every time you run it. If you say that you're Anne Dodsworth or Michael Suyama, for example, and your sales were good, then you may get a special message. However, who you say you are when asked to enter a login name isn't important to this exercise.

With Crystal Reports open, now open the report that you're going to use for the container report in this example. You do so by following these steps.

1. **Click the Open button on the Standard toolbar.**

   The Open dialog box appears.

2. **Navigate to the General Business folder, located at C:\Program Files\Seagate Software\Crystal Reports\Samples\Reports, and then double-click the folder.**

3. **Select the Employee Sales report and then click the Open button.**

   The employee sales report opens. However, you need to make one small format change first.

4. **Click the Section Expert button on the Standard toolbar.**

   The Section Expert dialog box appears.

5. **Select the Group Header #2: Employee.Last Name - A field from the Sections box and then click the Underlay Following Sections check box on the Common tab to remove the check mark.**

6. **Click OK to exit the Section Expert dialog box.**

7. **Click the Refresh button on the Standard toolbar.**

   The Refresh Report Data dialog box appears.

8. **Select the Prompt for New Parameter Values radio button.**

9. **Click OK.**

   The Enter Parameter Values dialog box appears, as shown in Figure 9-1.

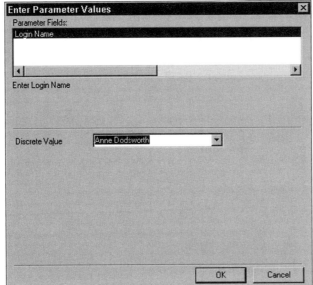

**Figure 9-1:**
The Enter
Parameter
Values
dialog box.

10. **In the Discrete Value drop-down list box, select the name of the sales-person you're masquerading as.**

    In this case, select the report for Anne Dodsworth.

11. **Click OK.**

    The preview of the Employee Sales report prints to the screen.

# Adding the Subreport

If you follow the instructions in the preceding section, you should have Employee Sales on-screen. Because the location of the subreport is easier to control if you're in the Design window, click the Design tab and scroll down so that you can see the Group Header #2: Employee Last Name - A field.

1. **Make the Group Header #2 section larger by dragging the boundary line down until the section is about ¾ inch high.**

**2. Choose Insert⇨Subreport from the menu bar.**

The Insert Subreport dialog box opens, displaying two tabs. You're in the Subreport tab, which has two options. You can either create a report on-the-fly by selecting the Create a Subreport radio button, or you can open a report that's already created by selecting the Choose a Report radio button. You want to use a report that's already created, so . . .

**3. Select the Choose a Report radio button.**

The Browse option is activated.

**4. Click Browse and then select the Employee Profile report in the General Business folder.**

**5. Click Open.**

The path to the Employee Profile report displays in the Report File Name text box. Figure 9-2 shows how the Subreport tab in the Insert Subreport dialog box looks at this point.

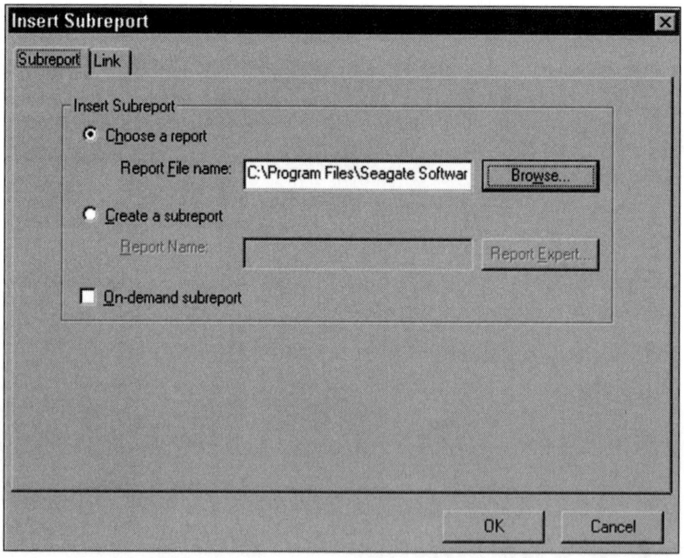

**Figure 9-2:**
The Subreport tab of the Insert Subreport dialog box.

**6. Select the Link tab in the Insert Subreport dialog box.**

In this example, you want to display with the report only the employee profile of Ms. Dodsworth, not the profile of every employee. Therefore, you have to link these two reports, which means that you need to find some common field between the two reports to find a perfect match. The list of available fields in the *container report* is on the left of the dialog box.

7. **Highlight the name of the field that you're going to use to connect the two reports and then click the right-facing arrow.**

   In this example, highlight Employee.LastName and click the arrow button.

   Employee.LastName moves to the right box in the Insert Subreport dialog box. You want to select only the data in the subreport that matches the data you enter on the parameter field (in this example, Last Name) when you view the employee sales quarterly report.

8. **Click OK.**

   A gray box appears with your mouse pointer. You're ready to place the subreport in your container report.

9. **Click to place the subreport on the report.**

   In this example, place the subreport in the GroupHeader #2 section, by moving the mouse pointer to the lower part of the Group Header #2 section and clicking one time. A rectangle appears in the Group Header #2 section, as shown in Figure 9-3.

Notice that three tabs now appear at the top of the report window. The usual tabs (Design and Preview) appear, as well as a new tab, Employee Profile.rpt. This tab is the Design tab for the Employee Profile subreport. A copy of that report now exists in the container report. Any changes made here will only change the inserted subreport, NOT the original report.

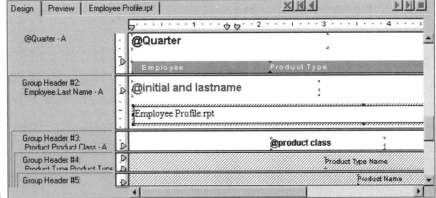

**Figure 9-3:** The subreport rectangle inserted in the Group Header #2 section.

Frequently, the data in a subreport supplements the data in the container report. You may, for example, have customer data in a container report and then use subreports to show the orders for each customer. In such cases, you need to coordinate the data in the container report with the data in the subreport by creating a link between the two reports so that the orders in each subreport match up with the correct customer.

# Viewing the Linked Subreport

After you place the subreport on the Design tab, you can preview the subreport in the container report by following these steps:

1. **Click the Print Preview button on the Standard toolbar.**

   The Enter Parameter Values dialog box appears. (If this dialog box does not appear, click the Refresh button on the Standard toolbar.)

   You can choose to be anybody on Xtreme's employee list.

2. **Click OK.**

   You see the preview of the subreport in the container report, as shown in Figure 9-4.

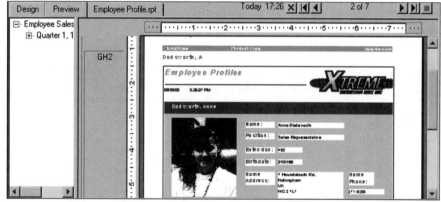

**Figure 9-4:**
The Subreport in the container report.

As you can see, the employee profile appears just below an employee's name and before that employee's individual sales numbers.

# Options for Subreports

As with most features in Crystal Reports, a myriad of subreport options are available for your use. In previous sections of this chapter, you follow one scenario for adding a subreport to a container report. In the foregoing example, the subreport is linked to the report. However, you can add a subreport that isn't linked. An unlinked subreport doesn't necessarily have any field that's associated with any field in the container report. Say, for example, you want to add a small report that shows the temperature in your top bicycle markets around the world. This data may come from a weather-office database and have no association with the data in your database, but you know that bike sales are dependent on the weather and that this information can be useful on a sales report.

 You can also choose to create a subreport at the time you insert it. To do so, you need to choose this option from the Insert Subreport dialog box. You must type a Report Name in the box and then click the Report Expert button to start creating the subreport.

You can also add more than one subreport to a container report. You simply open the container report and then repeat the steps for inserting a subreport for each subreport that you want in the container report. You can place sub-reports in separate sections in the report or side-by-side in one section.

# Part IV
# Putting On Some Finishing Touches

The 5th Wave          By Rich Tennant

"It's a ten step word processing program. It comes with a spell-checker, grammar-checker, cliché-checker, whine-checker, passive/aggressive-checker, politically correct-checker, hissy-fit-checker, pretentious pontificating-checker, boring anecdote-checker and a Freudian reference-checker."

# In this part . . .

Many great artists are not recognized as such in their lifetimes. In this part, you cannot be ignored. Great honors await those who read this part, for your reports will demonstrate the talents known only to a gifted few — at least until this book arrived. Polish the chrome, make a slight adjustment of the carburetor, and your report is ready for the Indy 500. As they say, 10 percent of the job takes 90 percent of the time. Well, by using the information in this part, you can take a long lunch and head home early — leaving everyone convinced you slaved for hours over your report. Ha! If only they knew your secret!

# Chapter 10

# Formatting Sections of a Report

● ● ● ● ● ● ● ● ● ● ● ● ● ● ● ● ● ● ● ● ● ● ● ● ● ● ● ● ● ● ● ● ● ● ● ● ● ● ● ● ● ● ● ● ● ● ●

*In This Chapter*

▶ Resizing a section

▶ Formatting sections with the Section Expert

● ● ● ● ● ● ● ● ● ● ● ● ● ● ● ● ● ● ● ● ● ● ● ● ● ● ● ● ● ● ● ● ● ● ● ● ● ● ● ● ● ● ● ● ● ● ●

*T*he way a report looks when printed is highly dependent on the format of the individual sections in a report. This chapter deals with making your report appear just right. (See Chapter 11 to find out how you can add real pizzazz to a report by combining the section formatting with other objects.)

In this chapter, I show you the techniques for changing the layout of sections of a report. These techniques make reading and highlighting certain aspects of a report much easier.

## Changing the Size of a Section

In Crystal Reports, each report you create has a minimum of five sections, which are the Report Header, Page Header, Details, Report Footer, and Page Footer. Crystal Reports allocates space for each of these sections. You can modify the space for all sections; however, judging what adjustments to the different sections may be necessary is difficult until you print a report. The Preview tab gives you an excellent representation of what the printed report will look like, but with the huge number of printers — each with its own quirks — the best way to test your formatting is to actually make a hard copy of your report.

The Design tab is the place to be if you want to make changes to the size of a section. On the left side of the window, in the gray area, each of the sections is labeled. Between the sections in the Report Layout area (the white area) are thick horizontal lines that represent the boundaries between the sections. These lines are the key to eyeballing adjustments because you can move your pointer to a line, hold down the left mouse button, and drag the line to adjust the height of the section. A simple example follows.

To change the height of a section, follow these steps:

1. **In any report, click the Design tab.**

   A typical report appears, as shown in Figure 10-1.

2. **Move the mouse over the boundary line that divides the sections and hold down the left mouse button. Keep away from the ruler bar on the left side!**

   When you do, the mouse pointer changes to a double-horizontal line with up-and-down pointing arrows. You are resizing the section above the mouse pointer.

   I recommend you stay to the right when doing this because other functions are performed by almost the same action if you're close to the ruler bar on the left.

3. **Drag the line up or down.**

   The entire line moves with your pointer.

4. **Release the mouse button where you want the line to be redrawn.**

   In Figure 10-2, the Details line is dragged down to increase the size of each of the Details sections.

To see what effect the changing of the Details section has (or any other change you make), click the Preview tab. The report looks magically double-spaced.

Be aware that the size of a section in the Design tab is the size of that section in the Preview tab, as well as when the report is printed. You made the Details section larger so that every record on the report takes up about half an inch. Whether fields exist in that space doesn't matter.

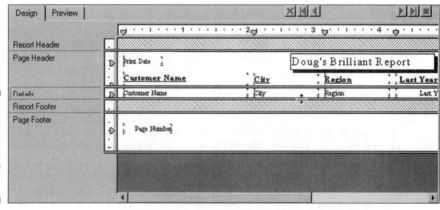

**Figure 10-1:**
A typical
report from
the Design
point of
view.

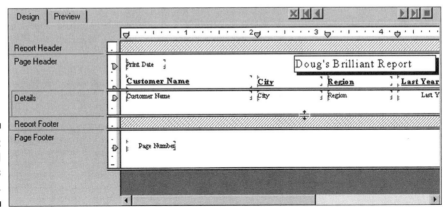

**Figure 10-2:**
The resized
Details
section.

You can also squeeze the Page Footer to a smaller size, as shown in Figure 10-3. Drag the Page Footer boundary line up as far as it will go. Notice that as soon as the boundary line touches a guideline or a field in the section, the line won't go any farther. Crystal Reports doesn't allow the boundary line to push around guidelines or fields. The field position RULES! If you want to make the section smaller, you must move the guidelines and fields first and then move up the boundary line.

Click the Preview tab to see the results, as shown in Figure 10-4. Then click near the bottom of the page to make the outline of the Page Footer appear.

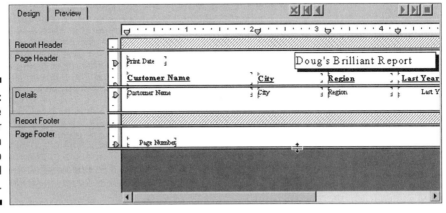

**Figure 10-3:**
The Page
Footer
section
squeezed to
a small
space.

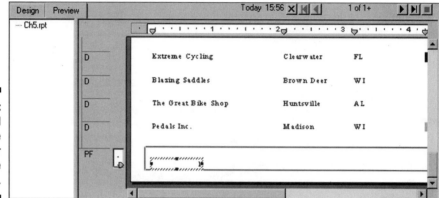

Design   Preview

**Figure 10-4:**
The reduced
size of the
Page Footer
on the
Preview tab.

# Automatically sizing a section

Crystal Reports includes the capability to automatically size a section for you. After all, computer software is supposed to make your job easier. Suppose you insert a large object, such as a graph or a picture, into a section of a report and then resize it to make it smaller. The section in which it's inserted stays at the expanded size, and you have to shrink it to eliminate any wasted white space in the printed report.

To automatically size a section, just follow these steps:

1. **Open any report in which you want to resize a section.**

2. **Insert a large object in a section and manually resize it to make it smaller.**

   In this example, I insert a logo into the Page Footer section.

3. **Right-click the section name in the left-margin space corresponding to the section you want to modify.**

   A menu appears, as shown in Figure 10-5.

4. **Choose Fit Section.**

   Figure 10-6 shows the line at the bottom of the page drawn up against the Xtreme Mountain Bike, Inc., logo object to eliminate any unneeded space in the printed report.

| Page Footer |
|---|
| Suppress (No Drill-Down) |
| Format Section... |
| Insert Line |
| Delete Last Line |
| Arrange Lines |
| Fit Section |
| Insert Section Below |
| Cancel Menu |

**Figure 10-5:**
The Page
Footer
shortcut
menu.

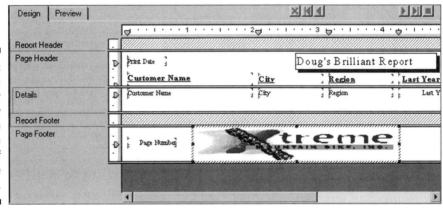

**Figure 10-6:**
The Page
Footer
automatically
resized to
make the
best use of
the available
space.

# Looking at the shortcut menu

If you follow the steps in "Automatically sizing a section" in the preceding part of this chapter, you right-click in the left margin of the section you want to adjust. When you do so, that section's shortcut menu appears and lists, among other things, the Fit Section option, which automatically shrinks up the size of a section to the lowest object in the section. However, you also need to know about several other options in that menu (refer to Figure 10-5).

If you're ever in doubt about what you can do to or on a particular object in Crystal Reports, simply right-click the object. A shortcut menu pops up, showing a concise list of what you're able to do. The main function of a short-cut menu is to provide a quick list of relevant actions that are available for the object(s) currently selected. On the shortcut menu, you see items, such as the following:

✔ **Name:** Appears at the top of the shortcut menu, naming the section with which the menu is associated. In Figure 10-5, Page Footer is the name at the top of the menu.

✔ **Hide (Drill-Down OK) and Suppress (No Drill Down):** Makes the object invisible on the report. If you choose Hide, the object can be made visible by the person viewing the report by using Crystal's drill-down capability. A *drill-down* is simply a means to hide and then display underlying information, as required, on a report. For example, if your report is grouped by Region and you hide the Details section, you get a summary report showing just the Region Header and Footer. You can see the Record details for a particular region by double-clicking the Group Name on the Preview tab. That way, rather than seeing all the detailed information for the region, you can hide the details and only see the summary information. Crystal Reports adds a tab at the top of the Report window to indicate the selected group — Alabama (AL) in this case, as shown in Figure 10-7. You can also drill-down on a graph, as described in Chapter 6.

By suppressing a section, as shown in Figure 10-8, the drill-down capability is not allowed. For example, if you're doing a report on salaries, you may use this capability. You can create a summary report that shows the salary cost by department, but the viewer of the report won't be able to drill-down and see the underlying salaries of each person in the department — which preserves confidentiality.

✔ **Format Section:** Takes you to the Section Expert in which you can see and change all the format options for all the sections on the report.

✔ **Insert Line:** Works in conjunction with two other options — Delete Last Line and Arrange Lines — and inserts a horizontal guideline into the section. If enough space for another row of text isn't available, Crystal Reports increases the size of the section.

✔ **Delete Last Line:** Removes the lowest guideline in the section unless fields are connected to it. This option also shrinks the section by deleting any white space in the section up to the guideline.

**Figure 10-7:**
The added
drill-down
tab appears
beside the
Preview tab.

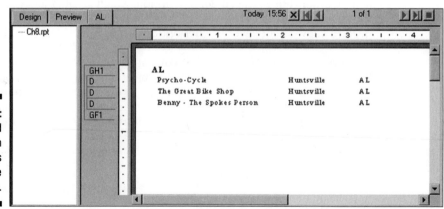

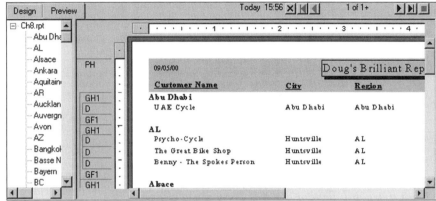

**Figure 10-8:**
The Report
header
suppressed
in Preview.

- **Arrange Lines:** Spaces the guidelines apart and adds any guidelines that are needed to fill up the rest of the section. The distance between the guidelines is the default point size that you've set for your fields. Figure 10-9 shows a series of guidelines correctly spaced to accept text 10 points high. To see the details (as shown in Figure 10-9), choose File⇨Options from the menu bar, click the Layout tab, and select the Show Guidelines in Design box.

- **Fit Section:** Removes any white space at the end of a section.

- **Insert Section Below:** Inserts a *subsection* under the section in which you right-clicked to bring up the shortcut menu. You use a subsection when you want to format a part of the section differently than the rest of the section. You may never need to use this concept in Crystal Reports, but if you do, at least you know how.

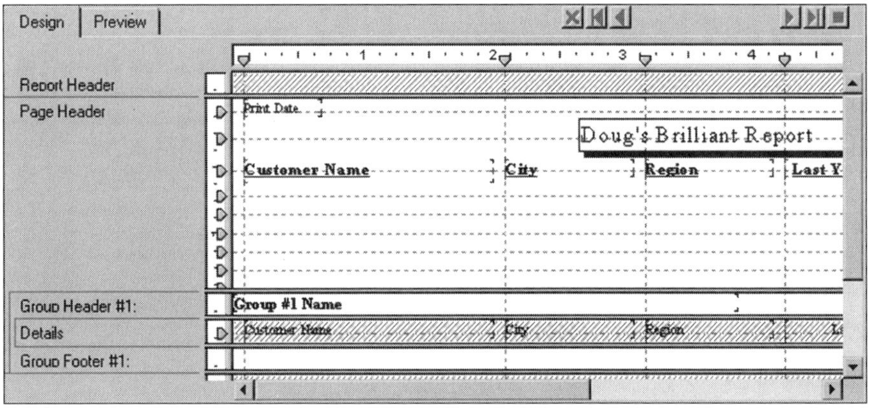

**Figure 10-9:**
A series of
horizontal
guidelines in
the Page
Header
section of
the report
design.

Suppose that you want to print each record in the Detail section of the report with more space between the records, making the record details easier to read. You can use the Insert Line option on the shortcut menu to do so. Just follow these steps:

1. **Right-click the left margin of the Details section of any report.**

   A shortcut menu appears.

2. **Click the Insert Line option as many times as you want.**

   The Details section looks something like the one shown in Figure 10-10.

Of course, you can add the space simply by dragging the line between the two sections, but the preceding method is more exact. Figure 10-11 shows the results (on the Preview tab) of adding lines to the Details section, leaving more room between each record.

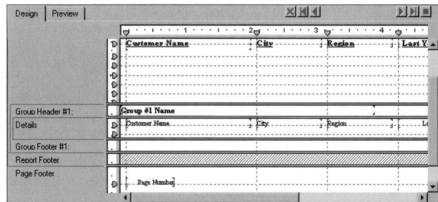

**Figure 10-10:** Guidelines added to the Details section.

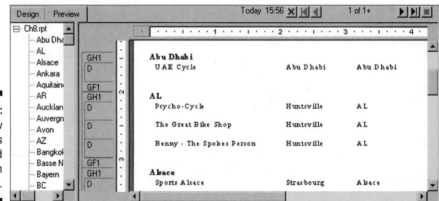

**Figure 10-11:** A preview with spaces added between records.

# Formatting Sections with the Section Expert

Because so many options exist for formatting sections, Crystal Reports includes a handy Section Expert to show you the way. You can open the Section Expert by using any of the following methods:

- ✔ Right-click any section name and choose Format Section from the short-cut menu that appears.

- ✔ Click the Section Expert button on the Standard toolbar.

- ✔ Choose Format⇨Section from the menu bar.

Figure 10-12 shows the Section Expert dialog box.

This dialog box is a busy one! On the left side is a listing of all the sections in your report. The name of the section where your mouse pointer was located when you opened the dialog box is automatically highlighted. At the bottom of the Sections list is a horizontal scroll bar that enables you to move left and right to read the entire section name, if necessary. The top of the dialog box contains the following buttons:

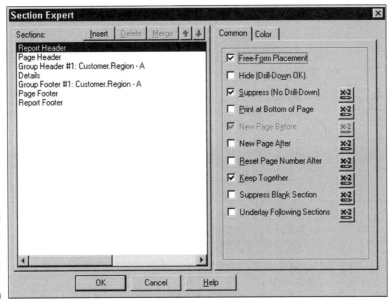

**Figure 10-12:**
The Section
Expert
dialog box.

✔ **Insert:** Inserts subsections into a report. For example, in Crystal Reports you can have several Page Footer sections, enabling you to print different page footers on certain pages of a report. These added sections can be formatted so that they're conditional — the same as the standard section — and will print based on a formula you enter in this dialog box (more about that later in this chapter). In Figure 10-13, a subdetail section has been added by clicking Details in the Sections listing and then clicking the Insert button. The original Details section becomes Details a, while the new subsection becomes Details b. When you click OK to close the dialog box, the new section appears in the report, as shown in Figure 10-14.

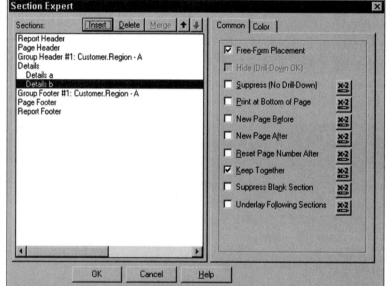

**Figure 10-13:**
The Section
Expert with
a new
Details
section
inserted.

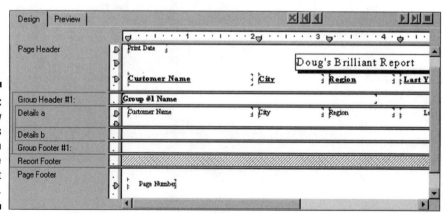

**Figure 10-14:**
The new
Details
section
added to the
report
design.

✔ **Delete:** Deletes any subsections that have been inserted into your report.

  *Note:* The Delete button is only active when a subsection is selected in the Sections list. This option deletes subsections only; it does not delete entire Group sections from the report.

✔ **Promote or Demote (up or down arrows):** Promotes or demotes sections that you previously added. By clicking a subsection, you can move it up or down in the report layout. You're unlikely ever to use this feature unless you become the Crystal Reports maven for your company and need to keep a few tricks up your sleeve to justify your bonus. Still, it never hurts to know what these features do.

✔ **Merge:** Use this command when you have multiple sections in an area and you want two of the sections combined into a single section. Click the section in which you want to merge the section that follows and then click the Merge button.

## *Using the Common tab*

On the right side of the Section Expert dialog box is the Common tab, which deals with options that are generalized to most sections. If you need to set something that's related to labels or colors, then you use the other tabs. The Common tab basically combines all the options that don't fit the other tabs, making it a catchall tab.

The list of formatting options on the Common tab corresponds to your selection under Sections on the left side of the dialog box. The options follow:

### *Free-Form Placement*

With Free-Form Placement, Crystal Reports lets you place objects anywhere in your report. Most of the time, you want this option turned on. Turning off Free-Form Placement causes Crystal Reports to insert guidelines at your default font-size spacing and forces the fields you add onto those guidelines. This harkens back to older versions of Crystal Reports that forced you to put fields on lines instead of anywhere you wanted.

### *Hide (Drill-Down Okay)*

This option is designed to stop the section from printing but not to stop drilling down. You can still double-click a summary field and get a drill-down tab in Preview. It's the same option you saw in the shortcut menu for each section.

### Suppress (No Drill-Down)

This option stops the section from being printed and stops a summary field from being drilled down. You can make this option conditional (notice the Formula button to the right). If you do, then in some cases the section is visible on the report and in others it is suppressed.

### Print at Bottom of Page

You can use this option to print sections as far down a page as possible. The genesis for this alternative is the good old invoice. Obviously, you want the total of an invoice to print at the very bottom of the page, leaving the rest of the page for the invoice details. You can make this option conditional.

### New Page Before

If you want to begin a new page before the section starts printing, click this option. You may want to use this feature after you insert groups into a report (listings by state, for example) to cause each group to print on a separate page. You can make this option conditional.

### New Page After

Select this option if you want a new page to start after the section is printed. The ideal use of this option is for a report's cover page. You can put all the information you need in the Report Header section and then force a new page to print after the header, ensuring that only the information you want is on the cover page. You can make this option conditional.

### Reset Page Number After

If you're using page numbering in your report — and you should be — you can adjust the counting of the pages by turning on this option. A good place to turn this on is in the Group Footer of a report that prints many pages per group of records. In a 50-page report that has 10 groups of records, every time a new group starts to print, the page number is reset to Page 1. Again, you can switch this option off conditionally.

### Keep Together

This option prevents Crystal Reports from printing any section across more than one page. If a full section with multiple lines doesn't fit at the bottom of a page, none of that section prints on that page — the entire section appears on the next page.

Say, for example, that a page can show 64 lines. Each detail record is 3 lines long, so 21 full records (3 x 21 = 63) can print on the first page. Although part of the last record (line 64) would otherwise print without its counterparts, Crystal Reports tells the section to stay together. That way, instead of the first line of record 22 printing on the first page, all 3 lines print at the top of the second page. This feature avoids having records split across pages, which is known as *widow/orphan protection*.

### Suppress Blank Section

If a section contains database fields that are sometimes empty, this option prevents Crystal Reports from printing white space. Have you ever created mailing labels from a database in which some addresses have a suite number and others do not? The labels without the suite numbers have a gap when they're printed. If you put the suite number in its own subsection and turn this option on, the records without suite numbers won't have the extra line where the blank field is. You can make this option conditional.

### Underlay Following Sections

This option allows the section in which it's turned on to be printed underneath the sections that follow. You can put a watermark graphic into a Page Header section that has the Underlay Following Sections turned on, and all the Details and Group Header and Footer sections that follow will print on top of the graphic. Another use is to allow a graph that's placed in a Group Header section to print beside the data in the Details section, rather than first printing the graph and then the data.

### Format with Multiple Columns

To use this option (which is only available in the Details section), you must highlight the Details section in the Section Expert dialog box. You use this option when you want the report to print in a multicolumn format. Rather than having the data print straight down the page, you can set up multiple columns and have the data flow from column to column. You can also have your data print across and then down the page, printing one record in each column, then printing a second record in the next column, then a third, and so on.

Select this option, and a new tab called Layout appears at the top right of the dialog box, as shown in Figure 10-15. This tab is where you specify the Width and Height of the Detail Size, the Gap required between the Details, the Printing Direction of the records, and whether you want the Group Headers and Footers to be included in the columns or not. You're most likely to use this option for name- and address-type reports (such as mailing labels).

## Using the Color tab

After formatting each of the sections with the settings previously mentioned, you can add color to the sections as an absolute format or as a conditional format. If you skipped earlier chapters in this book and need to figure out how to use conditional formatting, your best bet is to read Chapter 7 on formulas and Chapter 8 on conditional formatting. You don't have to be an expert on either one, but these chapters give you some ideas about how to construct formulas for this purpose.

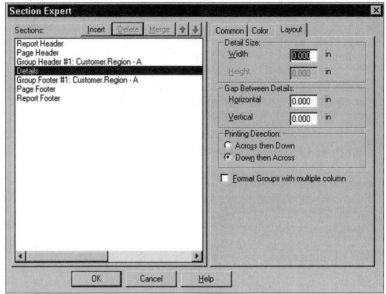

**Figure 10-15:**
The Layout
tab in the
Section
Expert
dialog box.

In Figure 10-16, the Section Expert dialog box appears with the Color tab displayed. The colors work in conjunction with whatever section you highlight. In other words, to set the background color for the Page Header, select Page Header in the Sections list and then click the Color tab.

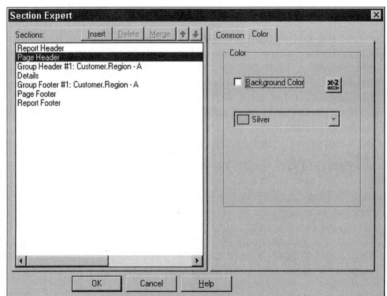

**Figure 10-16:**
The Section
Expert
dialog box
with the
Color tab
selected.

To add an absolute color to any section, follow these steps:

1. **Choose Format⇨Section from the menu bar (or click the Section Expert button on the Standard toolbar).**

   The Section Expert dialog box appears.

2. **In the Sections listing, click the section you want to format with a background color.**

3. **Click the Color tab.**

4. **Click to put a check mark in the Background Color box.**

5. **Click the pull-down arrow to see the color options and then select the color you want.**

6. **Click OK.**

In Figure 10-17, the Page Header section is colored silver.

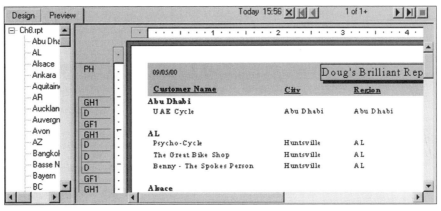

**Figure 10-17:**
The Page Header section is a darker color because silver is applied in the background.

## A conditional format formula

Suppose that you want to color every other record in the Details section, making the report easier to read. Here's how to create the formula to do so:

1. **Open the report that you want to format.**

2. **Choose Format⇨Section from the menu bar.**

   The Section Expert dialog box appears.

3. **Click Details.**

4. **Click the Color tab.**

5. **Click to put a check mark in the Background Color box.**

6. **Click the Formula button.**

When you click this button, the Format Formula Editor dialog box appears, as shown in Figure 10-18. I could go into all the details about entering a formula, but I won't. See Chapter 7 for more information.

Type the formula exactly as follows:

```
if Remainder (RecordNumber,2) <> 0 then Red else White
```

How does this formula work, you ask? The remainder (RecordNumber,2) takes the record number and divides it by two. If a remainder other than zero is present, then according to the formula the row prints in red (then Red). Otherwise, the row prints in white (else White). Figure 10-19 shows the formula properly entered in the Format Formula Editor text box.

7. **Click the Save and Close button to save the formula.**

The Formula Editor dialog box closes. The formula is added to the report.

To see the results of using this formula, click the Preview tab. Every other record is colored in, as shown in Figure 10-20. Very cool.

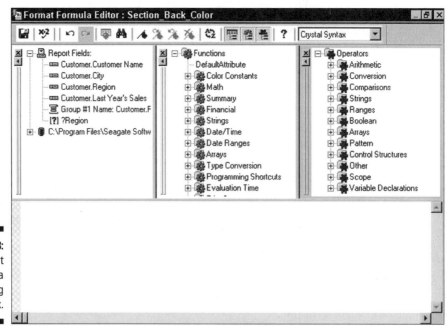

**Figure 10-18:**
The Format
Formula
Editor dialog
box.

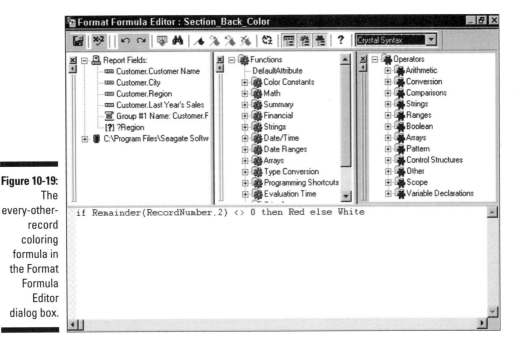

**Figure 10-19:**
The
every-other-
record
coloring
formula in
the Format
Formula
Editor
dialog box.

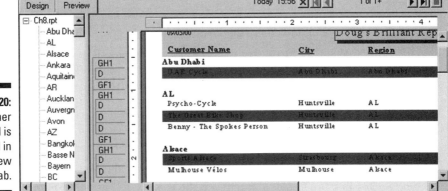

**Figure 10-20:**
Every other
record is
colored in
the Preview
tab.

## A conditional formula to color group results

By using a conditional formula, you can also format certain group sections in a color that distinguishes them from other sections. If you group your records by state or region and add a subtotal by group, you can enter a formula that changes the color of the section based on the value in the sum.

To add a conditional coloring formula to a group total, follow these steps:

1. **Open the report to which you want to add a conditional color.**

   For this example, use the report created in Chapter 5. The report is grouped by country, and a sum has been added to each group by using the Last Year's Sales field.

2. **On the Design tab, choose Format⇨Section from the menu bar.**

   The Section Expert dialog box appears.

3. **Select the Group Footer section of the report.**

4. **Click the Color tab.**

5. **Click to put a check mark in the Background Color option.**

6. **Click the Formula button.**

   The Format Formula Editor dialog box appears.

7. **Type if in the text box.**

8. **In the Report Fields list, find the Sum of Last Year's Sales under the Group Footer on Country and double-click it.**

   The following text is inserted:

   ```
   Sum ({Customer.Last Year's Sales}, {Customer.Country}),
   ```

9. **Type > 90000 then red else white.**

   The result looks like the formula shown in Figure 10-21.

   In plain English, what this formula says is that if the total of the values in the Last Year's Sales field by Country is greater than 90,000, then the Group Footer section prints in red. If not, then the Group Footer section prints in white.

10. **Click the Save and Close button.**

    The Format Formula Editor dialog box closes.

11. **Click OK to close the Section Expert dialog box.**

12. **Click the Preview tab to see the results, as shown in Figure 10-22.**

The coloring options are limited only by your imagination. However, if you get too wild with colors, you distract from the report itself. I suggest that you set a color scheme for your company so that every report has identifiable qualities, such as coloring group sums that fall below the company average and/or having a color for those groups with negative values.

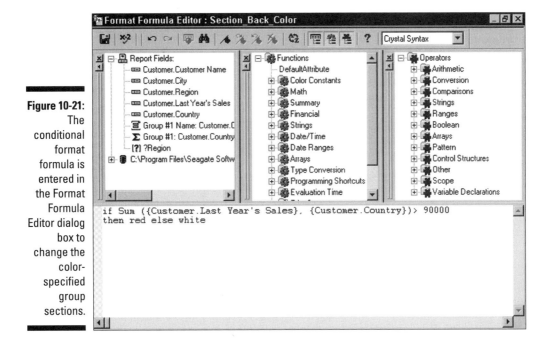

**Figure 10-21:**
The conditional format formula is entered in the Format Formula Editor dialog box to change the color-specified group sections.

**Figure 10-22:**
A group with sales greater than $90,000 printed in a different color.

# Chapter 11

# Creating Presentation-Quality Reports

- - - - - - - - - - - - - - - - - - - - - - - - - - - - - - - - - - - - - - - - - - - - -

- - - - - - - - - - - - - - - - - - - - - - - - - - - - - - - - - - - - - - - - - - - - -

*I*f you're not a creative person when it comes to formatting and designing report layouts, never fear! Seagate Crystal Reports includes ten predefined formats that you can apply to your report for eye-pleasing effects. If none of these formats turns you on, read the rest of this chapter to find out how to apply formats.

## Quickly Formatting a Report

Your report is done, complete with groups (refer to Chapter 5) and totals (refer to Chapter 7). Now that the substance is finished, you can add some veneer to your report.

Follow these steps to apply a quick format:

**1. Open a report you want to format by using the Style Expert.**

Figure 11-1 shows a report with little formatting.

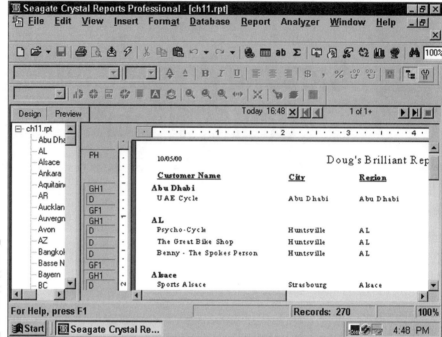

**Figure 11-1:**
A report
without
much
formatting.

## 2. Choose Format⇨Report Style Expert from the menu bar.

Crystal Reports displays a warning to alert you that applying a style is
not reversible with the Undo command. Don't worry — on a case-by-
case basis, you can always remove any format that isn't what you want.

## 3. Click Yes.

The Report Style Expert dialog box appears, as shown in Figure 11-2.

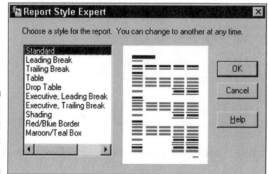

**Figure 11-2:**
The Report
Style Expert
dialog box.

4. **Select a style you want to apply to your report and click OK.**

   You can choose a style from the dialog box, apply that style, and if you don't like it, reopen the Report Style Expert and apply a new format. You don't have to worry about removing the previously applied format because the new format replaces it. To preview the format, click the format name; a representation of the format appears on the right side of the dialog box.

   Figure 11-3 shows the result of applying the Standard report style. I changed the zoom on the Preview tab to 50 percent to show you more of the report. If you don't know how to do this, see the next section of this chapter.

5. **If you want to try another style, again choose Format⟹ Report Style Expert and make a selection.**

   Figure 11-4 shows the Drop Table style applied to the report (at 50% zoom).

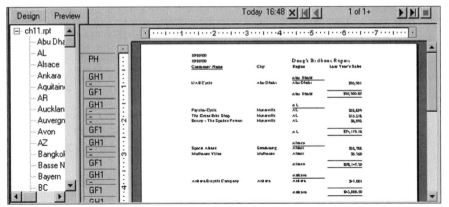

**Figure 11-3:** The Standard report style added to a report.

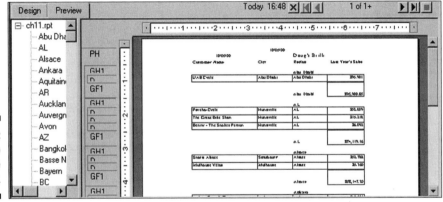

**Figure 11-4:** The Drop Table style in a report.

Try the rest of the formats in a report and see which one appeals to you. If you try them all without satisfaction, you can return to the original formatting by choosing File⇨Close. Crystal Reports asks whether you want to save the report with the changes. If you select No, the report closes without saving any changes you made after you opened it.

# Zooming In on the Report

When you're working hard to get a report to look just right, you can use the Zoom function to prevent straining your eyes. The Zoom function enables you to zoom in to take a close look at the formatting that you've applied and to zoom out to see how the report looks in full-page view.

The Zoom feature works best on the Preview tab because you're looking at live data. If you're trying to get the spacing just right, however, the Design tab — when zoomed — gives you an easy way to see exactly where an object is on the layout. Formatting on the Design tab is easier because you don't have to refresh the screen every time you make a change, as you do on the Preview tab.

You can adjust the zoom factor in two ways:

✔ Choose View⇨Zoom on the menu bar to bring up the Magnification Factor dialog box, as shown in Figure 11-5.

✔ Click the downward-pointing arrow near the right end of the Standard toolbar to open the Zoom Control drop-down list. Use this list to choose from several predetermined magnification percentages or type your own percentage in the box.

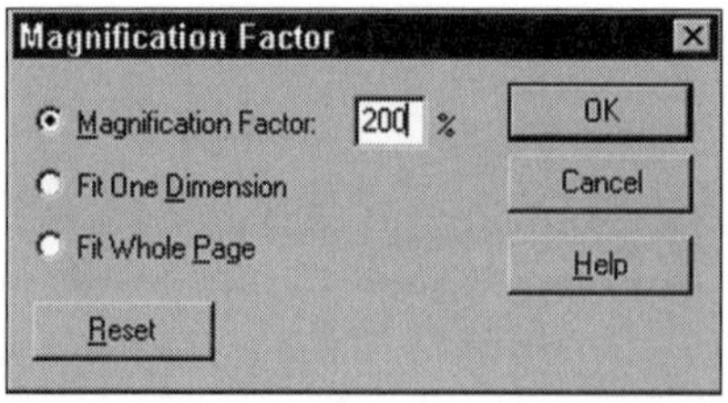

**Figure 11-5:** The Magnification Factor dialog box.

The first setting you can adjust in the Magnification Factor dialog box is the magnification factor — simply type a new value in the box. The valid zoom range is 25 percent through 400 percent. So to see your report at twice the default magnification, for example, type **200** in the box and click OK. Your report appears, as shown in Figure 11-6.

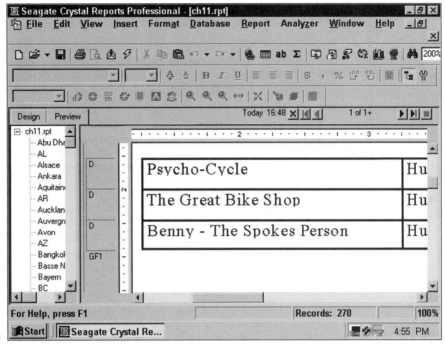

Figure 11-6:
The Design
tab zoomed
by a factor
of 200
percent.

Perhaps you think that if you change the magnification factor in one window, the magnification carries over when you switch to another window. It does not. Crystal Reports doesn't assume that you want a preview magnified. This approach makes sense because you may change the formatting on the Design tab and then want to see the change at a static magnification on the Preview tab. In this way, you can more easily compare apples to apples, so to speak.

The other magnification options are Fit One Dimension and Fit Whole Page. When you select the Fit One Dimension option, Crystal Reports fits the page on the Design or Preview tabs according to the width of the report. In other words, the report dimensions are controlled by the report objects and not by margin settings. The Fit Whole Page option causes Crystal Reports to adjust the report so that all the objects can be seen on-screen. In Preview mode, an entire page is shown.

In Figure 11-7, the Fit Whole Page option is selected on the Preview tab (shown at 21 percent). (If you use this option on the Design tab, the effect isn't very noticeable.)

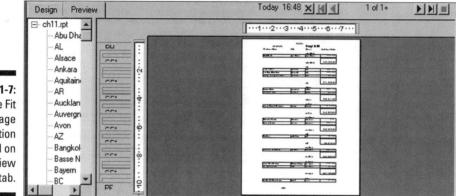

**Figure 11-7:** The Fit Whole Page option selected on the Preview tab.

To return the report view to the default setting, click the Reset button in the Magnification dialog box. The 100 percent magnification factor returns. Now that you know how to adjust the view of the report to better judge the effect of formatting, a discussion of the Special fields is in order.

# Working with Special Fields

A presentation-quality report requires types of information that aren't automatically part of the report. Because not every report requires the same Special fields, you need to decide what fields to include. Special fields are used to insert into a report information that isn't derived from an underlying database table or from a report formula.

To help you decide which of the Special fields to include in a report, see Table 11-1 for a description of each field. If you see a check mark in front of a Special field in the Field Explorer dialog box, then the field is already a part of the report.

| Table 11-1 | How Special Fields Operate |
|---|---|
| *Field* | *What It Does* |
| Page Number | Displays the current page number of the report. |
| Total Page Count | Displays the total number of pages in the report. |
| Page N of M | Displays the current page number along with the total number of pages in the report, such as *3 of 15*. This combines two previous fields into a nice statement. |

| Field | What It Does |
|---|---|
| Report Title | Displays the contents of the Title field from the Document Properties dialog box. You can use this dialog box to enter summary information, such as the title of the report, the subject, and the author. Chapter 18 covers the Summary Info options and this topic. |
| Report Comments | Displays the contents of the Comments field from the Document Properties dialog box. You can use this dialog box to enter summary information, such as the title of the report, the subject, and the author. Chapter 16 covers the Summary Info options and this topic. |
| File Path and Name | Displays the report file name and the path to where the file is stored. As computer users enter the era of the terabyte drive, determining the location of stored files becomes more of a problem. |
| File Author | Displays the contents of the Author field from the Document Properties dialog box. You can use this dialog box to enter summary information, such as the title of the report, the subject, and the author. Chapter 16 covers the Summary Info options and this topic. |
| File Creation Date | Displays the date the report was created. |
| Print Date | Displays the current date based on the clock in your computer. (You can change the date by choosing Report➪ Set Print Date.) |
| Print Time | Displays the time (based on the clock in your computer). |
| Data Date | Displays the date when the data in the report was last refreshed. |
| Data Time | Displays the time when the data in the report was last refreshed. |
| Modification Date | Displays the date on which the report file was last modified. |
| Modification Time | Displays the time when the report file was last modified. |
| Record Number | Displays the current record number as the report prints. This field is usually used in the Details section of a report. An example is shown later in this chapter. |
| Group Number | Displays the current group number. This feature can be used in the Group Header or Group Footer. See Chapter 5 for information on Grouping data. |

*(continued)*

### Table 11-1 *(continued)*

| Field | What It Does |
|---|---|
| Record Selection Formula | Displays the criteria used to select records included in the report. It will display in the Crystal Reports formula syntax that you see in the Record Selection Formula Editor. For more information see Chapter 4 on Record Selection and Chapter 7 on Formulas. |
| Group Selection Formula | Displays the criteria used in the Group Selection. This feature displays in the Crystal Reports formula syntax that you see in the Group Selection Formula Editor. The use of this formula is beyond the scope of this book. |

To insert a Special field in a report, follow these steps:

1. **Choose Insert➪Special Field from the menu bar.**

   The Field Explorer dialog box appears.

2. **If not visible, double-click the Special Fields item to display the entire list of fields, as shown in Figure 11-8.**

3. **Click the Special Field you want to insert and click the Insert to Report button on the toolbar in the Field Explorer dialog box.**

   The frame cursor is attached to the mouse pointer. When you move the mouse to a position where the field can be properly inserted, the place-holder appears as a grayed rectangle; if the field cannot be inserted at the location of the mouse, the placeholder appears as a circle with a line drawn through it.

4. **Position the mouse pointer in the section of the report where you want the Special Field information to appear and click the left mouse button to insert it.**

If you decide you don't want to insert the field you selected, press the Escape key before clicking in the report.

With any formats that you add (except those applied by the Style Expert), you can always revert to the original report status by choosing Edit➪Undo. The Undo command is dynamic because it reflects the last action taken. If you want to go back, you must execute this command immediately after adding a noxious format — pretty cool, huh?

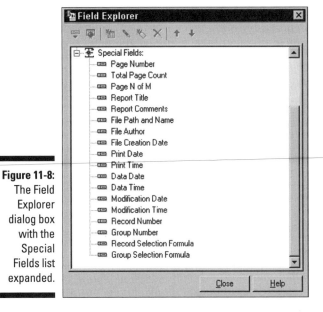

**Figure 11-8:**
The Field
Explorer
dialog box
with the
Special
Fields list
expanded.

# Inserting a Special Field

Before you insert a Special field into a report, consider where you want the information generated by the Special field to appear in the printed report. For example, the Date field probably belongs in the Report Header section or perhaps in the Page Footer section. Report information, such as the last modification date, report comments, and report title (not of the report itself, but of the computer filename) may belong in the Report Footer. As with most formatting in Crystal Reports, trying different locations and combinations is the best way to determine what works for your reports.

An additional consideration is that you can condition the printing of the Special field information and the way it's displayed by using a formula. (See Chapter 7 for more information about formulas.)

Follow these steps to insert the current date:

1. **Open the report in which you want a Date field inserted and click the Design tab.**

2. **Choose Insert⇨Special Field from the menu bar.**

   The Field Explorer dialog box appears.

3. **Click Special Fields and then, from the Special Fields list that appears, double-click the Print Date field.**

   The mouse pointer now appears as a gray box . This box indicates that the field placeholder is ready for insertion, as shown in Figure 11-9.

4. **Move the pointer to the section of the report in which you want the Special field to print.**

   In this case, the pointer is positioned in the Page Header section.

   If you move the pointer over an existing text field, the placeholder may disappear for a moment. Be patient, move the pointer to another area of the report and wait for the pointer to reappear.

5. **Click the left mouse button.**

   The field is inserted at that spot. Figure 11-10 shows the Print Date field inserted beside the title in the Page Header section of the report.

Previewing the report with the new field inserted yields the result shown in Figure 11-11.

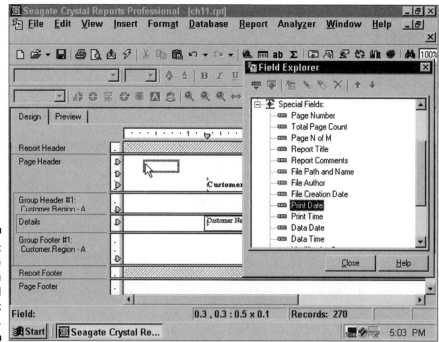

**Figure 11-9:**
The mouse
pointer with
a Special
Field box
attached.

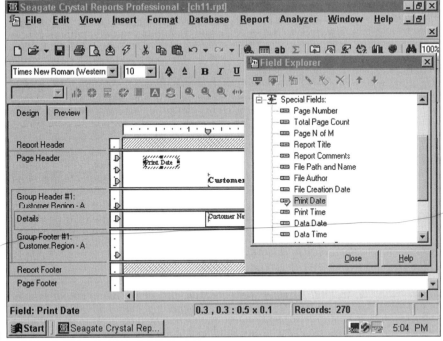

Figure 11-10:
The Print
Date field
inserted in
the Page
Header.

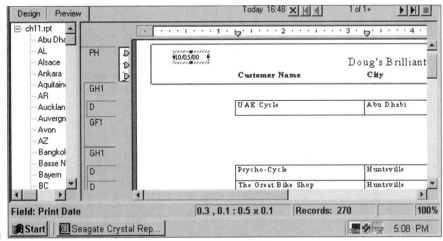

Figure 11-11:
The Print
Date field
visible in the
top-left
corner of
the report
on the
Preview tab.

# Adding a Record Number field

The Record Number field simply lists the number of each record in sequential order as it is printed in the report. Because this field generates a number for each record that's in the Details section, the best place to insert this field is in the Details section of the report. In Figure 11-12, the field is inserted to the left of the Customer Name field. This feature is used quite often in legacy reports (mainframe-style reports), usually in control breaks. That way, even though the records are split across many groups, the record numbering remains the same.

The Record Number field counts the number of records in the report and prints the number where you specify, as shown in Figure 11-13. The first record printed in the report, for example, is record Number 1, the second is Number 2, and so on.

## Adding information to the Report Footer

As mentioned earlier in this chapter, the placement of the Special field is as important as the information itself. Adding several pertinent pieces of information to the Report Footer makes identifying the report an easy task. In this example, you add the File Path and Name field and the Modification Date field to the Report Footer. Here's how:

1. **In any of the reports created earlier in this book, or in a report that you create, click the Design tab.**

2. **Choose Insert⇨Special Field from the menu bar.**

   The Field Explorer dialog box appears.

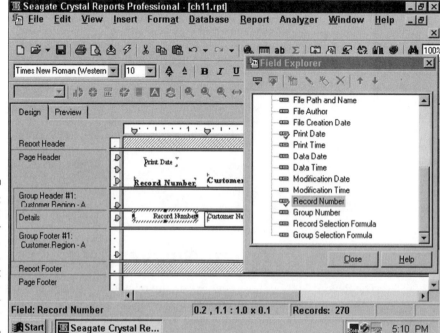

**Figure 11-12:**
The Record
Number
field
inserted to
the left
of the
Customer
Name field.

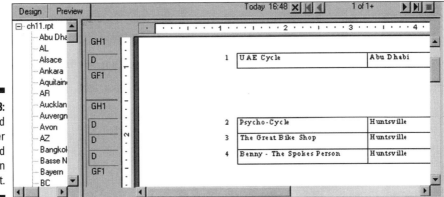

**Figure 11-13:**
The Record
Number
field
inserted in
the report.

3. **Select the File Path and Name field. (If the list of Special fields doesn't appear, click the plus sign [+] to reveal it.) Hold down the Ctrl (Control) key on your keyboard and select the Modification Date field.**

   After you complete this step, both fields should be highlighted.

4. **Insert the placeholders in the Report Footer section by clicking the Insert to Report button on the Field Explorer toolbar and then clicking the mouse pointer in that section.**

   The results are shown in Figure 11-14. The size of the fields is adjusted so that you can see them better.

5. **Click the Preview tab and then click the Last Page button to take you to the last page of the report. You may have to scroll near the last record of the report to see the fields.**

   The inserted fields appear, as shown in Figure 11-15.

**Figure 11-14:**
The File
Path and
Name
and the
Modification
Date are
inserted in
the Report
Footer
section of
the report.

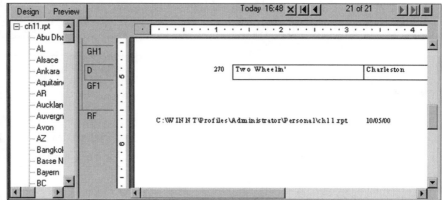

**Figure 11-15:**
The File
Path and
Name field
and the
Modification
Date field
inserted in
the Report
Footer.

# Formatting Special fields

Although you may find that the default font, color, and other format attributes are fine as presented, that isn't likely. To make changes, simply right-click the particular field or value on the Preview tab. Figure 11-16 shows the shortcut menu that appears.

**Figure 11-16:**
Right-click
any Special
field to open
the Format
Field
shortcut
menu.

Select Format Field to open the Format Editor dialog box, as shown in Figure 11-17. The tabs that are available depend on the type of field you're formatting.

The formatting possibilities are seemingly endless! The abundance of formatting adjustments that you can make to a field makes discussing them all nearly impossible. Just for the fun of it, however, click the Font tab, as shown in Figure 11-18. I've changed the Font to display in Arial, 12 point, italic numbers.

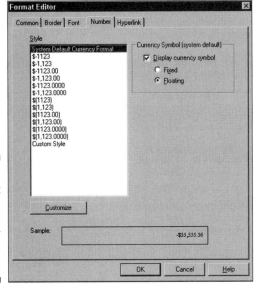

**Figure 11-17:**
The Format
Editor dialog
box, with
the Number
tab
selected.

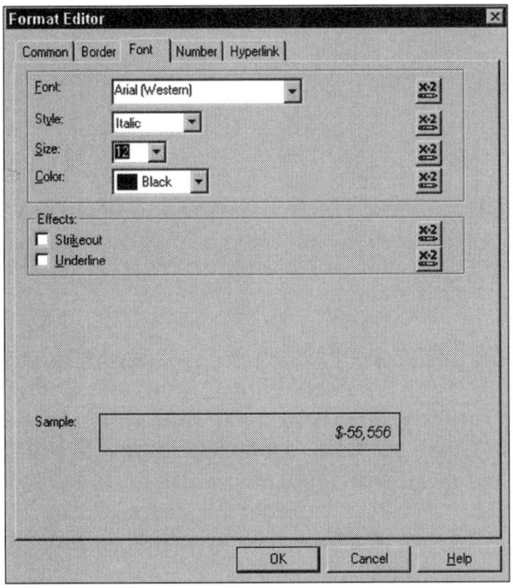

**Figure 11-18:**
The Font tab
selected in
the Format
Editor dialog
box.

When you adjust font style, Crystal Reports shows you the effect in the
Sample box at the bottom of the dialog box.

A point to consider is that the Underline option in the Format Editor dialog box works together with the Border options. In other words, you can have both an underline and a border at the same time.

As is true with most format settings, the application of a particular format can be conditioned by a formula. Click the Formula button (X+2) to open the Formula Editor dialog box and enter the conditions. (For more on formulas, see Chapter 7.)

## Formatting a Date field

A Date field can be formatted in a variety of ways, too. To see the formatting options, follow these steps:

1. **Right-click one of the following:**
   - The Date field
   - The Design tab
   - The actual date on the Preview tab

2. **In the shortcut menu that appears, select Format Field to open the Format Editor dialog box.**

3. **Click the Customize button.**

   The Custom Style dialog box appears with the Date tab displayed, as shown in Figure 11-19.

At the bottom of this dialog box is a Sample box that reflects any changes you make. The default setting that Crystal Reports uses is derived from the date setting established by the Windows operating system, as shown in the Style box of the Format Editor dialog box.

If you prefer to have your own format, however, you certainly can. An easy change to make is to select the Windows Long format, which changes the date to something like Tuesday, March 16, 2000, rather than to a numerical format. To choose this format, click the drop-down arrow in the Date Type box and select the format or go wild and select Custom. If you select Custom, you can change the order of the date numbers, the exact format of each of the components — Month, Day, and Year — and so on.

If you change the date format from short to long, you must reformat the Date field in the report by stretching it to display the entire date.

You can format all the special fields you insert in a report. When you right-click a field, the shortcut menu that appears is specific to the field you select. Experiment with the different formats until you're satisfied with the results.

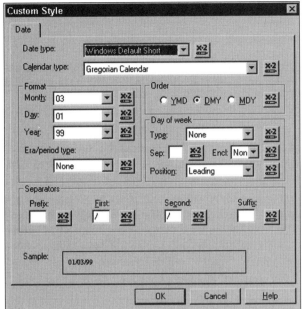

**Figure 11-19:**
The Date
tab in the
Custom
Style dialog
box.

# *Combining a text object with a Special field*

Knowing how to execute the formatting that's discussed in this section sets you apart from novice Crystal Reports users. You may know how easy popping a Special field into a report is (as described earlier in this chapter), but what if the person reading the report doesn't know what the Special field numbers represent? For example, because the Total Page Number field can be mistaken for just about anything, you — the report creator — have the duty to include explanatory text for each Special field entry.

When the Record Number field was added, Crystal Reports included the name of the field in the Page Header because the field was added to the Details section. The other Special field that was added to the report was added to a section other than Details so the Title field was not inserted automatically. Yet, knowing the identity of each object is crucial for everyone dealing with the report.

You may think that you can simply add a text object so that it precedes or follows the Special field and then enter the description of the field. But Crystal Reports has a more elegant solution, which is to combine the Special field and the text object.

In this example, I create a text object and then insert a Special field into it. In any report that has a Special field, you can do the same by following these steps:

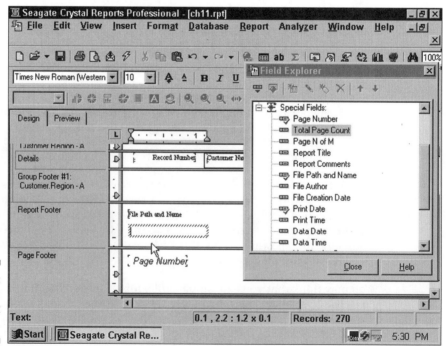

**1. Click the Text Object button on the Standard toolbar and insert a text box in the Report Footer section of the report, as shown in Figure 11-20.**

**2. Type** Total Pages:

Now, the pièce de résistance. . . .

**3. Click and drag the Special field so that the left edge of the Special field is inside the text object, just to the right of the words. After it's lined up, release the mouse button.**

The Special field is inserted into the Text Object box, as shown in Figure 11-21. Don't worry if the name of the field [Total Page Count] jumps down to the next line in the text box. That happens because the name of the field is so long compared to the size of the actual number that'll be displayed. You can adjust the field size later.

**4. Click the Preview tab to see this esoteric formatting trick in action.**

The report appears, as shown in Figure 11-22. The Preview tab is zoomed to 150 percent to see the result better.

**Figure 11-20:**
Inserting a
new text
object.

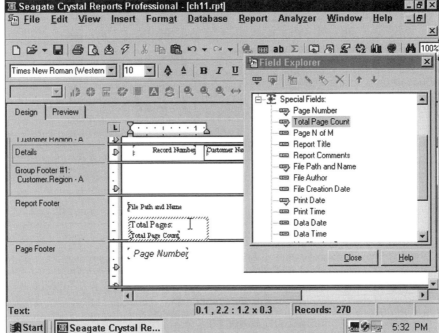

**Figure 11-21:**
The Total
Page Count
field
inserted into
the Text
Object box.

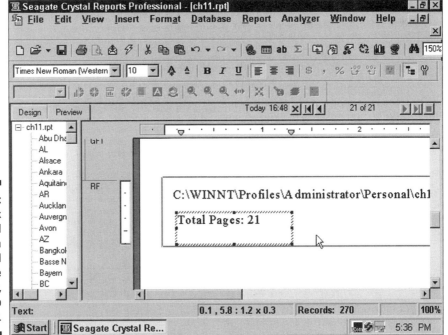

**Figure 11-22:**
A text box
combined
with a
Special field
on the
Preview tab,
zoomed to
150 percent.

By combining a Special field and a text box, you have more flexibility in terms of options than you ever have by creating two separate objects. You can even combine two database fields rather painlessly. Just drag and drop them into a text object, and off you go.

# Inserting Lines and Boxes

Lines and boxes can enhance particular values in a report and are a snap to add to the layout. If you add a line object in a group summary, Crystal Reports assumes that you want it inserted in every group summary in the report.

## Drawing a line

You can add a line in one of the following ways:

 ✔ On the Supplementary toolbar, click the Insert Line button. (See the "Using the Supplementary toolbar" sidebar in this chapter for more information on how to work with this toolbar.)

 ✔ Choose Insert➪Line from the menu bar.

The mouse pointer transforms to look like a small pencil on the screen. Now you can draw the line by holding down the left mouse button and dragging the mouse. Working in the Design tab makes this easier.

To add a line to a Group Footer, follow these steps:

 1. **Click the Design tab in your report.**

 2. **Click the Insert Line button on the Supplementary toolbar.**

    The mouse transforms into a pencil.

 3. **Position the pencil tip where you want the line to start.**

    In this example, you want a line that separates the Details listing from the Group Footer section. The line is drawn at the top of the Group Footer section.

 4. **Click the left mouse button and drag the pencil to the right to where you want the line to end, as shown in Figure 11-23.**

 5. **To appreciate the beauty of this format, click the Preview tab.**

    Figure 11-24 shows the Preview tab.

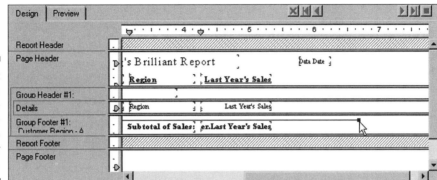

**Figure 11-23:**
Drawing a line at the top of the Group Footer section.

**Figure 11-24:**
A preview of a line dividing the Details listing from the Group Footer information.

The line you see in Preview is too long because I got carried away as I was drawing it. Just like any other object, you can click the line and use the sizing handles on either end to change its length.

---

# Using the Supplementary toolbar

Users of Version 6.0 and later have an additional toolbar just for adding enhancements to reports. To see the toolbar, click the icon that looks like a golden wrench at the far right on the second toolbar from the top of the screen, directly under the Zoom button. With the mouse pointer on the icon, the pop-up text reads "Toggle Supplementary Toolbar." Clicking the icon displays the toolbar in the lower-left corner of the screen, just above the Windows Start button. Move your mouse pointer over each icon on the toolbar, and Crystal Reports displays the pop-up description for each icon.

**Note:** All the toolbars are at your command. Choosing View➪Toolbars displays a dialog box from which you can toggle off and on all four Crystal Reports toolbars.

A drawn line can be horizontal or vertical only; angled lines aren't possible. The benefit is that you can be certain that any lines you draw are perfectly aligned.

## Formatting a line

You can adjust lines after they're in place. You begin any line object with the original line (as demonstrated in the preceding section) and then build from there.

To change the format of a line in a report, follow these steps:

1. **Right-click the line to open the shortcut menu, as shown in Figure 11-25.**

   Opening this menu is a bit tricky. Just make sure that the end of the mouse pointer is right on top of the line.

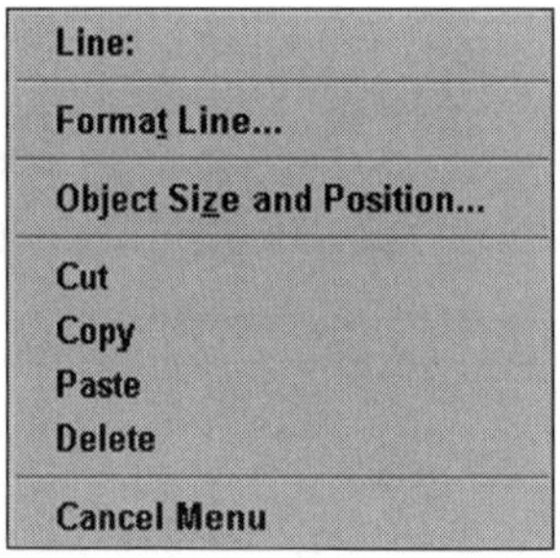

**Figure 11-25:**
The shortcut
menu for
line
formatting.

```
Line:
Format Line...
Object Size and Position...
Cut
Copy
Paste
Delete
Cancel Menu
```

2. **Select Format Line.**

   The Format Editor dialog box appears, as shown in Figure 11-26. This dialog box is one of the few in which you have no sample field to gauge the format you select before applying it to the report — the buttons show you the width.

3. **To change the line width, click the line size you want.**

   The number (in points) is displayed to the right.

4. **(Optional) If you don't want to use Black, select a color preference by clicking the drop-down arrow in the Color box.**

5. **(Optional) If you want the line to print at the bottom of the section (like an accounting statement), select the Move to Bottom of Section When Printing box.**

6. **Click OK to close the dialog box.**

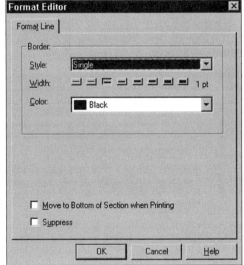

**Figure 11-26:**
The Format
Editor dialog
box for line
formatting.

If you misdraw the line, one thing you can do — and the magnification feature makes it easy — is grab the handles at either end of the line and lengthen or shorten the line to match the length of the field.

## Drawing a box around an object

Drawing a box around a group of records is especially tricky if you try to draw a box that crosses sections of the report. So drawing a box involves a little planning. The best way to draw a box is to select the point where you want the upper-left corner, click and hold the mouse button, and then draw the box by dragging the lines across and down to the point where you want the lower-right corner.

To draw a box around an object or objects, follow these steps:

1. **Open the report and click the Design tab.**

   In this view, it's easier to see the lines that define the sections in the report.

2. **Choose Insert⇨Box on the menu bar or click the Insert Box button on the Supplementary toolbar.**

   The mouse pointer transforms into a pencil shape.

3. **Click at the point where you want the upper-left corner of the box to start and then drag it across and down to the right, to the point where you want the lower-right corner to be.**

4. **Release the mouse button.**

   Congratulations! You've just drawn a box, as shown in Figure 11-27.

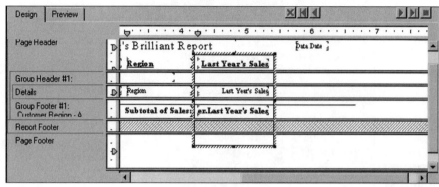

**Figure 11-27:**
A box drawn around the fields in the Last Year's Sales column.

You may format the box by clicking it to bring up the sizing handles and then right-clicking to open the shortcut menu. Select Format Box and then select the line type, color, and thickness. You can even add a drop shadow.

# Inserting a Picture or Logo into the Report

As soon as your coworkers see the other nifty formats you can add to your reports, they're bound to ask you to insert a picture or logo. After you add all the other attributes, you're ready for that finishing touch — the company graphic. And why not? The big deal with Windows is its capability to read bitmapped files across all applications. But before you can insert a picture or logo, it must exist in a format Crystal Reports can accept, such as .BMP (a bitmap), .TIFF, .JPEG, or .PNG. The Paint program included with Windows creates files in .BMP format.

To insert your company logo in a report, follow these steps:

1. **Open the report in which you want to insert a picture or logo and click the Design tab.**

   Depending on where you want the picture inserted, you may have to resize the section to accommodate the new picture object. However, Crystal Reports adjusts the size of the section for you if you position the upper-left corner of the picture object in a section that is too small for the entire object. For example, if you want the picture to be in the Page Header beside the title, position the pointer to the right of the title and click. Figure 11-28 shows the picture outline at the point where Crystal Reports adjusts the section size to make the picture fit.

2. **Choose Insert⇨Picture from the menu bar (or click the Insert Picture button on the Supplementary toolbar).**

   The Open dialog box appears. You may have to switch folders or drives to locate the file you want to insert. Crystal Reports includes a bitmap of the Xtreme Mountain Bike Company logo in the Program Files\ Seagate Software\Crystal Reports\Samples\Databases folder named Xtreme, making this file easy to use as an example.

3. **Click the file you want to insert and then click the Open button.**

   The Open dialog box closes. The mouse pointer, with a gray-outlined box attached (as shown in Figure 11-28), indicates the size of the picture or logo.

4. **Position the upper-left corner of the box at the point where you want the logo inserted and then click the left mouse button to insert the picture, as shown in Figure 11-29.**

   Crystal Reports pushes the Page Header open to make room for the logo.

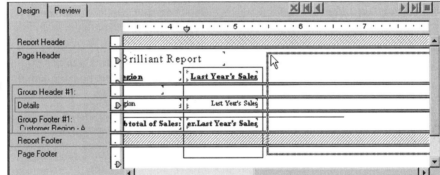

**Figure 11-28:**
A picture outline before being inserted.

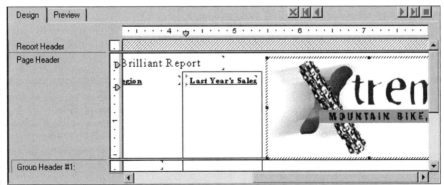

**Figure 11-29:**
Additional space is automatically provided for the logo.

# Inserting an OLE Object

An OLE (Greek — or is it geekspeak? — for Object Linking and Embedding) object is different from any ordinary picture or logo file because it's an active file. That is, an OLE object is usually a file created in another application, such as Microsoft Paint. If the object is not OLE and needs editing, you normally have to go to the trouble of making the edit in Paint, deleting the old object from your report, and then reinserting it. Whew! Too much like work. To make life easier, using OLE, you can click the object, and the application that created the object starts up so that you can make changes directly.

To insert an OLE object, follow these steps:

1. **Open the report in which you want to insert the OLE object and click the Design tab.**

2. **Choose Insert⇨OLE Object from the menu bar.**

   The Insert Object dialog box appears.

   You can use an existing object or create a new one, and you can embed a wide variety of OLE objects in a report, ranging from a picture to a spreadsheet.

3. **For an existing object, select the Create from File radio button and then type the complete filename in the box or click the Browse button to locate the file.**

4. **Click to select the Link box if you want the link to be maintained and the object automatically updated if changes are made to it.**

5. **Click OK and insert the object into the report.**

   With the link established, if you change the object in its native program (such as Excel), the changes are automatically reflected in Crystal Reports.

To activate the OLE, double-click it. If you insert a spreadsheet, for example, Excel starts within Crystal Reports. Very cool.

## Linking versus embedding

If a *linked* object (a company logo, for example) is added to a report and the logo is changed in a different program, the new logo appears the next time you run the report.

If an *embedded* object is added to a report, even if the object (file) changes (if someone nukes the logo file, for example), the changes are not made in the refreshed report.

# Adding a Hyperlink

As Web connections become permanent features in computer use, hyperlinks become as common as page numbers in documents. A hyperlink added to a report makes it easy for someone reading a report to click the link and go to an Intranet document or a Web site. You can use hyperlinks to point a reader to a document that explains or gives detail for an item in a report, or to point to an e-mail address. Finally, a hyperlink can connect to another report, making it an on-demand subreport.

To add a hyperlink, follow these steps:

1. **Click the object to which you want to add a hyperlink.**

   This could be a simple text object that reads "Click here to go to our Web site."

2. **Right-click to open the short-cut menu.**

   If a hyperlink is already part of the object, the menu includes the item, Go to Hyperlink.

3. **Click Format Text, Graphic, or whatever item is appropriate for the object.**

   The Format Editor dialog box appears.

4. **Click the Hyperlink tab, as shown in Figure 11-30.**

   Depending on the type of object selected, a number of links can be created. In this example, a Web site on the Internet is selected.

5. **Depending on the target of the hyperlink, enter the address as follows:**

   - **Web site:** Type the complete address, such as: `http://www.howtosoftware.com`.

     When the object is clicked, your Web browser opens and goes directly to the Web site indicated in the link.

   - **E-mail address:** Type the address as `Dwolf@howtosoftware.com`, for example.

     When the object is clicked, your default e-mail program starts and inserts the linked address into the To field of the e-mail address line.

   - **File:** Click the Browse button to locate the file in your company network. If the file is a Crystal Report file, the file runs as an On-demand report when the object is clicked. If the file is a Word document, Microsoft Word starts when the object is clicked and the document appears.

6. **Click OK to finish the hyperlink.**

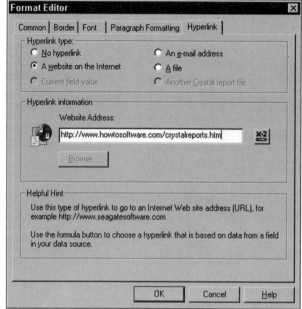

**Figure 11-30:**
The Format
Editor dialog
box with the
Hyperlink
tab
selected.

You can add a formula to the link, which lets Crystal Reports determine whether the link is active. The conditions of the formula must be met, however, before the report reader can access the link.

With the capability to add hyperlinks to your reports, you broaden the range of your report dynamics.

# Using Auto Arrange to Format Reports

Auto Arrange centers and repositions the fields so that they are equally spaced across the page. To use the Auto Arrange feature, you must first insert the fields you want in the report and add groups and other formatting. Then choose Format➪Auto Arrange. Crystal Reports warns you that this command cannot be undone. If you have not saved the report, you may want to do so before continuing so that you have a copy that hasn't been rearranged. Otherwise, click OK and the report is arranged.

Every aspect of Crystal Reports can be modified in some way, but the key is not to overdo the formatting. If a report is too "busy," it takes away from the message that you're trying to convey. However, if *obfuscation* is your goal, you can accomplish it easily with the formatting options.

# Part V

# Creating Specific Types of Reports

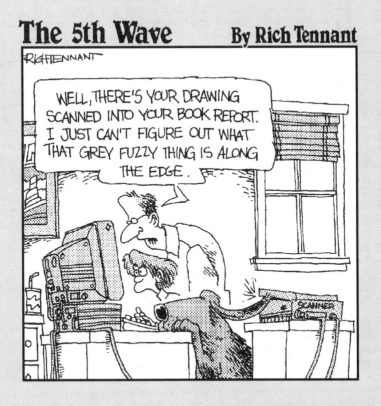

The 5th Wave          By Rich Tennant

WELL, THERE'S YOUR DRAWING SCANNED INTO YOUR BOOK REPORT. I JUST CAN'T FIGURE OUT WHAT THAT GREY FUZZY THING IS ALONG THE EDGE.

# In this part . . .

$V$ ariety is the spice of life, and in reporting, it's no different. In this part, the thyme, sage, saffron, curry, and fenugreek all become a part of your flavorful report repertoire — metaphorically, at least. Seagate Crystal Reports has a wide variety of report types from which you can choose. This part is devoted to helping you cook a report that's sure to cure the common cold and land you that corner office with a key to the executive washroom. By matching the report type with the needs of those in your organization, you will gain the reputation of a master report chef. Stand aside, Wolfgang Puck, a new report maker has come to town.

# Chapter 12

# Creating a Cross-Tab Report

**C**ross-Tab objects are one way to present your data. The usual Crystal Reports lists your data in Groups. For example, if you want to report your product sales, you can group first by Product Name and then by Region. That way, you can see the number of Descent bikes sold in the Regions AL, BC, CA, and so on. Then, if you want to compare the sales of Descent bikes to Mozzie bikes in the Region CA, you have to flip some pages or create another report that's grouped first by Region and then by Product Name. To save you this trouble, Crystal Reports gives you Cross-Tab objects.

Cross-Tab objects can be thought of as a Summary-style report that allows you to group in two directions on a page — horizontally and vertically.

In this chapter, you create a simple Cross-Tab report, which can be a great analytical tool and a way to identify trends.

## Identifying the "By" Word

A *Cross-Tab* is an arrangement of fields in which the data can be compared in order to identify trends. Pollsters — those best friends of politicians — use cross tabulations of voter interviews to see which issues create a response *by* age, *by* location, or *by* whatever demographic or psychographic category the respondent fits. Campaign directors then design TV and direct-mail ads so that their candidate's image is acceptable to those targeted respondents. If the directors are good at reading Cross-Tabs, they get their candidate elected.

When you use Cross-Tabs, the operative word is *by* because the genesis of a Cross-Tab is sales *by* region, products *by* customer, votes *by* precinct, and so on. If you think that a report will be more valuable if it includes data that can be defined as something *by* something else, you're in Cross-Tab Land.

In business, the same principle applies. With an existing or new product, the survey research can be cross-tabulated to determine which customer profile is most likely to purchase a product. You can even determine the price range that's acceptable to the customer. In this chapter's example, I create a Cross-Tab to determine which suppliers sell products in which regions.

A Cross-Tab is difficult for people to handle conceptually, so think of something like this:

|         | *Beer* | *Wine* | *Total* |
|---------|--------|--------|---------|
| Males   | 100    | 20     | 120     |
| Females | 15     | 75     | 90      |
| Total   | 115    | 95     | 210     |

This table is a Cross-Tab that analyzes sales by gender and alcohol preference. You can find out a great deal by taking a quick look at a Cross-Tab.

In Crystal Reports, a Cross-Tab is an object, not an entire report. Therefore, a Cross-Tab can be inserted at a particular place in the report or combined with a summary report (see Chapter 13). A Cross-Tab can be inserted into the Report Header or Footer or into the Group Header or Footer. Where you place the Cross-Tab object is crucial. If you insert the Cross-Tab in the Report Header or Footer, the Cross-Tab object is displayed only once and includes every record in the report. On the other hand, if you insert the Cross-Tab in the Group Header or Footer, the Cross-Tab considers only the records in that particular group and is displayed before or after every group of records.

# Creating a Cross-Tab Object in a New Report

A Cross-Tab object is arranged by rows and columns. If you've worked with a spreadsheet, you've seen this concept at work. When you select a Database field for inclusion in a Cross-Tab, each value in the Database field is given its own row or column. The column header or row header is the value of the field.

Before discussing how to add a Cross-Tab to an existing report, start with a new report to see the entire process. In the following steps, the Xtreme database is used to create an example report with three products and two regions selected. The Cross-Tab shows the number of each product sold by region. The Xtreme database is included with the installation of Crystal Reports or can be downloaded from the Seagate Software Web site.

To create a Cross-Tab in a new report, follow these steps:

1. **Choose File⇨New from the menu bar.**

2. **In the Report Gallery dialog box that appears, select Using the Report Expert radio button, then select Cross-Tab from the Choose an Expert list, and then click OK.**

   The Cross-Tab Report Expert dialog box appears.

3. **Click the Database button to open the Data Explorer dialog box.**

4. **Click Database Files and then double-click Find Database File.**

   The Open dialog box appears. The Xtreme database is located in C:\Program Files\Seagate Software\Crystal Reports\ Samples\Databases.

5. **Select the Xtreme database and then click Open.**

   The Data Explorer dialog box displays with the Xtreme database tables listed, as shown in Figure 12-1.

6. **Select the Customer, Orders, Orders Details, and Product tables and then click Add to include them in the report.**

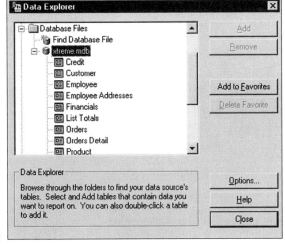

**Figure 12-1:**
The Data Explorer dialog box with the tables from the Xtreme database.

7. **Click Close.**

   The Links tab in the Cross-Tab Report Expert dialog box appears with Crystal Reports establishing the table links for you, as shown in Figure 12-2.

8. **Check the links that Crystal Reports creates to make sure that all tables are linked correctly and then click Next.**

   The Cross-Tab tab of the Cross-Tab Report Expert dialog box appears, as shown in Figure 12-3.

   The next few steps are key to adding the Rows and Columns and then the Summarized fields. You can start by adding the Rows field, to hold the names of the products.

9. **In the Available Fields box on the Cross-Tab tab, scroll to the table name Product, double-click it to see the fields in the table, and then select the Product Name field.**

10. **Click the Add Row button.**

    The name Product.Product Name appears in the Rows box. Next, you want to add the Columns field.

11. **In the Available Fields box on the Cross-Tab tab, scroll to the Customer table, double-click it to reveal the fields in the table, and then select the Region field.**

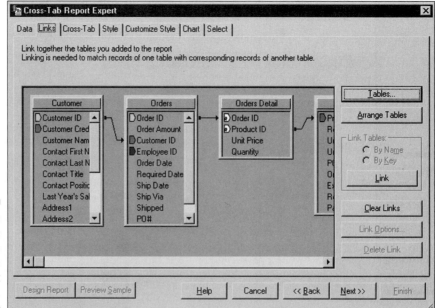

**Figure 12-2:** The Links tab in the Cross-Tab Report Expert.

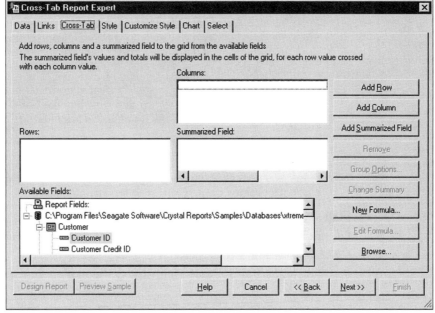

**Figure 12-3:**
The Cross-
Tab Report
Expert
dialog box,
with the
Cross-Tab
tab
selected.

12. **Click the Add Column button.**

The Customer.Region name appears in the Columns box.

Next, you want to add a Summarized Field. The purpose of this Cross-Tab is to see the total number of orders that contain each product by region, so adding the Product Name field in the Summarized Field box yields the result.

13. **In the Available Fields box, select the Product Name field and click the Add Summarized Field button.**

The Cross-Tab tab should resemble Figure 12-4.

Note that Crystal Reports changes the name of the field in the Summarized Field box to Count of Product.Product Name. This change makes sense because the Cross-Tab shows the total number of orders that contain each product by region.

In addition to the Cross-Tab tab previously mentioned, the Cross-Tab Report Expert dialog box offers the following tabs to help customize your Cross-Tab report:

- **Data:** Use this tab to choose a database and then the tables from that database.

- **Links:** Use this tab to link or unlink tables. Linking tables is covered in more detail in chapter 14.

- **Style:** Lets you experiment with, and choose from, a number of predefined styles for the report grid, as shown in Figure 12-5. For purposes of the example, stay with the default style.

- **Customize Styles:** Offers you a great deal of control over what's included in the Cross-Tab report and how it's displayed (see Figure 12-6). For this example, no changes are needed.

- **Chart:** Lets you include a chart with the Cross-Tab report. No need to do this for the example.

- **Select:** Lets you narrow the number of items that appear in the rows or columns of the Cross-Tab report.

14. **Click Next to display the Select tab.**

    For this example, you only want data for three products from two regions.

15. **Scroll through the Available Fields list to the Region field, select it, and click Add.**

    The Customer.Region field is added to the Select Fields box on the right. You can select the Customer.Region field from either the Report Fields section or the Customer Table section.

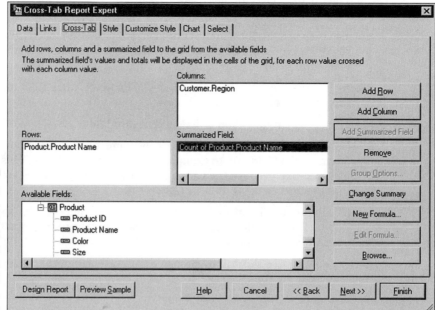

**Figure 12-4:** The Cross-Tab Report Expert dialog box with a Summarized Field added.

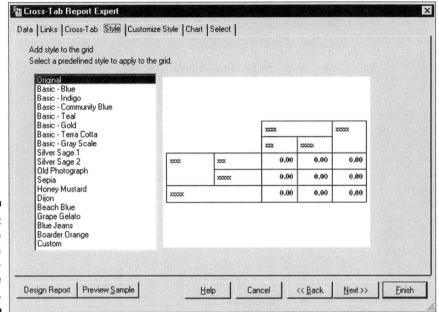

**Figure 12-5:**
The Style
tab with a
list of Cross-
Tab style
types.

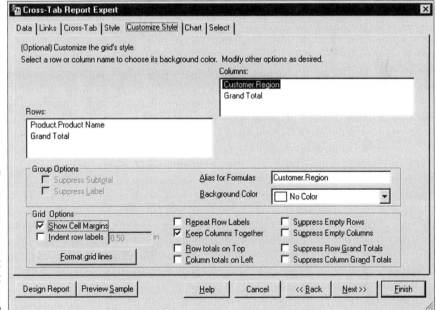

**Figure 12-6:**
The
Customize
Style tab on
the Cross-
Tab Report
Expert
dialog box.

16. **Underneath the Browse Data button, open the drop-down list and select Is One Of.**

    Another drop-down list box appears.

17. **Click the arrow in the drop-down list box to open it.**

    The Regions appear.

18. **Select the regions you want, one at a time.**

    For this example, select AL and CA. As you select one, it gets added to the box below the list box. Next you want to select the products.

19. **Scroll through the Available Fields list to the Product Name field, select it, and click Add.**

    The Product.Product Name field is added to the Select Fields box on the right.

20. **Underneath the Browse Data button, open the drop-down list and select Is One Of.**

    When you do this, another drop-down list box appears. Open it and the Product Names appear.

21. **Select the products you want, one at a time.**

    For the example, select Active Outdoors Lycra Glove, Active Outdoors Crochet Glove, and the Guardian U Lock. As you select one, it gets added to the box below the list box. The completed dialog box looks like the one shown in Figure 12-7.

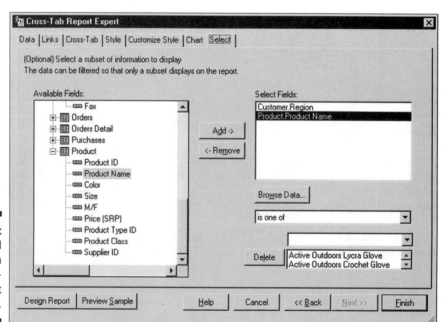

**Figure 12-7:**
A completed
Select tab in
the Cross-
Tab Expert
dialog box.

**22. Click Finish.**

> After a moment, Crystal Reports crunches the data and presents you with the Cross-Tab, as shown in Figure 12-8.

Note that when you create a Cross-Tab by using the Cross-Tab Expert, the Details section is automatically Hidden. No individual database records are displayed in the report — only the Cross-Tab appears. However, you can always add fields to the report, if you desire. In this example, after you create the Cross-Tab, display the Details section and add fields to it.

Crystal Reports inserts the Cross-Tab into the Report Header, but you can move it to the Report Footer if you want.

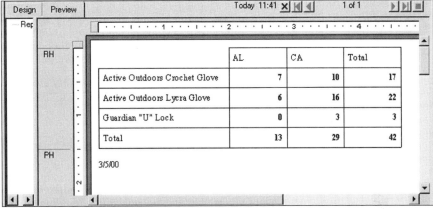

**Figure 12-8:** A brilliant Cross-Tab appears in the Report Header. The row of product names is resized to show the entire name.

| | AL | CA | Total |
|---|---|---|---|
| Active Outdoors Crochet Glove | 7 | 10 | 17 |
| Active Outdoors Lycra Glove | 6 | 16 | 22 |
| Guardian "U" Lock | 0 | 3 | 3 |
| Total | 13 | 29 | 42 |

3/5/00

# Inserting a Cross-Tab into an Existing Report

If you already created a report and want to add a Cross-Tab to it, start in the Design tab. (The Design tab makes adding objects so much easier.) You can insert the Cross-Tab in either the Report Header or Footer or in any Group Header or Footer. You can open the Cross-Tab dialog box in two ways:

- On the Supplementary toolbar, click the Insert Cross-Tab button.
- Choose Insert➪Cross-Tab.

Take a look at the Format Cross-Tab dialog box (as shown in Figure 12-9), which is nearly the same as the Cross-Tab Report Expert dialog box (refer to Figure 12-4). The difference between the two is in the tabs at the top — this one has only three.

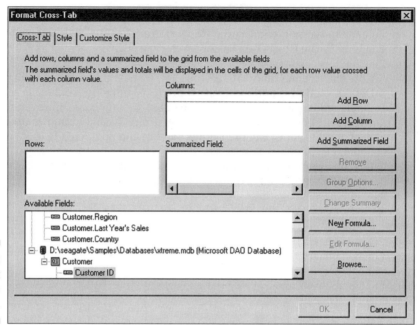

Fill in the Rows, Columns, and Summarized Field boxes as needed for your new Cross-Tab.

You can use the Add Row, Add Column, or Add Summarized Field buttons to add fields to a Cross-Tab, or you can simply drag-and-drop the field from the Available Fields list to the Rows, Columns, or Summarized Field boxes.

To insert a Cross-Tab, follow these steps:

1. **After adding the fields you need, click OK or click either the Style tab or the Customize Style tab to make further adjustments and then click OK to insert the Cross-Tab.**

   The Cross-Tab is attached as a rectangle to the mouse pointer; you insert the Cross-Tab the same way you insert a field.

2. **Insert the Cross-Tab object into the desired section of the report by moving the mouse pointer to that section and clicking the left mouse button.**

   Cross-Tab objects can be placed in Report Headers or Footers or in Group Headers or Footers. They cannot be placed in the Page Header or Footer or in the Details section.

**3. Click the Preview tab to see the report with the Cross-Tab.**

The example in Figure 12-10 is a Cross-Tab with Product.Product Name as Columns, Customer.City as Rows, Orders.Order Amount as the Summarized field, and the Basic Indigo Style selected. I inserted the Cross-Tab object into the Region Group Header of a Customer Phone list report. Notice that the Column names don't show up very well. I tell you how to fix that in the next section of this chapter.

| Design | Preview | | Today 9:00 | 4 of 4+ | |
|--------|---------|---|-----------|---------|---|
| GH1 | CA | | Active Outd | Active Outd | Guardian " | Guardian A | Gua |
| | | Irvine | $2,299.71 | $14,815.30 | $0.00 | $0.00 | |
| | | Newbury Park | $459.90 | $6,506.58 | $175.20 | $43.80 | |
| | | San Diego | $5,410.25 | $5,813.42 | $5,912.96 | $43.80 | |
| | | Santa Ana | $0.00 | $1,312.11 | $51.40 | $0.00 | |
| | | Total | $8,169.86 | $28,447.41 | $6,139.56 | $87.60 | |
| GH2 | | Bike Shop from Mars | 805-375-0110 | | | | |
| GH2 | | Changing Gears | 714-450-7009 | | | | |
| GH2 | | Off the Mountaing Biking | 714-450-3622 | | | | |

**Figure 12-10:**
The Cross-Tab object in the Report Header.

If you have incomplete data, you may end up with blank rows or columns. If that happens, you have to fine-tune your record selection so that the report doesn't contain records with partial information. To have Crystal Reports suppress empty rows or columns, right-click the Cross-Tab object, select Format Cross-Tab from the shortcut menu, and then click the Customize Style tab in the dialog box that appears. The features of the Customize Style tab are covered at the end of this chapter.

## Reformatting the layout

You can reformat the layout of the Cross-Tab tab by clicking and dragging. To resize a column, simply resize any field in the column. If the column name is very long compared to the summarized number in the column, you can make the Column name field taller and allow the name to wrap onto a second or third line. By referring to Figure 12-10, you see that the names of the products are truncated or cut off because of the length of the field. Figure 12-11 shows the table with the Product Name field enlarged. You can also reformat the numbers by right-clicking them and choosing a format option from the shortcut menu.

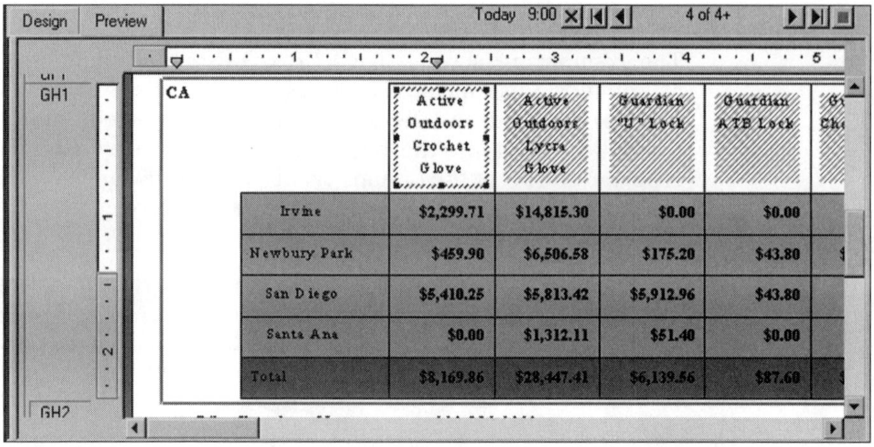

**Figure 12-11:**
The Product
Name
field is
lengthened
to reveal the
entire name.

## Removing the grid

In addition to being able to format individual numbers and resize the columns in a Cross-Tab object, you can turn off the grid outline that defines the Cross-Tab object. To do so, follow these steps:

1. **Right-click the table to open the shortcut menu.**

   The shortcut menu says Cross-Tab at the top.

   *Note:* When you right-click the Cross-Tab, Crystal Reports may think you're trying to modify a single field rather than the entire Cross-Tab. To select the entire Cross-Tab for editing, try right-clicking the top-left corner of the Cross-Tab.

2. **Choose Format Cross-Tab.**

   The Format Cross-Tab dialog box appears.

3. **Click the Customize Style tab.**

4. **Click Format Grid Lines to open the Format Grid Lines dialog box.**

5. **Select the Show Grid option to remove the check mark and turn off the grid around the cross-tab.**

6. **Click OK to close the dialog box and then click OK in the Format Cross-Tab dialog box.**

## Pivoting the Cross-Tab object

Crystal Reports has the capability to pivot the rows with the columns to quickly provide a different view of the data.

To pivot the Cross-Tab object, follow these steps:

1. **Right-click the Cross-Tab object so that the entire object is selected.**

   You want to click in the upper-left corner of the Cross-Tab object, above the first row.

2. **From the shortcut menu that appears, as shown in Figure 12-12, choose Pivot Cross-Tab.**

   The rows and columns change places, as shown in Figure 12-13.

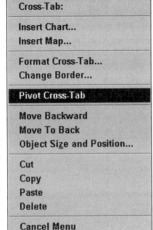

**Figure 12-12:**
The pop-up menu for the Cross-Tab object.

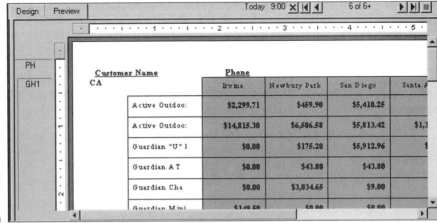

**Figure 12-13:**
The Cross-Tab object is pivoted, changing the positions of the rows and columns.

# Customizing the Cross-Tab Object

One of the tabs in the Cross-Tab dialog box is the Customize Style tab. If you decide to make some adjustments after you preview the Cross-Tab, click the Cross-Tab object, right-click to open the shortcut menu, and then choose Format Cross-Tab to bring up the Format Cross-Tab dialog box. Click the Customize Style tab to display it, as shown in Figure 12-14.

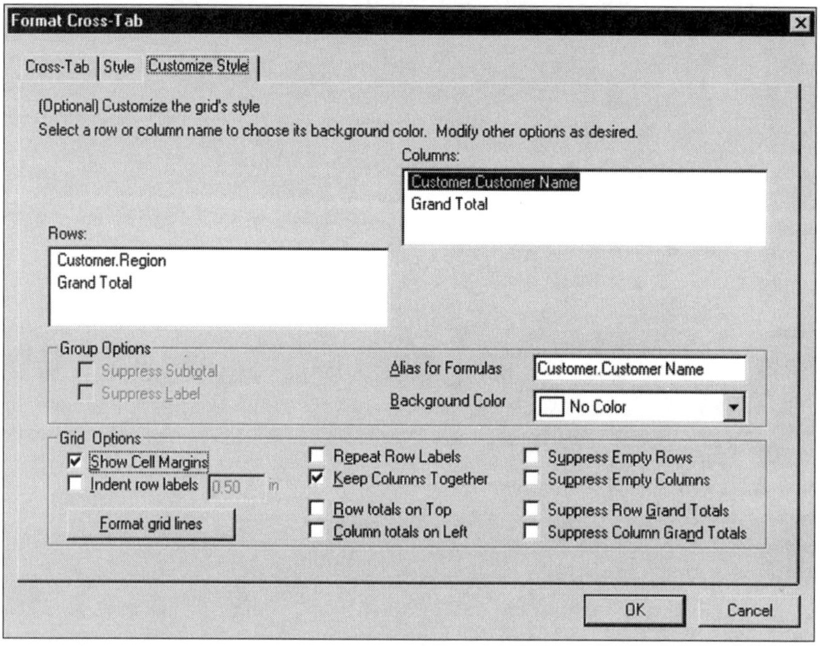

**Figure 12-14:** The Customize Style tab of the Format Cross-Tab dialog box.

Use the Customize Style tab to format your Cross-Tab's grid with background color, gridlines, and cell margins. For example, you may want certain items in the Cross-Tab to have a different background color in order to highlight those values. The Customize Style tab offers the following options:

- **Columns:** Displays the columns you select for your Cross-Tab. Select the field for which you want to customize the style.

- **Rows:** Displays the rows you select for your Cross-Tab. Select the field for which you want to customize the style.

- **Suppress Subtotal:** Use this check box to suppress the subtotal for a selected field. You must first have two fields selected in either the Rows list or the Columns list.

✔ **Suppress Label:** Use this check box to suppress the label of a suppressed subtotal field. This check box is only active after the Suppress Subtotal check box is selected.

✔ **Alias for Formulas:** Enter an alias name for the selected row or column field. The field's original name is shown in this box by default. Using an alias is an advanced feature of Crystal Reports not covered in this book.

✔ **Background Color:** Use this list to pick the color you want for the background of the selected row or column field.

✔ **Show Cell Margins:** Select this check box to have the program automatically format the spacing between the cells of the Cross-Tab. When this check box is not selected, any extra space (white space) between the cells of the Cross-Tab is eliminated and the contents of the cells are adjusted to use as little space as possible in your report.

✔ **Indent Row Labels:** Select this check box to indent row labels on your Cross-Tab. Use the inches box to specify the size of the indent you want to see.

✔ **Format grid lines:** When you click this button, the Format Grid Lines dialog box appears. In this dialog box, you can define whether the grid lines are shown or not, as well as the color, style, and width you want the grid lines to have. Figure 12-15 shows the dialog box for formatting the grid lines.

✔ **Repeat Row Labels:** Select this check box for the program to repeat row labels on every page for Cross-Tabs that print across more than one page.

✔ **Keep Columns Together:** Select this check box for the program to keep columns together on every page for Cross-Tabs that print across more than one page.

✔ **Row Totals on Top:** Select this check box if you want row totals to appear at the top of the Cross-Tab rather than at the bottom (the default position).

✔ **Column Totals on Left:** Select this check box if you want column dimensions to appear on the left of the Cross-Tab rather than on the right (the default position).

✔ **Suppress Empty Rows:** Select this check box for the program to remove empty rows from the Cross-Tab. When this check box is selected, any rows in which fields contain zero values are hidden.

✔ **Suppress Empty Columns:** Select this check box for the program to remove empty columns from the Cross-Tab. When this check box is selected, any columns in which fields contain zero values are hidden.

✔ **Suppress Row Grand Totals:** Select this check box for the program to remove the grand total from rows in the Cross-Tab.

✔ **Suppress Column Grand Totals:** Select this check box for the program to remove the grand total from columns in the Cross-Tab.

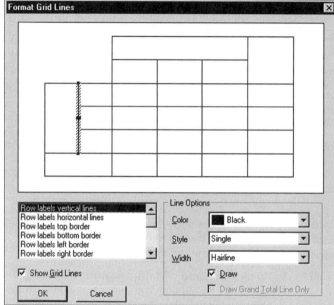

**Figure 12-15:**
The Format
Grid Lines
dialog box
opened
from the
Customize
Style tab.

# Design Report versus Preview Sample

What's the difference between Design Report and Preview Sample in the Cross-Tab Expert? Design Report creates the report and puts you in the Design tab. Preview Sample allows you to tell Crystal Reports how much data to include in the report and then shows you the report in the Preview tab.

Preview Sample is great to use when you create a report that includes tons of data. Maybe it's a quarterly transaction report of all orders and easily contains 100,000 records. You can speed up the report design process by using Preview Sample and designing the report by using a smaller number of records.

If you want to use this feature, click Preview Sample.

If you want to preview the report with all records, click OK. If you want to limit the number of records, select the First 100 Records radio button, enter the sample number you want, and click OK.

After you finish designing the report and want to show all records, simply click the Refresh Report Data button on the toolbar or choose Report➪Refresh Report Data.

# Chapter 13

# Creating a Summary Report

● ● ● ● ● ● ● ● ● ● ● ● ● ● ● ● ● ● ● ● ● ● ● ● ● ● ● ● ● ● ● ● ● ● ● ● ● ● ● ● ● ● ● ● ● ●

*In This Chapter*

▶ Creating a summary report

▶ Suppressing data

● ● ● ● ● ● ● ● ● ● ● ● ● ● ● ● ● ● ● ● ● ● ● ● ● ● ● ● ● ● ● ● ● ● ● ● ● ● ● ● ● ● ● ● ● ●

*A*fter you complete a report, you sometimes want to condense its information. For example, if you have hundreds of records in the Details section, the individual records may not be as important as the summary operations you've created — although someone else may want to delve in and take a look at the individual records. No need to create two reports; all you need to do is use drill-down on the summary information to get the details. In this chapter, I show you the best ways to present the report in a summarized manner.

## Looking at a Summary Report

You cannot create a summary report without first having, for lack of a better word, a *full* report that includes records in the Details section and (this is important) a group and a summary field.

You can consider a *summary report* to be the high-level overview of a complete detail report. Rather than seeing the underlying individual records as you do in a detailed report, you see the summary information only.

To create a summary report, follow these steps:

1. **Open the report you want to modify.**

   Make sure that the report has at least one group already created. If the report doesn't have a group, you must create one, as described in Chapters 2 and 5. The report in Figure 13-1 groups the Customer Names by Region.

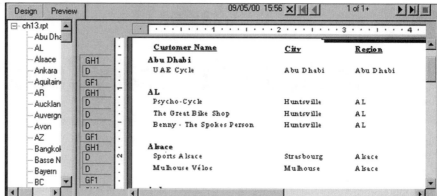

**Figure 13-1:**
Details
showing on
the report.

2. **Click the Design tab and open the Section Expert in one of these three ways:**

- Click the Section Expert button on the Standard toolbar.

- Choose Format⇨Section.

- Move the mouse pointer to the left margin, right-click to open the shortcut menu, and then choose Format Section. The Section Expert dialog box appears, as shown in Figure 13-2.

See Chapter 9 for information about the options contained in this dialog box.

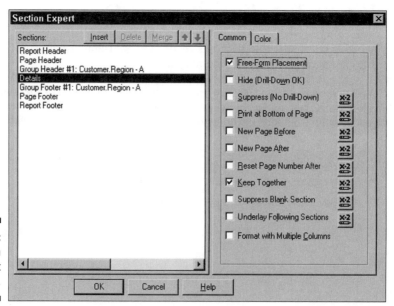

**Figure 13-2:**
The Section
Expert
dialog box.

3. **Select Details in the Sections list on the left side of the dialog box**.

   The options listed on the Common tab on the right side of the dialog box depend on the section selected on the left. You can select whatever options you want.

4. **Click the Hide (Drill-Down OK) option and click OK to return to the Design tab.**

5. **Click the Refresh button on the Standard toolbar.**

6. **Click the Preview tab to see the results, as shown in Figure 13-3.**

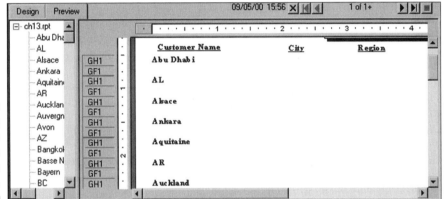

**Figure 13-3:**
A Summary Report! The Details are hidden now.

You can also hide sections of the report by moving the mouse to the left margin in the section you want to change and right-clicking the mouse. The pop-up menu appears, as shown in Figure 13-4. Choose Hide (Drill-Down OK) to achieve the same effect as in the preceding set of steps.

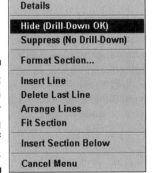

**Figure 13-4:**
The pop-up menu for hiding sections of the report.

# To Drill or Not to Drill, That Is the Question

Forgive the bad allusion to Shakespeare — I just can't resist showing off my liberal arts education. When you open the Section Expert dialog box, as described in the first set of steps in this chapter, you have two options regarding the way Crystal Reports formats the section. In the example in the preceding section, you choose the Hide (Drill-Down OK) option. If you use that method, anyone looking at the summary report can double-click the summary number and get the underlying records to display in a new Drill-Down tab.

Try this trick yourself: Double-click a subtotal in your report. The new Drill-Down tab appears, displaying the name of the group chosen and the detail records, as shown in Figure 13-5.

To close this Drill-Down tab, click the red X by the page control buttons.

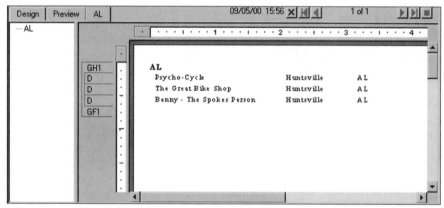

**Figure 13-5:** Double-click a summary, and the drill-down tab appears.

If you don't want anyone to see the underlying records, you can select the Suppress (No Drill-Down) option in the Section Expert dialog box. This option can come in handy for a payroll report, for example, in which each record lists the salary of employees. People may need the summary data but not the individual record data. By using this option, you can suppress the information and make it inaccessible from the report.

The Suppress option overrides the Hide option, so if you mistakenly have them both turned on, the Suppress option is in charge.

As you move the mouse pointer over the various components of a report in Preview mode, the mouse pointer may transform into a magnifying glass. That's your clue that the object underneath the pointer can be drilled down.

# Chapter 14

# Linking to Other Databases

• • • • • • • • • • • • • • • • • • • • • • • • • • • • • • • • • • • • • • • • • • •

*In This Chapter*

▶ Understanding linking concepts

▶ Working with links

▶ Using SQL joins

• • • • • • • • • • • • • • • • • • • • • • • • • • • • • • • • • • • • • • • • • • •

*I*n the esoteric world of database design, one table does not a database make. (*Esoteric,* in this case, means "understood by a chosen few," which now includes you.) Although you can create a database with just one table, most databases are made from collections of tables. When database administrators design and create the tables, they create relationships between the tables. The relationships between tables are made from fields that are identical to fields in another table. In Crystal Reports, you can create additional links that are made from fields in one table that are similar, sometimes identical, to fields in another table. In this chapter, you explore the ins and outs of linking database tables and files.

## Linking Concepts

The simple linking concept is that if you've selected fields from multiple tables for the report and you don't tell Crystal how the tables link, your reports won't work. However, much more is involved in linking than that simple statement implies. As examples, Tables 14-1 and 14-2 show an order table and a customer table, respectively.

| Table 14-1 | An Order Table | |
|---|---|---|
| *Order #* | *Customer #* | *Product* |
| 055 | 467 | Pupas |
| 056 | 258 | Butterflies |
| 057 | 333 | Pupas |
| 058 | 258 | Caterpillars |
| 059 | 467 | Moths |

| Table 14-2 | A Customer Table | |
|---|---|---|
| *Customer #* | *Address* | *City* |
| 258 | 5050 Parkland Road | Indianapolis |
| 333 | 657 Maple Plain | Pittsburgh |
| 467 | 95443 High Hills Plaza | Tucson |

If customer number 258 places an order, you can enter all of that customer's information in the order table. For example, you can take an order, complete the customer's address, and add the phone number. By using links, however, you save yourself unnecessary steps by simply inserting the customer number. The database then goes to the customer table, finds the matching number 258, and finds the address for you. You enter 258, and the database finds the address, 5050 Parkland Road. By using this technique, you type the address only one time — not on every order, every invoice, and every letter.

The database designer created the relationship between the two tables so that the customer's address is stored in one location in the database. This is an example of how the relationships in the database help you connect to the correct data while you create reports with Crystal Reports. In Crystal Reports, these relationships are called "links."

Links make data in one table accessible to data in another table. If you don't link the customer number from the Order table to the customer number in the Customer table, you cannot find the customer address. When you later create a report, you cannot print the customer address on the report if the tables aren't linked via the customer number. When you design a database, you create the links between fields so that you can easily find the data you're looking for.

# Normalizing a database

The process of making a database as efficient as possible, by not storing redundant data, is called *normalizing.* A well-designed database is normal. (Our only hope is that we all can be somewhat normal.)

By having a normalized database, the person who enters a certain type of data enters that type only one time, in one table. When that data is needed in conjunction with other information, the database goes out and looks up the data. That's where the links come in.

Tables 14-1 and 14-2, the Order table and the Customer table, are linked by a common field: the customer number. The linking field usually has the same kind of data in it (in this case, a number), and the data is usually the same length (in this case, three digits). The linking field usually is a primary key in a table, as described in the following section.

# Keying primarily

A *primary key* is a field in a database that serves as a unique identifier for each record; you have a primary key, for instance. Someone wanting to find information about you may look up your Social Security number, which is a unique number for each individual. (Hopefully, no two people have the same Social Security number.) In the sample tables shown in the "Linking Concepts" section earlier in this chapter, you look up a customer based on the customer number. The customer number is the primary key for the customer table.

A primary key usually has an *index* or is an *indexed field,* which means that a database, by using a number of techniques, can quickly look up a record on an indexed field. Using primary keys to link tables with indexed fields makes your database fast and efficient.

How does an index work? Its name gives the secret away. Just as an index in a book makes looking up specific information easier, a database index makes looking up data faster and easier. An index may organize the same data in several different ways, enabling you to easily find matches among hundreds of records.

Some of the databases on which you do reports automatically index a primary key. Other databases don't have indexing capabilities. If you can, work with your database administrator to make sure that each database table has an index. Doing so not only improves the performance of your database but also improves the speed at which you can generate reports.

Suppose that you *query* (ask) the database to display the name and address of customer 258 and then display a list of all the customer's orders. The computer looks at order number 055 in the order table and then asks whether that's an order number for 258. Because the answer is No, that order isn't included in the answer to your query. The computer moves on to the next record. Is order number 056 an order for customer 258? Yes. That record is included in the answer. The computer matches the orders to customer number 258. Those orders are 056 and 058. Even though the orders aren't sequentially related to customer numbers, the computer finds the records matching your request by using the links between the tables.

What Crystal Reports calls "links" between tables may be made up of *keys*, including primary keys and foreign keys. Sometimes you hear the terms "joins" or "relationships" rather than links.

# *Working with Links*

To view the links already established in a report in the Xtreme database, follow these steps:

1. **Open a report by clicking the Open button on the Standard toolbar.**

    The Open dialog box appears.

2. **Navigate to the folder by following C:\Program Files\Seagate Software\ Crystal Reports\Samples\Reports\General Business.**

3. **Double-click the General Business folder and then double-click the Inventory report.**

    The report opens.

4. **Open the Database menu and select Visual Linking Expert.**

    The Visual Linking Expert dialog box opens.

In the Visual Linking Expert dialog box, shown in Figure 14-1, you see the underlying tables from which this report collects its data. The Product, Purchases, and Product Type tables from the database used for this report appear with small arrows indicating the links between them. For example, you can see that the Product ID field in the Product table is linked to the Product ID field in the Purchases table. By using these links, you can navigate through the tables to collect and match information from any of the linked tables.

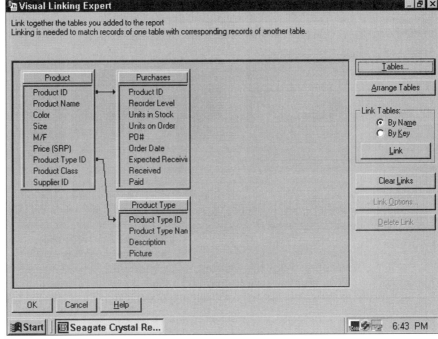

**Figure 14-1:**
The Visual
Linking
Expert
dialog box
with
Inventory
Report
tables and
links
displayed.

If you're unable to see all the tables, click the scroll bars that appear at the bottom and side of the Visual Linking Expert dialog box to view tables not shown in the window or click the Maximize button for the window.

You may notice a pattern with linked fields. For instance, all the linked fields in this example have identical names; they just appear in different tables. If you take a closer look, you see that the linked fields also have the same characteristics. The data length is the same, as is the data type. The linked field names are not always identical, but they often are. What is more important is that the data in the field can be matched.

## Browsing through fields

In the Product table in the Visual Linking Expert dialog box, click the Product ID field. Right-click the field and then click the Browse Field option from the shortcut menu to display the data in the field in a separate Product.Product ID dialog box, as shown in Figure 14-2. This box shows the type of data in the field; in this example, the data is a Number type. The values displayed are some of the Product ID's in the database. Click Done to close the dialog box.

Now do the same thing with the Product ID field in the Purchases table. See! It's the same type of field, Numeric, and the data values are the same. Looks as if these two fields would do a great job of linking these two tables together.

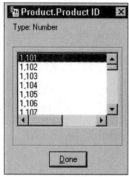

**Figure 14-2:**
The
Product.
Product ID
dialog box
showing
Browsed
data.

This information is useful if you want to create links between tables. You can link between two string type fields in which the string consists of 50 characters in both fields and the fields contain identical information. In some circumstances, you may be able to link when one field has a string of 20 characters and another has a string of 50 characters (for example, when you want to link an address field from one database in which the field is defined as 20 characters with the address field from a different database that allows 50 characters).

You cannot link numeric data with string data. *Numeric* data can be used in a mathematical calculation, such as a date field, a value, a measurement, or currency. *String* data, although it may include numbers, isn't used as part of a mathematical calculation.

When you finish perusing the Browse Field dialog box, simply click the Done button to close the dialog box. You're ready to create your report.

## Looking at links

The arrows between the tables in the Visual Linking Expert dialog box show you the links. When you click a link line to select it, the line is highlighted to show that it is selected and the text in the linked tables is highlighted. You can then easily see the links.

When you link tables in Crystal Reports, you have to know a few important concepts. One concept is that you have a primary table and a lookup table. The primary table has a link to a field in the lookup table. Using that link, a query of the primary table goes to the matching record in the lookup table to find the correct data. The *primary* table is the table you link *from;* the *lookup* table is the table you link *to.*

In the Visual Linking Expert dialog box, the Product table is a primary table. From this table, you link to the Product Type table via the Product Type ID field. The Product Type table is the lookup table.

## *Exploring the Visual Linking Expert buttons*

The buttons along the bottom and side of the Visual Linking Expert dialog box enable you to initiate different activities. Table 14-3 describes these buttons, which you use to complete a report.

| Table 14-3 | Buttons in the Visual Linking Expert Dialog Box |
|---|---|
| *Button* | *What It Does* |
| OK | Accepts the links you've created. Click this button when you have all your links set up the way you want and you're ready to create a report. |
| Cancel | Cancels your activity in the Visual Linking Expert dialog box. |
| Help | Accesses context-sensitive help. When you click this button, Help information is displayed in the Visual Linking Expert dialog box. |
| Tables | Opens the Choose Tables to Use in Visual Linking dialog box. You can then select the tables you want to link to create your report. |
| Arrange Tables | Arranges all the tables in the Visual Linking Expert dialog box. Click this button to arrange tables after you add several tables and want them automatically arranged. |
| Link Tables | Links the tables displayed in the Visual Linking Expert dialog box if they have not already been linked. Select the By Name or the By Key radio button to automatically create logical links between those tables. Select name, and the program looks for matching names, such as Product ID. Select key, and the program finds matching primary keys. After you select name or key, click the Link button. If Crystal Reports can't create links, a message appears, telling you that links are not possible. |
| Clear Links | Click this button to erase all the links arranged in the Visual Linking Expert dialog box. |
| Link Options | Specifies options for the link. When you select a link line and click Link Options, the Link Options dialog box opens. You can then choose which index you want to use and select other options about the selected link. |
| Delete Link | Deletes a link after you select a link line. |

## Using link options

Some of the link options are only available for non-SQL based reports. If you are using an SQL-based report, some of the items in this dialog box are grayed out.

When you link two fields from two tables, more than one index may be on the link. Crystal Reports selects one of the indexes available to use for the link. You may want to change the index to improve the report performance or to make indexes consistent for one report.

If you want to adjust the index used for the link, open the Link Options dialog box by following one of these methods:

✔ Click the link line and then click the Link Options button in the Visual Linking Expert dialog box.

✔ Right-click a link line. When the menu appears, choose Options.

✔ Double-click the link line.

The Link Options dialog box opens, and you see the following features:

✔ **From/To Description:** The top box provides a description of the link and indicates the table the link travels from and the table the link travels to.

✔ **Index in Use:** This box tells you the index that's in use. Click the drop-down arrow to see any other options. If you select the No Specific Index option, Crystal Reports selects an index for you when you display the report in the preview window. If the database you are using comes from an SQL data source, <No Specific Index> displays. In a non-SQL data source, you expect to see the indexes you can use for the link in this drop-down box.

✔ **Fields in Index:** This box lists the fields in the index.

✔ **Allow Partial Text Matches:** This check box lets you make partial text matches. This feature can be useful when you try to link, for example, one field with 50 characters and another with 20 characters and with similar data in the fields. Click this box to allow a match on the partial text in the fields rather than an exact match of the text as, for example, when you have an address field from one database defined as 20 characters and an address field from a different database defined as 50 characters. Allowing a partial text match enables you to match "10789 Rancho Pen. Bv" with "10789 Rancho Penasquitos Boulevard."

*Note:* A partial text match works only when the string in the lookup table is longer than the string in the primary table.

✔ **When Linking to Two Files from This File:** This box provides the following three options that enable you to determine how you want to link two records from these tables. Select the radio button (the circle next to the text — it looks like an old-fashioned car radio button) to choose the option you want. These options are available only on data files (non-SQL data sources).

- **Look Up Both at the Same Time:** Looks up one record in the primary table (Table A) and a matching record in the lookup table (Table B). Crystal Reports looks for the next matching record in one lookup table and then for the next matching record in the next lookup table (Table C) until it finds all the matching records. This process is repeated for every record in the primary table (Table A).

- **Look Up All of One, Then All of Others:** Directs Crystal Reports to look up each record in the primary table (Table A) and then all the matching records in the lookup table (Table B). After all the matching records are found in Table B, Crystal Reports looks for all the matching records in the second lookup table (Table C). The program goes back to the primary table and repeats this process with each record in the primary table. In other words, it links first from Table A to Table B, and then from Table A to Table C.

- **Look Up All the Combinations of the Two Files:** For each record in the primary table (Table A), looks for a matching record in the lookup table (Table B), after which it finds all the matching records in the next lookup table (Table C). After all the matching records in Table C are found, the process is repeated with the next record in the first lookup table (Table B). After all the matches are found for that record in the first lookup table (Table B), the process is repeated on the next record in the primary table (Table A).

✔ **SQL Join Types:** This box is addressed at the end of this chapter, in the section "Using SQL Joins."

## *Creating links*

Creating links between tables is as easy as drawing a line with your mouse. In any report, you can open the Visual Linking Expert dialog box and manipulate the linking process. You can create a link to the new table in two ways: by manually drawing a link or by clicking the Link button.

In the example Inventory report, open the Visual Linking Expert dialog box as follows:

1. **Open the Database menu and choose the Visual Linking Expert.**

   The Visual Linking Expert dialog box appears, showing the report tables and the existing links.

2. **Click the Clear Links button.**

   A dialog box appears, asking whether you're sure you want to delete.

3. **Click Yes.**

4. **Move the mouse pointer to the Product table (in this example), click the Product ID field, and hold down the mouse button.**

5. **Drag the mouse pointer to the Product ID field in the Purchases table.**

   A linking pointer appears that looks like a zigzagged line with an arrow on one end. Make sure it is below the field, not in the gray highlighted area on top of the Product ID field or the link will not be drawn.

6. **Release the mouse button.**

   A link is created between the Product ID fields in the two tables.

The other option is to use the Link button. Use this method to create the link between the Product and the Product Type tables. In the Link Tables area, select the By Name radio button and then click the Link button.

All the fields you would expect to link now have a link between them (refer to Figure 14-1 to see links between the Product, Purchases, and Product Type tables). Crystal Reports calls this Smart-linking. Smart-linking should be used with caution because it may create links between fields that are named the same but do not contain the same type of data. Not all fields with the same name have the same data.

## Deleting a table from the report

In this section, you find out how to delete a table by deleting (in the example) the Orders table, which isn't necessary for the report.

To delete tables and links at the same time, follow these easy steps:

1. **Choose Database⇨Remove from Report.**

   The Remove from Report dialog box appears with the list of databases included in the report.

2. **Select the table you want to remove from the report.**

3. **Click the Remove button.**

4. **Repeat Steps 2 and 3 for each table you want to remove.**

5. **Click Done when you're done.**

These steps also automatically remove any links you had between the tables.

# Using the Visual Linking Expert dialog box to add tables

You can add tables by using the Visual Linking Expert dialog box. To do so, follow these steps:

1. **In the Visual Linking Expert dialog box, click the Tables button.**

   The Choose Tables To Use In Visual Linking dialog box appears.

2. **Click the Add Table button.**

   The Data Explorer dialog box appears.

3. **Find the table(s) you want to add from the list.**

   In this example, select the Orders Detail table.

4. **Click the Add button.**

   The selected table appears in the Invisible Tables box in the Choose Tables To Use In Visual Linking dialog box, which is behind the Data Explorer dialog box.

5. **Repeat Steps 2 and 3 until you've added all the tables you need.**

6. **Click Close.**

   The Data Explorer dialog box closes, returning you to the Choose Tables To Use In Visual Linking dialog box. Notice in Figure 14-3 that the tables you added shifted automatically to the Visible Tables box. However, the difference between Invisible and Visible isn't important right now and is not covered in this book.

**Figure 14-3:**
The Choose Tables To Use In Visual Linking dialog box with the Orders Detail table ready to be linked to the others.

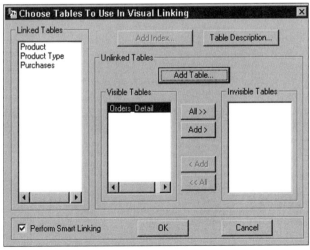

7. **Check the Perform Smart Linking box and then Click OK.**

   If you choose to NOT Perform Smart Linking, you have to draw in a link. Refer to the "Creating links" section earlier in this chapter to see how to do so.

   The Orders Detail table is now linked to the Product table using the Product ID field.

## Creating a report after you select tables

After you select all the tables you want for your report and remove any you don't want, click OK in the Visual Linking Expert dialog box.

Return to the Design window for your new report. The Field Explorer dialog box is open, ready for you to select the fields you want and to insert them in the Design window (see Figure 14-4).

**Figure 14-4:**
The Field
Explorer
dialog box.

Because you linked the four tables in the Visual Linking Expert dialog box, you can create a report with fields from any of the four tables. By using these three tables, you can create a report that lists the Orders Detail, Product, Product Type, and Purchases.

## Using SQL Joins

The information in this section is important because, according to the creators of Crystal Reports, 60 percent of their customers use SQL databases.

Don't worry — you don't have to be an expert in SQL to be able to use SQL joins. Some of this information is handy reference material if you're making an SQL connection.

*SQL,* or Structured Query Language, is the underlying language used in many databases. (Some people just say "S-Q-L," and others pronounce it "sequel." Either way, they're referring to Structured Query Language.) Although the language is fairly easy to understand, a discussion of it is beyond the scope of this book. For more in-depth information, take a look at one of the many available books about the SQL language, including *SQL For Dummies,* 3rd Edition, by Allen G. Taylor (IDG Books Worldwide, Inc.). In addition, many colleges and technical schools offer classes on the subject. If you're familiar with working with databases in Access, you know that you can create a query and then view the SQL language written to produce that query.

Crystal Reports enables you to link SQL tables to create reports and to specify the kind of join you want to use to link them. The type of join you specify determines in what order the lookup is made between tables. The order of the lookup also determines how records are joined in the results. For example, in an equal join, all matching records are returned in the report. However, in a left-outer join, when the arrow starts with the left table and points to the right, you see all the records in the table on the left and only the matching records in the table on the right. SQL join types are listed in the Link Options dialog box. To use these join types, you must add a table via *Open Database Connectivity (ODBC),* the Microsoft standard for connecting client/server systems.

## Adding tables via ODBC or non-ODBC

ODBC is the Microsoft standard for Open Database Connectivity, and Crystal Reports supports that standard. Adding a database of this type to a report follows a bit different route than adding other types of databases.

You add an ODBC database to an existing report by following these steps:

1. **Open the database menu and choose Add Database to Report.**

   The Data Explorer dialog box appears.

2. **Double-click the database you want to add to the report.**

3. **Click the Close button.**

   The next screen you see depends on the database you select. If you're using a secured database, you're asked for your user name and password.

From the SQL Server Login dialog box, click the Options button to select the Database, Language, Application Name, and WorkStation ID.

# Crystal Reports and SQL

Although SQL is primarily a query language, it also has capabilities for creating, managing, and organizing tables in a database. Usually used in a client/server application, SQL sends statements to an SQL database server. The statements ask (or query) the database to return certain information. The SQL database server receives the SQL request for information, analyzes the request, finds the requested information, and then returns that data to the source of the query statement.

Because Crystal Reports provides a graphical user interface (GUI, pronounced gooey) with which to query an SQL database, the program creates the actual SQL statement with the information that you provide in the various dialog boxes. With Crystal Reports, you don't have to be a programmer to get results. It's one of many SQL-compliant application products that use SQL for querying a database.

*Note:* Check with your database administrator if you're connecting to a different database. Other databases that can be read by Crystal Reports by using ODBC are shown in Table 14-4.

| Table 14-4 | ODBC Drivers |
|---|---|
| *Database* | *ODBC Data Source* |
| IBM DB2/2 | CRDB2 |
| SQL Server | CR SQLBase |
| Oracle 7 | CR Oracle 7 |
| Oracle 8 | CR Oracle 8 |
| Informix | CR Informix |
| Informix 9 | CR Informix9 |
| Gupta | CRGUP |
| Sybase System 10/11 | CR Sybase System 10 |

Some SQL databases let you connect without using ODBC. Because so many options exist, I suggest you see your database administrator to find out how your organization connects to the database.

# Using SQL join types

A description of how to delve into the nitty-gritty of SQL is beyond the scope of this book. You can use Table 14-5, however, as a guide to help you select the SQL join type you want to use. If you're experienced with SQL, the table already makes sense; if you're not, however, take this table to your nearest SQL guru to help you make sense of the various SQL join types. My educated guess is that you will only ever use the first two SQL join types listed: Equal and Left Outer.

| Table 14-5 | | Defining the SQL Join Types |
|---|---|---|
| *SQL Join Type* | *Symbol* | *What It Includes* |
| Equal join | = | All records in which the linked field value is an exact match |
| Left outer join | *= | All records in which the linked field value is an exact match, plus a row for every record in the primary table whose linked field has no match in the lookup table |
| Right outer join | =* | All records in which the linked field value is an exact match, plus a row for every record in the lookup table whose linked field has no match in the primary table |
| Greater join | > | All records in which the linked field value in the primary table is greater than the linked field value in the lookup table |
| Less join | < | All records in which the linked field value from the primary table is less than the linked field value in the lookup table |
| Greater-or-equal join | >= | All records in which the linked field value from the primary table is greater than or equal to the linked field value in the lookup table |
| Less-or-equal join | <= | All records in which the linked field value from the primary table is less than or equal to the linked field value in the lookup table |
| Not-equal join | != | All records in which the linked field from the primary table is not equal to the linked field value in the lookup table |

# Creating SQL Expression Fields

In order to create an SQL Expression Field, the data source used in the report must be an SQL database. When you connect to this type of database, the SQL Expression editor is added to the Field Explorer dialog box. Figure 14-5 shows the Field Explorer dialog box, with the Expression editor included.

**Figure 14-5:**
The SQL Expression Fields selection in the Field Explorer dialog box.

To create the SQL Expression, follow these steps:

**1. In the Field Explorer dialog box, click the SQL Expression Fields item.**

**2. Click the New button on the toolbar.**

The SQL Expression Name dialog box appears.

**3. Type a name for the expression and click OK.**

For this example, type Book.

The SQL Expression Editor dialog box appears, as shown in Figure 14-6.

You build and edit your SQL expression in the large white SQL Expression box. You can work here in a number of ways with SQL expressions:

- You can select individual components from the Fields, Functions, and Operators tree boxes at the top of the SQL Expression Editor dialog box, and the program enters them directly into this box.

- You can type your SQL expression in the box.

- You can use the above two methods together.

- You can paste into the box SQL expressions that you cut or copy from other reports or from the Help system.

- You can cut or copy from the box SQL expressions to use in other reports or in printed documents.

• You can paste field values into your SQL expressions via the Browse Data button. This button is not active unless a field is selected; it appears on the SQL Expression Editor toolbar.

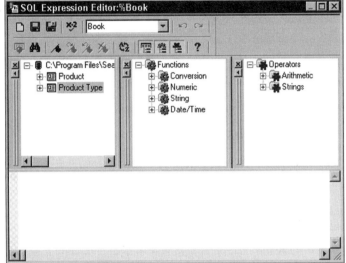

**Figure 14-6:**
The SQL
Expression
Editor
dialog box.

4. **After creating the expression, click the Save and Close button.**

   The expression is listed in the Field Explorer dialog box, and you can insert it into the report.

The Help section of Crystal Reports has a series of SQL expressions that you can use as examples for your own expressions. In addition, the Seagate Software Web site includes more example expressions, which you can cut and paste into your own expressions.

# Integration with Microsoft Office Products

Seagate Crystal Reports takes advantage of the Microsoft Add-In technology by offering a Report Creation Wizard that you can use with Microsoft Excel and Microsoft Access. The Seagate Software Report Creation Wizard offers familiar report design capabilities directly within your Microsoft Office applications — you can create a Crystal Reports report from your data without leaving Excel or Access.

## Create reports from Microsoft Excel spreadsheet data

By using the Add-In for Excel, you can create reports using data from a Microsoft Excel spreadsheet. You can choose and limit the Excel data you want available in the report. To maintain consistency with the data, *any data changes in Excel are updated automatically* in Seagate Crystal Reports. The capability is compatible with Excel Versions 97 and 2000.

You may need to install the Microsoft Excel Add-In through Excel's Add-In Manager before you can use it. If you installed Excel after Seagate Crystal Reports, refer to the following procedure. If, however, you installed Excel before Seagate Crystal Reports, the Add-In is installed automatically.

*Note:* If the Excel Add-In is automatically installed and you choose to remove it, you must install it manually (using the following procedure) and then use the Microsoft Add-In Manager to uninstall it. After the Crystal Report Wizard is added to Excel, you can select it anytime you use Excel.

To install the Crystal Report Wizard in Excel, follow these steps:

1. **In Excel, choose Tools➪Add-Ins.**

2. **In the Add-Ins dialog box that appears, click Browse.**

3. **In the Browse dialog box that appears, search for the file Crptxls.xla and click to select it.**

   Crptxls.xla is installed in the \Program Files\Seagate Software\ Report Designer Component directory by default. The file may have been moved to another directory by a system administrator.

4. **Click OK.**

   The Crystal Report Wizard is added to the Add-Ins dialog box and is selected by default.

### Installing the Crystal Report Access Add-In

You may need to install the Microsoft Access Add-In through the Access Add-In Manager before you can use it. If you installed Access after Seagate Crystal Reports, refer to the following procedure. If, however, you installed Access before Seagate Crystal Reports, the Add-In is installed automatically.

*Note:* If the Access Add-In is automatically installed and you choose to remove it, you must install it manually (using the following procedure) and then use the Microsoft Add-In Manager to uninstall it.

After the Crystal Report Add-In is added to Access, you can select it anytime you use Access.

To install the Crystal Report Access Add-In, follow these steps:

1. **In Access, choose Tools➪Add-Ins➪Add-In Manager.**

   The Add-In Manager dialog box appears. The Add-Ins option is available only after a database has been opened in Access.

**2. Click Add New.**

Search for the file Crptaccwz2k.mde (or Crptaccwz97.mde if you're using Microsoft Access 97) in the Open dialog box and click to select it.

Crptaccwz2k.mde is installed in the \Program Files\Seagate Software\ Report Designer Component directory by default. The file may have been moved to another directory by a system administrator.

**3. Click Open.**

The Crystal Report Access Add-In is added to the available Add-Ins list in the Add-In Manager dialog box.

# Part VI

# Disseminating Reports without a Hitch

The 5th Wave          By Rich Tennant

"The new technology has really helped me get organized. I keep my project reports under the PC, budgets under my laptop and memos under my pager."

# In this part . . .

Would you rather be rich or famous? No, "both" is not an option in answer to this question. Seagate Crystal Reports has the capability to take your reporting *masterpieces* and share them with the world! Herein lies the ticket to fame. Imagine . . . your report is distributed to every salesperson in the company. Or, better yet, it's posted to that Orwellian device known innocently as the World Wide Web. Undoubtedly, the end is near. Better get that report done before Armageddon, or there will be heck to pay. Your report is spreading everywhere at the speed of light! Supplicants are sending you e-mail from all over the world acknowledging your greatness. This is your moment in time! *Music up, lights fade to a single spotlight on a lone worker at a computer terminal. On the desk, a copy of the IDG Books catalog and* Crystal Reports 8 For Dummies. *The look on the face of the worker resembles Caesar crossing the Rubicon. . . .*

# Chapter 15

# Distributing Reports

. . . . . . . . . . . . . . . . . . . . . . . . . . . . . . . . . . . . . . . . . . . . . . . . . . . . . .

. . . . . . . . . . . . . . . . . . . . . . . . . . . . . . . . . . . . . . . . . . . . . . . . . . . . . .

*I*n this chapter, you see how to share your reports with a variety of software programs other than Seagate Crystal Reports. After you create a magnificent report, you naturally want to share it with the world! You can share your handiwork with other people in three general ways:

✔ Send a Crystal Reports file so that others can open the file in their copy of Crystal Reports.

✔ Export the report to a specific format, such as Microsoft Word or Microsoft Excel.

✔ Export the report to an HTML document, so others can view it in a Web browser, such as Netscape Navigator or Internet Explorer.

## What Is an Export File?

All computer programs are composed of files, and all computer programs create files. Crystal Reports creates report files. Underlying all files is a common data structure that other programs with the proper settings can understand. An *export file,* therefore, is simply a Crystal Reports file that has been translated into a structure that other programs can read and interpret. Some programs can interpret all the aspects of Crystal Reports files, and others cannot.

When you export a report file, you can retain some or all of the fancy formatting you previously created, depending on the program to which you're exporting the report file.

# Exporting Reports

Exporting a report file requires similar steps each time. You always select the *file format* (the data structure) into which you want to export the report file, and then you choose the physical destination for the translated report.

Follow these steps to export a report:

1. **Open the report you want to export from Crystal Reports.**

   In this example, I use the Brilliant Report created in Chapter 11.

 2. **Click the Export button on the Standard toolbar to open the Export dialog box.**

3. **Select the format for exporting the report.**

4. **Select the destination for the report and click the OK button.**

   Crystal Reports exports your report to the specified location and in the specified format.

## Choosing a file format

Every time you export a report file, you must specify a report format. Table 15-1 lists some of the formats you can use and gives you information to help you decide which file format to choose. The main thing you have to know for this process to work is what type of software the other person has.

| Table 15-1 | | Export Formats |
|---|---|---|
| *Software Application* | *Format* | *File Can Be Read By* |
| Crystal Reports | .RPT | Crystal Reports or Seagate Info |
| Word processing | .DOC, .RTF | A word processing program (Word for Windows reads .DOC files; almost all word processing programs read Rich Text Format [.RTF] files) |
| Spreadsheet | .XLS, .WKS | Spreadsheet programs (Excel reads .XLS files; Lotus reads .WKS files) |
| Lotus Notes | Any format | Lotus Notes |
| Exchange | Any format | Microsoft Exchange |

| Software Application | Format | File Can Be Read By |
|---|---|---|
| ODBC | Data | An ODBC data source set up through an ODBC administrator |
| HTML | HTML | Netscape, Internet Explorer, and other Web browsers |

For example, if all the employees in your office have Crystal Reports on their systems, export the file in Crystal Reports format. This format is sometimes called *native format* (referring to the product you're using to distribute the report, not to aborigines).

If your office uses Microsoft Exchange and all your coworkers have Microsoft Office (but not Crystal Reports), you can export the report in one of the Microsoft formats. Choose either Excel (XLS) or Word (DOC).

## *Choosing the report destination*

You also have to decide on the destination of the report that you're exporting. Table 15-2 lists the export-destination options and where the report goes when you select a certain option.

| Table 15-2 | Export-Destination Options |
|---|---|
| **Export Destination** | **What It Does** |
| Application | Generates the report and launches the application that can read the format you choose. If you are exporting to Word for Windows, Word will start with the report displayed. |
| Disk file | Saves the report to a disk file. When you select this option, a dialog box opens in which you can select the destination file. The file can be exported to a hard disk on your system or to a disk in drive A (or any other drive). |
| Exchange folder | Stores the report in a Microsoft Exchange folder. A dialog box opens in which you select the destination folder. |
| Lotus Domino database | Exports the report to a Lotus Notes database. |
| Microsoft Mail (MAPI) | Attaches the report to an e-mail message. Crystal Reports supports MAPI, the Microsoft Mail format used for either Exchange or Microsoft Mail. (For more information about MAPI, see the section "Mailing a Report," later in this chapter.) |

If you're exporting a report file to Excel (XLS), for example, you select Disk File as your destination. When the dialog box opens for you to select the destination file, select the filename you want, such as Dougrpt, and click OK.

If you work in a company that uses Microsoft Exchange, select Exchange Folder as the export destination. A dialog box opens in which you designate which Exchange folder is the destination folder.

## Exporting to Excel format

If you're networked and other users don't have Crystal Reports, you can export reports in other file formats directly to their machines. If you're in a small shop, however, you may have to use *sneaker net* (the system of physically carrying a disk to another computer, otherwise known as *troglodyte net*) to get a file from your machine to another. Or if you plan to attend a meeting, you may need to bring the report with you on a disk. Either way, you can export the report to an Excel file on a floppy disk.

With a report open in Crystal Reports, follow these steps:

1. **Click the Export button on the Standard toolbar.**

   The Export dialog box opens.

2. **Click the drop-down arrow in the Format box to display export format choices and then select Excel 7.0 (XLS).**

3. **Click the drop-down arrow in the Destination box to display destination choices and then select Disk File.**

   Figure 15-1 shows what the Export dialog box looks like after you complete these selections.

**Figure 15-1:**
The Export dialog box, with the Excel 7.0 format and the Disk File destination selected.

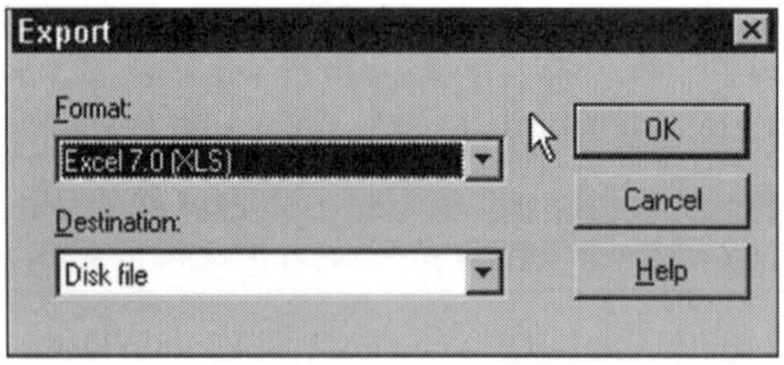

Export

Format:
Excel 7.0 (XLS)

Destination:
Disk file

OK

Cancel

Help

4. **Click OK.**

   The Choose Export File dialog box appears. Your next step is to choose the destination for the report file.

**5. Click the Up One Level button to the right of the Save In list box.**

Continue clicking this button until My Computer appears in the Save In box, as shown in Figure 15-2.

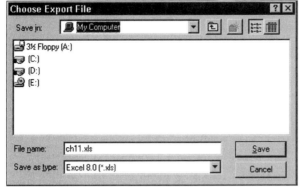

**Figure 15-2:**
The Choose Export File dialog box with My Computer selected.

**6. Before you take another step, make sure that you have a 3½-inch floppy disk in drive A.**

**7. Select the 3½ Floppy (A:) option and then click the Open button.**

The Choose Export File dialog box remains on-screen with Drive A files displayed, if there are any. The Open button changes to Save.

**8. Click the Save button.**

The Exporting box appears. This box isn't a dialog box; it simply displays during the exporting process.

You can easily tell whether the export worked. Follow these steps to see whether the file is on drive A:

**1. Choose Start➪Programs➪Windows Explorer.**

Windows Explorer opens.

**2. Select the 3½ Floppy (A:) option.**

The file you exported is displayed on the right side of the Explorer window. Figure 15-3 shows that this exported file is a Microsoft Excel worksheet.

The exported Excel file may not be what you expected. Notice in Figure 15-3 that all the columns (A, B, C, and so on) are the standard width and that the City column (which is the second column in the report) is in the fourth column of the spreadsheet. What gives? Crystal Reports attempts to lay out the report on the page as close as possible to the original field placement. Because the City field is 2 inches from the left margin, it is put in a column about 2 inches from the left side of the spreadsheet.

| | A | B | C | D | E | F | G | |
|---|---|---|---|---|---|---|---|---|
| 1 | | | | | Doug's Brilliant Report | | | |
| 2 | 10/05/00 | | | | | | | |
| 3 | **Customer Name** | | | **City** | **Region** | | | **Last Year** |
| 4 | | | | | | | | |
| 5 | **Abu Dhabi** | | | | | | | |
| 6 | UAE Cycle | | | Abu Dhabi | Abu Dhabi | | | $9 |
| 7 | | | | | | | | |
| 8 | **Number of Customers:** | | | 1 | **Subtotal of Sales:** | | | $95 |
| 9 | **AL** | | | | | | | |
| 10 | Psycho-Cycle | | | Huntsville | AL | | | $: |
| 11 | The Great Bike Shop | | | Huntsville | AL | | | $: |
| 12 | Benny - The Spokes Person | | | Huntsville | AL | | | $ |
| 13 | | | | | | | | |

◄ ◄ ► ►◄ **A Brilliant Report** / ◄ ► ►◄

Ready

🔰Start | 📷Seagate Crystal ... | 🗀Temp | ❌Microsoft Excel ... | 🖼🐢 9:35 PM

**Figure 15-3:**
The Ch11 report in Microsoft Excel worksheet format.

Try exporting to Excel 7.0 (XLS) (Extended) format instead. Figure 15-4 shows the format options available in the Format Options dialog box.

**Format Options** ☒

☑ Column Headings
☑ Use worksheet functions to represent subtotal fields in report

─ Set column width ─
○ Constant column width [10]
◉ Column width based on objects in area [Details ▼]

─ Format ─
◉ Non-Tabular format
○ Tabular format (Arrange all objects in one area into one row)

[ OK ] [ Cancel ]

**Figure 15-4:**
The Format Options dialog box in Microsoft Excel Extended.

These options include Column Headings and Use Worksheet Functions to Represent Subtotal Fields in Report, a formula to represent subtotals rather than just pasting the number in the cell. The columns are also based on the width of the fields in the Details section. Click OK and take a look at this report in Excel, as shown in Figure 15-5.

You may also export the file so that it opens immediately in Excel. In the Export dialog box, select one of the Excel formats and then select Application as the destination. Click OK to start the export. When the export is finished, Excel opens and the newly exported report appears. Use the File and Save As options in Excel to save the report as an Excel file.

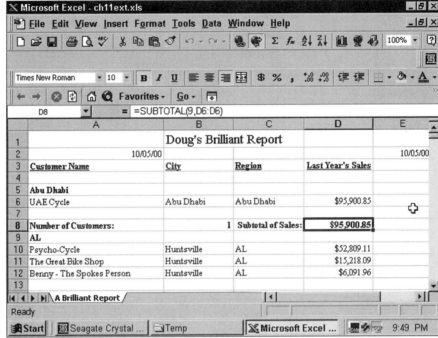

Figure 15-5:
The Ch11
report in
Microsoft
Excel
worksheet
format.

# Exporting to Microsoft Word format

When you export your Crystal Reports report to a Microsoft Word file, you convert the file to a .DOC document. By doing so, all Word users have ready access to your report. If you want to export a report into a Word document, open a report in Crystal Reports and follow these steps:

1. **Click the Export button on the Standard toolbar.**

   The Export dialog box appears.

2. **Click the drop-down arrow in the Format box to display the export format choices, and then select the Word for Windows document format.**

   You have to click the scroll button to move to the bottom of the list.

3. **Click the drop-down arrow in the Destination box to display the destination choices and then select Disk file.**

   The Choose Export File dialog box appears with a suggested name and destination for the file.

4. **Click Save.**

   The file is exported.

5. **Start Word and open the file, as shown in Figure 15-6.**

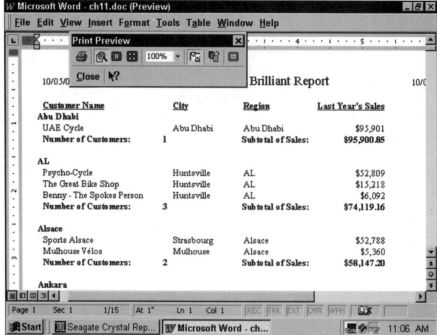

**Figure 15-6:**
The
exported
file in Word.

You may also export the file so that it opens immediately in Word. In the Export dialog box, select the Word for Windows format and then select Application as the destination. Click OK to start the export. When the export is finished, Word opens and the newly exported report appears. Use the File and Save As options in Word to save the report as a Word file.

## Exporting the Report Definition

Ever wish you could get a printout of how your report is built, because you want to know where all the fields are, what all the formulas are, and what the record selection is? Then export the report to the Report Definition format. The following steps tell you how:

**1. Click the Export button on the Standard toolbar.**

The Export dialog box appears.

**2. Click the drop-down arrow in the Format box to display the export format choices and then select the Report Definition format.**

The list is in alphabetic order; look under the R's.

3. **Click the drop-down arrow in the Destination box to display the destination choices and then select Disk file.**

   The Choose Export File dialog box appears with a suggested name and destination for the file.

4. **Click Save.**

   The Report definition file is created.

5. **Start Notepad or any text editor and open the file, as shown in Figure 15-7.**

## *Exporting to an ODBC data source*

With Crystal Reports, you can export reports to any ODBC data source. *ODBC,* or Open Data Base Connectivity, is a Microsoft standard for communications between applications and databases. (You may think that it stands for Obfuscation Daily By Computer.) You may ask yourself why you would want to export reports to an ODBC data source, anyway. Here are a few reasons:

✔ You can change data from a centralized database into a format that you can use in a local database. For example, you can change data from a Microsoft SQL Server to data you can use with Microsoft Access on your local database.

✔ Conversely, you can change data from a local database to data that is compatible with a centralized database. For example, you can change data from a Paradox database on your machine to data you can use with Oracle on a centralized database.

✔ You can convert a report to a new database table that can be used as a separate data set. Then you can create reports from that set of data.

When you export to ODBC, the assumption is made that you have an ODBC data source set up through ODBC Administrator for Crystal Reports. In that case, your ODBC data source is on the Export Format list. If not, follow the steps in the following section.

## *What's an ODBC data source?*

Using ODBC is like travelling through Europe with someone who knows every language in the world and can translate to every person you meet. In the same way, Crystal Reports can use ODBC to read all kinds of databases. The ODBC translator uses its translator library to interpret what the database says. Each database speaks to ODBC through its specific library files.

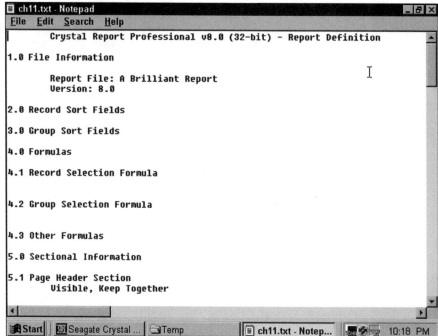

**Figure 15-7:**
The Report
Definition.

Files with the .DLL extension are library files used for translating between application programs. When you set up a database to be read by using ODBC, you have to know which library files to use for the destination database. Table 15-3 shows the database name and the ODBC data source as they appear in the Export dialog box. Selecting the correct data source ensures that you're using the correct libraries.

| Table 15-3 | Library Files |
|---|---|
| *Database* | *ODBC Data Source* |
| IBM DB2/2 | CRDB2 |
| *Database* | *ODBC Data Source* |
| Microsoft SQL Server 6.x | CRSS |
| Oracle 7 | CROR7 |
| Informix 7 | CRINF7 |
| SQLBase | CRGUP |
| Sybase System 10/11 | CRSYB |

Use this table as a guide when you're deciding which library file to use in your ODBC connection.

To export to an ODBC data source, begin with a report open in Crystal Reports, and then follow these steps:

1. **Click the Export button on the Standard toolbar.**

   The Export dialog box appears.

2. **Click the drop-down arrow in the Format box to display the export format choices and then select an ODBC format.**

   Use the scroll buttons to move to the ODBC options. The information in Table 15-3 can help you select the correct ODBC format. In this example, select ODBC-CRSS for SQL Server.

   *Note:* When you're working with ODBC, the Destination section is grayed out.

3. **Click OK.**

   If the ODBC data source specifies a particular database, the report is exported to that database. Otherwise, the Select Database dialog box appears.

4. **Select the database to which you want this report added as a new table.**

   The database name is highlighted.

5. **Click OK.**

   If the ODBC data source you highlight requires a logon ID and password, the Log On dialog box appears.

6. **Type your ID and password and then click OK.**

   The ODBC Table Name dialog box appears.

7. **Type the name for the new table in the database and click OK.**

   Crystal Reports exports the report as a new table in the destination database.

## Saving a report with/without saved data

The easiest way to give somebody else the report is, of course, to just give them the .RPT file with the data saved with it. They can then open the report in Crystal Reports to look at it. If you *save the data with the report,* you save the definition plus all the records that make up the report. The saved data does not include the source tables or the databases from which you selected individual records.

If you're the sales manager for a company, for example, you may want to send your salespeople the weekly sales report with the saved data. With their copy of Crystal Reports, they can look at and analyze that data without having to connect to the database to run the report themselves. Or, you may send them just the report (with no saved data), which they can run to get their own data. Either way, this feature is a powerful one for any business.

If you save the report without the data, the following results apply:

✔ Your report requires less disk space.

✔ The program you use to open the report has to retrieve data before it prints the report. In other words, the person receiving the definition must have access to the database.

If you save the report with data, the following results apply:

✔ Your report requires more disk space.

✔ The program you use to open the report doesn't have to retrieve data before printing the report, because that data is already part of the report.

*Note:* Along with the preceding considerations, you should know that when Crystal Reports saves data with a report, the data is compressed so that it takes up less disk space. When you open the report, Crystal Reports decompresses the data.

By default, Crystal Reports is set to save the data with the report. To change this option to NOT save the data with the report, follow these steps:

1. **Choose File from the menu bar.**

2. **Click the check mark to the left of the Save Data with Report default option to turn it off.**

3. **Choose File⇨Save to save the file.**

   With the Save Data with Report option turned off, as shown in Figure 15-8, only the report design gets saved.

You can use this menu to save a file in one of three ways:

✔ **Save:** Saves the active report to a disk, under its current name. All changes you make to the report overwrite the preceding version of the report.

✔ **Save As:** Saves the report to a disk, under a new name. This option is handy when you want to save an original copy separately from the copy to which you make changes. When you choose this option, you have two files (under different names): the untouched original and the report you changed.

✔ **Save Data with Report:** Saves the underlying data that accompanies the report. The data saved with the report is sort of a snapshot of how the data looked when you ran the report. You still have to use File⇨Save or File⇨Save As to create a saved report file, however.

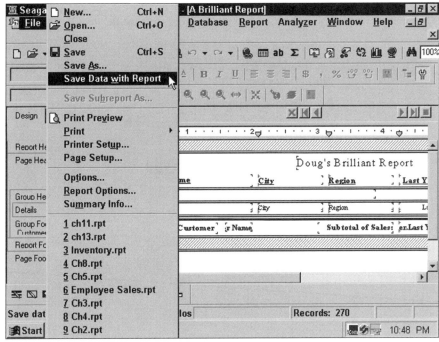

**Figure 15-8:**
The File
menu, with
a report file
open.

# Mailing a Report

Each electronic-mail system is unique. Because of the differences in how mail systems work, you are given generic exporting instructions in this section. The figures shown in this section are from a real-life example, although you have to use your own mail-application program.

Whenever you combine the activities of one program with another, things get a little complicated. You need to know about some caveats and assumptions about exporting to e-mail. Both Microsoft Mail and Microsoft Exchange use MAPI. Crystal Reports supports exporting to MAPI and to Lotus Notes.

*MAPI* is simply a standard for e-mail; it's the Microsoft Mail API (application programming interface), which many companies use. VIM, another standard for getting mail, has a different format. VIM was created and is maintained by Lotus.

Follow these steps to mail a report:

1. **Click the Export button on the Standard toolbar.**

   The Export dialog box appears.

2. **Click the drop-down arrow in the Format box to display the export format choices and then select Crystal Reports (RPT).**

   Use the scroll button to move to this selection.

3. **Click the drop-down arrow in the Destination box to display the destination choices and then select Microsoft Mail (MAPI).**

   Figure 15-9 shows the selections in the Export dialog box.

**Figure 15-9:**
The Export
dialog box,
with Crystal
Reports and
Microsoft
Mail
selected.

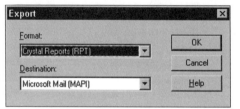

4. **Click OK.**

   When you export a report to e-mail, one of two things may happen: Crystal Reports may ask you to log on to your e-mail application in the usual way, or your e-mail application may automatically open. Continue sending mail as you normally do in your e-mail application.

# Faxing a Report

You can fax a Crystal Reports report directly to a fax machine if you have a fax application, such as Microsoft Fax or Delrina WinFax, installed on your system. You must have a fax application installed before you can use this Crystal Reports feature.

Follow these generic steps to fax directly from Crystal Reports:

1. **Open Crystal Reports and then open the report you want to fax.**

2. **Choose File⇨Printer Setup from the menu bar.**

   The Print Setup dialog box appears.

3. **Click the drop-down arrow next to the Name box for a list of all available printers.**

4. **Select the fax driver and click OK.**

   Figure 15-10 shows the screen with a fax printer driver selected.

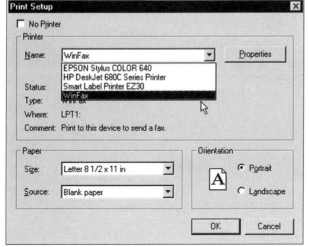

**Figure 15-10:**
A fax driver
selected as
the printer
destination.

5. **Choose File⇨Print⇨Printer from the menu bar.**

   The Print dialog box appears, indicating that the print job is being sent to your chosen fax driver, as shown in Figure 15-11.

   This example is being sent to WinFax on LPT1.

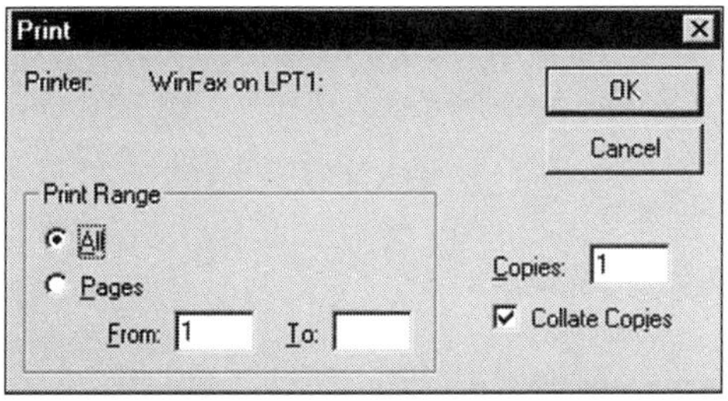

**Figure 15-11:**
A fax printer
driver
selected
as the
destination
for the
report.

6. **Click OK.**

   The dialog box for your chosen fax driver appears. Every fax application is different but generally you can select a cover page, fill in the number to which you're faxing, and complete other required information.

7. **Select the option that lets you send the fax from your fax application and click OK or the Send button.**

   Your computer dials the fax machine and when connected, Crystal Reports generates the report and sends it to be printed on the recipient's fax machine.

# Web Reporting

A lot of companies circulate information to employees, customers, and even the general public by using Internets and intranets. By posting your reports to the World Wide Web, you can provide access to information that previously required human attention to receive. No more faxing or mailing reports; simply tell your salespeople or customers to point their browsers to your Web site.

## Exporting to HTML

The World Wide Web uses a standard language — *HTML* (or HyperText Markup Language) to create graphical pages. You once had to learn to rewrite your reports in HTML to make them usable on the Web. Not so anymore. Crystal Reports exports its reports directly to HTML format! And with the capability to add Hyperlinks to a report, you can create a report that has an e-mail feedback link or links to other Web sites that are relevant to your report. To export a report to an HTML format, follow these steps:

1. **Open the report you want to export.**

2. **Click the Export button on the Standard toolbar.**

   The Export dialog box appears, enabling you to select two things: the format and the destination for the report file.

3. **Click the drop-down arrow in the Format box and scroll through the list until you see the format that's compatible with your Web browser.**

   In this example, select HTML 3.2 Extended or—new in Version 8—DHTML (which is Dynamic HyperText Markup Language), as shown in Figure 15-12.

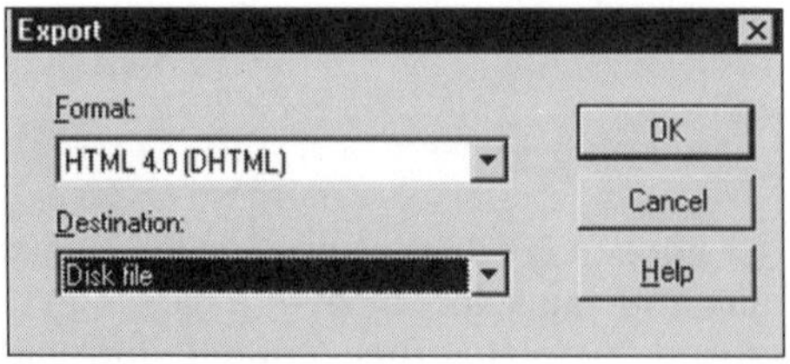

**Figure 15-12:**
The Export dialog box, with HTML format and Disk File destination selected.

| Export | |
|---|---|
| Format: | OK |
| HTML 4.0 (DHTML) | Cancel |
| Destination: | Help |
| Disk file | |

4. **Click the drop-down arrow in the Destination box to display the destination choices for the .HTML file and then select Disk File.**

The Export to Directory window appears. Accept the default, which in this case is the Crystal Reports folder, or enter a new destination.

5. **Click OK.**

Crystal creates a directory of files, the .HTML files, and any graphics and charts stored as .JPG files. Click any .HTML file in the directory, and your browser displays that page of the report.

## Checking your Web page

You can also export the report so that your browser opens it immediately. Follow the steps in the preceding section, except that in the Export dialog box (after selecting HTML as the format) select Application in the Destination box. Crystal Reports saves the report to a default folder location. After the export is finished, your browser starts and the exported file appears, as shown in Figure 15-13.

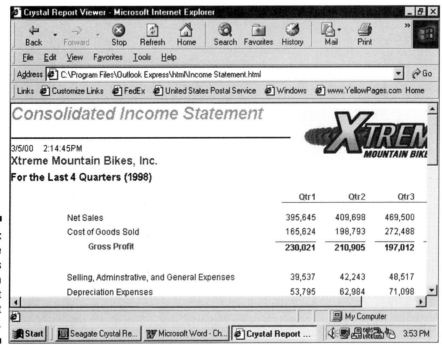

**Figure 15-13:** The sample report as seen in Microsoft Internet Explorer.

# Chapter 16

# Setting Your Options

● ● ● ● ● ● ● ● ● ● ● ● ● ● ● ● ● ● ● ● ● ● ● ● ● ● ● ● ● ● ● ● ● ● ● ● ● ● ● ● ● ● ● ● ● ● ● ● ● ● ●

● ● ● ● ● ● ● ● ● ● ● ● ● ● ● ● ● ● ● ● ● ● ● ● ● ● ● ● ● ● ● ● ● ● ● ● ● ● ● ● ● ● ● ● ● ● ● ● ● ● ●

*I*f you've worked with computers, you may recognize the term *default.* But it's not your fault if you don't; default refers to an automatic setting in computer software, such as the setting for the size of text you add to a Crystal Reports report. With a default setting, every time you add a text object to a report, for example, you can direct Crystal Reports to make the text 18 points high. That way you don't have to format every piece of text every time you add text to a report. In this chapter, you discover a variety of default settings that can make creating your report much easier.

The Crystal Reports environment consists of settings that determine how every report is formatted. You can enter a setting, for example, to format all numbers with two decimal places. Of course, you can override the setting, if necessary, to change the format to whatever you need. The point is that when you create a report, you can have most of the settings you want already in place, rather than having to add them to every new report. These settings take effect from the time you change them. They do not affect objects already on an existing report. If you add a new object to an old report, however, the new settings do affect that object.

Check out the default options in Crystal Reports by choosing File⏎Options. The Options dialog box appears, as shown in Figure 16-1. Take a moment to look at this dialog box and the environment settings for Crystal Reports.

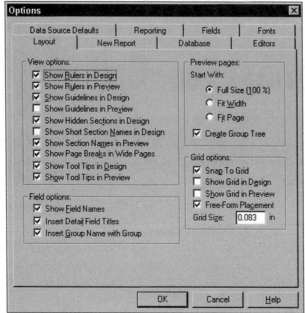

**Figure 16-1:**
The Options
dialog box.

*Note:* If an option is turned on, a check mark appears in the box beside it. Click the option to add or remove the check mark.

Crystal Reports saves the settings you make in Options if you gracefully exit it. If you make changes in Options and then crash out of Crystal Reports or the power goes out, the changes you make are not saved. If you make a lot of changes, exit from Crystal Reports right away and then restart it.

# The Layout Tab

Refer to Figure 16-1 to see the Options dialog box with the Layout tab displayed. Select the following options to set the layout defaults you want to use when you create reports:

- **View Options:** You can turn on or off any of these settings, which include rulers and guidelines in both the Design tab and the Preview tab.

    The section names referred to in the View options are the names in the gray area to the left of the report layout area. A short section name can be used in the Design tab to give more screen space to the Report Layout area. Figures 16-2 and 16-3 show the different ways the section names can be displayed. The mouse pointer indicates the section name in each figure.

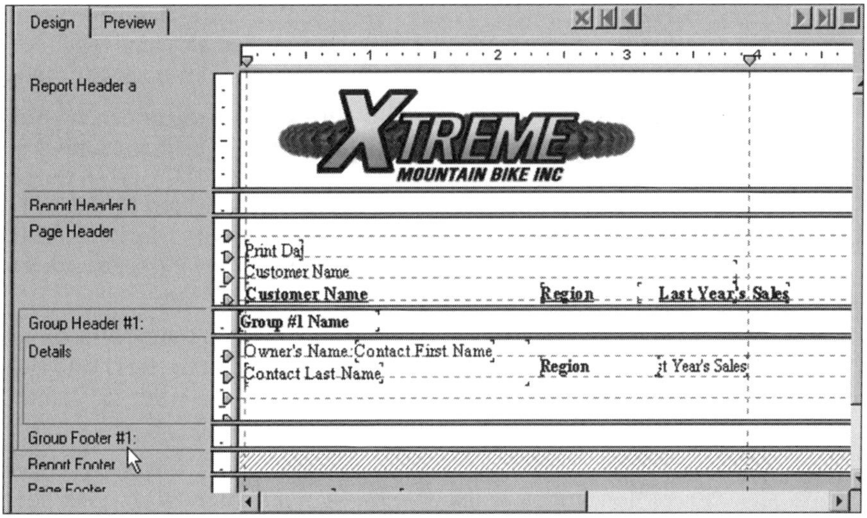

**Figure 16-2:**
A long section name on the Design tab.

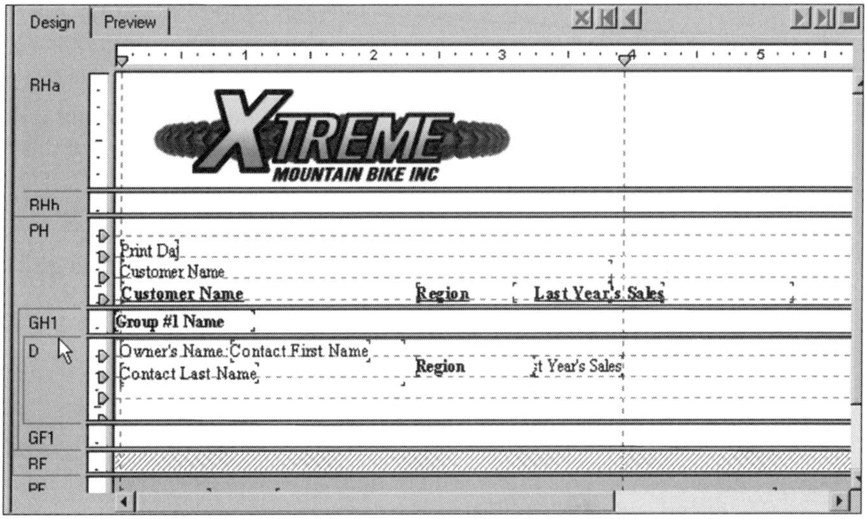

**Figure 16-3:**
An abbreviated section name on the Design tab.

✔ **Preview Pages:** In Crystal Reports, you can work in the Design tab or the Preview tab. The Preview tab gives you a view of the report that includes live data and, consequently, is as close as you can get to seeing how the report will look without printing it. Use the Preview Pages settings to determine the way the report is initially displayed when you first preview a report. You can use the Zoom feature to change the size of the report in Preview at any time.

The Group Tree shows your report groups in an easy to use window on the left side of the Preview tab. You can toggle it on or off when you're in the Preview tab.

- ✔ **Field Options:** You have the option of seeing the placeholders for the fields with their field names or a series of XXXs for text and 555s for numbers. I like leaving the Show Field Names option turned on.

   The Insert Detail Field Titles option is already on when you create a new report. When you insert a database field, the field name is inserted as a heading above the Details section where you inserted the database field. The idea is that you can easily determine which field is where in your report. If you use this setting in concert with the Show Field Names option and you insert a database field, the field name appears as the header and in the Details section, as well.

   You may want to leave on the Insert Group Name with Group setting, too, because it adds the name of the group to the Group Header section whenever you add a group to your report. (Refer to Chapter 5 for more information about group names.)

- ✔ **Grid options:** Crystal Reports automatically turns on the Snap To Grid option, and — in my opinion — that's where you should leave it. When you insert an object into a report, Crystal Reports moves the object so that it's aligned with a grid of horizontal and vertical lines. This feature gives the report a well-spaced layout, without your having to struggle with each object. If you want, you can have the underlying grid visible in both the Design and Preview tabs.

   If you have the Free-Form Placement option turned on and you have numerous guidelines, you can place fields between guidelines. If this option is turned off, you can move fields only from one guideline to another. Check out the Free-Form Placement option by playing around with it.

The grid size determines the spacing between the individual grid lines. The smaller the number, the more closely packed the lines.

# The New Report Tab

The New Report tab is used to determine two things: where new reports are saved and where reports you're mailing are sent by default. This tab offers the following options:

- ✔ **Report Directory:** To open the Choose Directory dialog box, as shown in Figure 16-4, click the Browse button in this area to display the path to where your reports are stored. With Version 8, Crystal Reports follows Microsoft's convention and directs the default location to the My Documents folder.

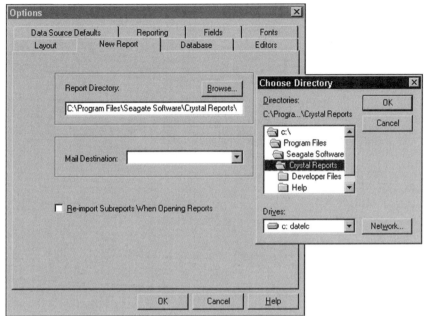

**Figure 16-4:**
Select the
New Report
tab and
click the
Browse
button.

> ✔ **Mail Destination:** This setting determines where a report is sent by
> default when you want to use electronic mail to send it.
>
> ✔ **Re-Import Subreports When Opening Reports:** You can also have
> Crystal Reports update the design of any subreports upon opening. The
> default is off, forcing you to update the subreport manually if design
> changes have occurred.

# *The Database Tab*

Use the Database tab to set SQL/ODBC database options, the method you want
to use to sort and display table and field names, and other advanced options.
Just click the Database tab to open the dialog box shown in Figure 16-5.

The Database tab offers the following options:

# Show

These options let you specify what you see when looking for database tables in the Data Explorer.

- ✓ **Tables:** Enables reporting on database tables in your SQL/ODBC data sources.

- ✓ **Views:** Enables reporting on virtual tables in your SQL/ODBC data sources.

- ✓ **System Tables:** Enables tables that are typically used by the system administrator only but are available for use if you have the appropriate permissions.

- ✓ **Synonyms:** Enables reporting on virtual tables that are available on some hosts.

- ✓ **Stored Procedures:** Enables reporting on the result sets from stored procedures if you're using SQL systems that support stored procedures.

- ✓ **Table Name LIKE:** Enables you to enter the SQL LIKE function to specify the kinds of table names you want to appear in the Data Explorer. You can use the underscore character (_) and the percent sign character (%) as wildcards with this function. The underscore character specifies any single character, and the percent sign signifies any character string. For example, DAV_ matches DAVE only, while DAV% matches both DAVE and DAVID. The table name LIKE C% would display only those tables that have a table name beginning with the letter C.

✔ **Owner LIKE:** Works exactly like the Table name LIKE box except that the LIKE function here is used to select the Owner (or Creator or Alias) of the table, not the table name itself. For example, Owner LIKE C% would display only those tables that have an owner beginning with the letter C.

✔ **Reprompt User When Connecting:** Opens the Allow Reporting On dialog box before it opens the Data Explorer. This dialog box enables you to specify the types of data you want to appear in the Data Explorer. All the options from the Show section of the Database tab appear in the Allow Reporting On dialog box.

## List tables and fields by

In this area, you can specify the text that you want the program to use for tables and fields by setting the following options:

✔ **Name:** Identifies tables and fields by using the actual name, for example, "Customer" table and "Customer Name" field.

✔ **Description:** Identifies tables and fields by using the description that you specify, for example, "Our Clients" table and "The names of all our customers" field.

✔ **Both:** Identifies tables and fields by using both the name and the description that you assign, for example, "Customer - Our Clients" table and "Customer Name - The names of all our customers" field.

## Sorting

These options let you specify in what order the tables and fields will display in the Field Explorer and other field lists when you create a report.

✔ **Sort Tables Alphabetically:** Displays tables throughout the program, sorted in alphabetical order (rather than in the order they appear in the database). This is the default setting, and I recommend it.

✔ **Sort Fields Alphabetically:** Displays fields throughout the program, sorted in alphabetical order (rather than in the order they appear in the database table). This option is not the default, but I think it makes finding the fields you want to insert much easier.

# Advanced

These options are for the really knowledgeable database people. The default settings are fine.

✔ **Use Indexes or Server for Speed:** Uses the available indexes/servers to speed the record selection process. If this check box is not selected, the record selection process may be much slower.

*Note:* If an index has a name that's different from the database it indexes, you need to identify the index for the program. You do this by using the Link Options dialog box, which you can access via the Visual Linking Expert, as explained in Chapter 14.

✔ **Perform Grouping On Server:** Performs grouping on the server (server-side processing). Server-side processing allows you to set up a report that performs the majority of its processing on the server and pushes only relevant details to your computer. Server-side processing provides you with a number of benefits:

- Less time connected to the server

- Less memory needed to process the report on your computer

- Lower transfer time from the server to the client

Server-side processing works only for reports based on SQL data sources. (You cannot, for example, use server-side processing for a report based on a query, because a query is not an SQL data source.)

This option is not selected by default; but if you use SQL data sources, you want to select it.

✔ **Use Default Alias:** Uses the default alias for each database that you activate. The default alias is the name of the database in one word without the extension. For example, the default alias for the database Craze.mdb is "craze." Use this option if you are usually satisfied with the default alias and do not want to have to accept or change the alias whenever you activate a database.

Deselect this check box to display the Alias Name dialog box whenever you activate a database. You can accept the default alias or enter a new one in the Alias Name dialog box.

✔ **Translate DOS Strings:** Assumes that any character code it finds in a dBASE string field is an ASCII code and then translates that code to a corresponding ANSI value, so that the same character that appears in dBASE appears in your report.

*Note:* If you deselect this check box and you use upper ASCII characters in your dBASE string fields, the special characters are the same in your report as they are in the dBASE string field.

✔ **Case-Insensitive SQL Data:** (This one is interesting.) Searches for strings in your SQL data without checking the case. For example, if your report contains SQL data, and the data is of mixed case (red, RED, Red), a case-sensitive search for "red" returns only "red." If you select this check box, the same query returns red, RED, and Red, when you use red as a record-selection value. This option is selected by default.

✔ **Translate DOS Memos:** Assumes that any character code it finds in a dBASE memo field is an ASCII code and then translates that code to a corresponding ANSI value so that the same character that appears in dBASE appears in your report.

*Note:* If you clear this check box and you use upper ASCII characters in your dBASE memo fields, the special characters aren't the same in your report as they are in the dBASE memo field.

✔ **Auto-SmartLinking:** Links your tables automatically when you're using the Visual Linking Expert.

✔ **Cartesian Product:** Produces all possible combinations of the original data. This option is not selected by default.

*Note:* The Cartesian Product option applies to OLAP data sources and does not apply specifically to other direct-access data sources. This option ensures that a report shows all values of all dimensions (as opposed to all values of the first dimension by a value of the second dimension, which is the result if this option isn't selected).

✔ **Perform Query Asynchronously:** Uses asynchronous queries. The program normally sends an entire query to the database server. Selecting this option, however, allows the program and the ODBC database server (if it supports asynchronous queries) to transfer data back and forth. An advantage of using this option is that you can cancel queries during processing more easily. This option is not selected by default.

✔ **Select Distinct Data for Browsing:** Shows the first 500 distinct (unique) records when you browse the contents of a database field. When Select Distinct Data for Browsing is not selected, browsing returns the unique values in the first 500 records.

*Note:* Because most SQL servers do not support selecting distinct records for long data types, such as memo and blob fields, selecting and browsing distinct records are not supported for such fields.

# The Editors Tab

In Crystal Reports you can set the formatting default view of the text in the Formula Editor or in the SQL Expression Editor. It's simply a way to make reading the entries easier on your eyes. I increase the size of the font for the Formula Editor to at least 14 points. Figure 16-6 shows the Editors tab.

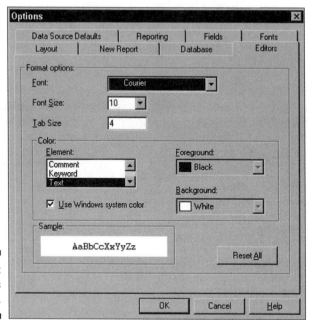

**Figure 16-6:**
The Editors
tab.

# *Data Source Defaults Tab*

If your reports are consistently from the same type of data and the databases are stored in the same folder, you can set the default file type and folder location. That way, every time you start to create a new report, you don't have to do the point-and-click routine in the Data Explorer to locate your data. The Data Source Defaults tab, as shown in Figure 16-7, offers the following options:

- **Data Directory:** To set the default database folder location, click the Browse button and click your way to the folder.

- **Database File Filter:** This field is important if you're accessing databases that have file extensions different from the one listed. You may not be familiar with file extensions because they are virtually invisible in the Windows environment, but they're still with us from the DOS days. Simply put, any file you create on your computer is stored with the name you gave it, followed by a period and a three-character extension. If you open the folder in which you expect to see the database and it doesn't appear, check with the database creator to find out whether you need to add a different file extension in this field.

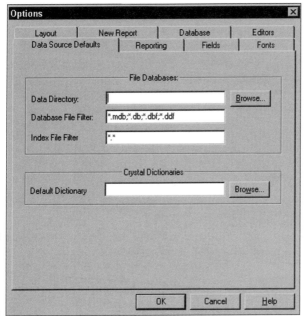

**Figure 16-7:**
The Data
Source
Defaults tab.

- ✓ **Index File Filter:** Use this option to include only those file types you want to make accessible. If you set the filter to Paradox (*.px), for example, the program displays only files with that extension in the Attach New Index dialog box and other boxes that offer you index options. Indexes are of major importance in establishing links between multiple databases.

- ✓ **Default Dictionary:** This option directs a report designer to select a Crystal Dictionary from which to create the report. Dictionaries provide a customized view of the database. If you use dictionaries, you can designate a folder location and a file name.

# The Reporting Tab

The Reporting tab, as shown in Figure 16-8, has some more-sophisticated settings that you probably won't need until after you use Crystal Reports awhile. For now, simply keep in mind that you have the following options available:

- ✓ **Date-Time Field:** You can choose to convert the date-time field in your database to a string or to a date, or you can keep it exactly as it is originally. If you select the Convert to String option, for example, fields in your database that are combined date-time fields are converted to string fields.

- ✓ **Convert NULL Field Value to Default:** This option handles the conversion of NULL-value data in a field to a specific value (numbers to zero, strings to a space).

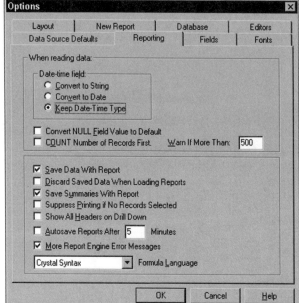

**Figure 16-8:**
The Options
dialog box,
with the
Reporting
tab
displayed.

✔ **COUNT Number of Records First:** This setting is important if you work with extremely large SQL databases. Why? Because when you're in the process of designing or previewing a report, you don't have to have a multitude of records in the report to determine whether the design is giving you the report you want. Crystal Reports gives you the opportunity to retrieve only a portion of the records.

✔ **Warn If More Than:** This option works in concert with the COUNT Number of Records First option. Enter a number in this field to set the maximum number of records you want to display during the design phase.

✔ **Save Data With Report:** I recommend that you select this option because most of the time you want the data included with your report. If you don't, you can simply choose File⇨Save Data with Report to toggle off the command. For more information about saving or not saving data with a report, refer to Chapter 15.

✔ **Discard Saved Data When Loading Reports:** When you open a Crystal Reports report, you usually want the underlying data to accompany it, although you may want the data not to be part of the report. If you select this option, the formatting and other settings remain.

✔ **Save Summaries With Report:** If this option is turned off, the summaries have to be recalculated every time you open a report. I don't know why you would deselect this option, but you can!

✔ **Suppress Printing If No Records Selected:** The default setting has Crystal Reports print the report, whether or not any records are present. Use this option to change that.

- ✔ **Show All Headers On Drill Down:** When turned on, this option shows all the headers above the section being drilled down on the Drill Down tab.

- ✔ **Autosave Reports:** This feature periodically saves your report so that you cannot accidentally lose your work. On large reports in which you save the data with the report, you may want to set a long time between saves.

- ✔ **More Report Engine Error Messages:** This check box is for techie types who need to know why the special code they added to a report by using the Report Engine doesn't work. This option opens the floodgates on the Crystal Reports messages for run-time reports. Rather than hold back any errors, *all* the errors are shown. The option to display all error messages is already selected when you see the Crystal Reports Design tab, but you get to decide what the run-time user sees by using this option.

- ✔ **Formula Language:** In Version 8, you can select the default formula language, which is switchable when you actually create a formula.

# The Fields Tab

The Fields tab, as shown in Figure 16-9, lists the types of fields you can insert in a report. This tab enables you to set up the default format of the fields you insert.

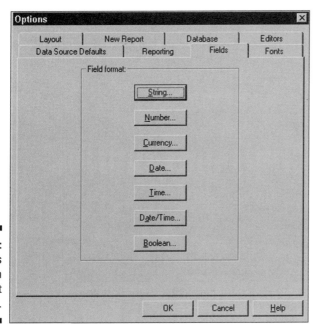

**Figure 16-9:** The Fields tab, with Field Format buttons.

Each of the field types has its own particular formatting attributes. Therefore, when you click a Field Format button, the Format Editor dialog box specific to that field appears. For example, clicking the String button opens the Format Editor dialog box, as shown in Figure 16-10.

A *string field* is made up of characters that are not considered to be numbers or dates. That doesn't mean that the field can't have numbers or dates — it simply means that Crystal Reports treats as character strings any characters not specifically formatted as dates or numbers. Crystal Reports doesn't make this decision, however. The data type comes from the database itself.

To open the Format Editor dialog box, as shown in Figure 16-11, click the Number button on the Fields tab of the Options dialog box (refer to Figure 16-9). The Format Editor dialog box appears, displaying four tabs: Common, Number, Border, and Hyperlink. You use the Number tab to determine such settings as the number of decimal places to display, the degree of rounding that occurs, and the way negative numbers are displayed. Click the Currency Symbol box to set the manner in which numbers are displayed relative to the type of currency symbol that's included. When you change the format, that change is immediately reflected in the Sample preview box at the bottom of the dialog box.

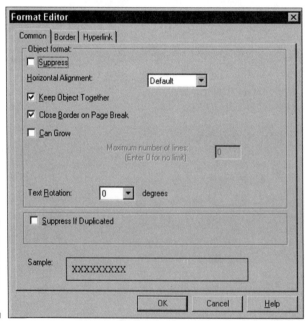

**Figure 16-10:**
The dialog box for the String field type.

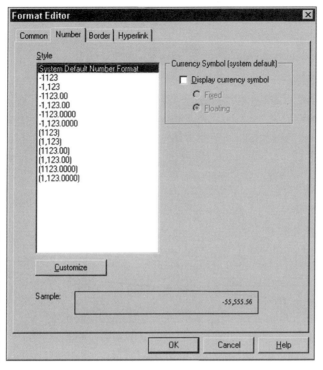

**Figure 16-11:**
The Format
Editor dialog
box, with
the Number
tab
selected.

On the Border tab in the Format Editor dialog box, you can automatically add elements, such as drop shadows or single- or double-line borders, every time you insert text objects. If you've established a consistent style for every text object you insert, you can use this tab to make those settings automatic.

The remaining buttons on the Fields tab are of the same nature: You use them to set the automatic format for the type of field associated with the button.

# The Fonts Tab

The Fonts tab gives you the tools to set the automatic (or *default*) font sizes and types for each of the objects listed in the Options dialog box. You use this tab in conjunction with the Fields tab to develop the look you want in your reports. Clicking an object button on the Fonts tab opens the Font dialog box, as shown in Figure 16-12.

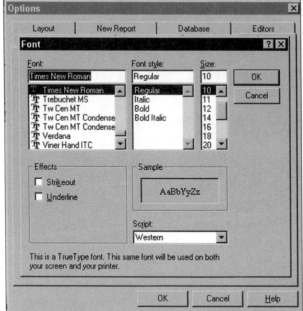

**Figure 16-12:**
The Font dialog box opens after you click any of the object buttons.

In the Font dialog box, you can select the preferred font and size for each of the objects you insert in a report. As you try different fonts and sizes, the change is reflected in the Sample preview box.

To check the settings you make for each type of object on your report, click through all five buttons on the Fonts tab.

# Part VII
# The Part of Tens

The 5th Wave By Rich Tennant

"I'm sure there will be a good job market when I graduate. I created a virus that will go off that year."

# In this part . . .

In April 1990, I happened to be at a writers' conference in which another unknown, relatively poor author named Dan Gookin was attending. He told me of an idea he had about writing a real beginner's book on DOS, including humor, with the cover name *DOS For Dummies*. I told him that was a great idea and that I bet no publishers would do it — their groupthink would be that no person would self-identify as a *Dummy*. He replied that the title had indeed been sniffed at by several major publishers. Well, history agrees with Dan and me — over 3.5 million copies of *DOS For Dummies* have been sold, and Dan no longer worries about paying the rent.

So the Part of Tens, a Gookin original, lives on. In this Part of Tens, I try to convey some of the more important concepts regarding planning and executing your reports. Hand the "Ten or So Questions to Ask Before You Create a Report" to your boss the next time she demands a report but doesn't convey any guidance. Ask for the answers before starting. Then, with the report under construction, look at the enhancement ideas to create a dynamic report.

# Chapter 17

# Ten or So Questions to Ask Before You Create a Report

. . . . . . . . . . . . . . . . . . . . . . . . . . . . . . . . . . . . . . . . . . . . . . . . . . . . . . . . .

*In This Chapter*

▶ Finding the special purpose for your report

▶ Determining what to include in your report

▶ Getting your report out to the audience

. . . . . . . . . . . . . . . . . . . . . . . . . . . . . . . . . . . . . . . . . . . . . . . . . . . . . . . . .

*Y*our boss comes into your office in a rush stating that she needs a sales-by-salesperson report right away! Now what do you do? Remain calm. You need to ask the person requesting a report, boss or not, the following questions.

## How sensitive is the information in the report?

Is the person requesting this report allowed to access the data? Does the report contain any confidential information?

Although writing down the purpose of the report may seem like a useless exercise, doing so is very important because it allows you to focus on what should be in the report and how the information should be displayed. Asking questions also allows report recipients to know whether this is the report they want or whether they should reexamine the purpose of the report.

More and more, companies and institutions are careful about security issues, such as who sees what data. In a hospital, a corrections facility, a school, or a business, some information may not be available to all people. In a company, a person may require security clearance to see certain data. Some financial data may be distributed only to certain people. Some information may be proprietary. Keep these security issues in mind when you create a report.

# From what databases, views, or tables do you need to include information in this report, and what fields do you want to include in the report?

Data for a report may come from different sources. Record the databases, tables, or views that hold the data you need. You may need to know the exact directories that hold information. You may need to know what network to access. You may need a password to obtain access to some data.

If creating your report involves more than one table, you need to link the tables. The Visual Linking Expert can be helpful to you.

# Do you want all the records in the report or a subset?

Women only? Over 60 years old? Transactions for March?

Many reports are run on a monthly, quarterly, or yearly basis. You need to know this information before you create your report. If you don't know, you may find yourself waiting for 15 minutes for a report preview to display because you're looking at data for the last 10 years. Whether you're looking for data from a certain region, a certain gender, or a certain time period, you're better off if you can reduce the number of records in your report. The Select Expert can be helpful to you.

# How do you want the data grouped?

Find out whether to group the data by region, by date, or by alphabet. Some reports may have several groups. For example, a report may be grouped by state, then by gender, and then by age.

# How do you want the data sorted?

Usually, the two choices for sorting are ascending or descending order. In addition, you need to know whether the data should be sorted in ascending or descending order by amount, by alphabet, or by some other criteria. As with groups, you may sort alphabetically by state and then sort by amount within those groups.

# What summary calculations do you want in the report?

Monthly totals? Grand totals? Averages? Find out whether you need to count the records in the report, get a running total, add summaries at the end of the groups, and so on. Consider whether you want summaries after every group.

# What text do you want to appear in the report header, page header, page footer, report footer, or other text?

Record the text you want to display in each of these report sections. Decide on which pages you want to display this text. You may want to display some text on the first page but not on the others. Find out whether any other text is required. You may need to describe some of the summary calculations. You may need to add some quotes or expressions.

# Do you want certain data to stand out?

You can make data stand out by using flags, special formatting, or conditional formatting. If the person for whom you're creating the report wants the data to stand out, find out how.

This step is for the more-sophisticated, presentation-quality report. Will the report be printed? Will the report be distributed on a network? Do you have a color printer? You can make totals greater than 10,000 appear in red. If you're presenting in black-and-white, then you may want to make totals greater than 10,000 appear in reverse image. Based on the report's purpose, you can make the critical data stand out.

# How should the report be distributed and to whom?

You may have a network, where all the reports are distributed to an Exchange folder or to Lotus Notes. You may want reports uploaded automatically to a company intranet page. Perhaps you are distributing a report to a group that doesn't have access to Crystal Reports. Find out whether you need to export the report so that it can be read by another software product.

Again, the security issue raises its head. Can anybody see the information in this report or is it proprietary, or confidential? You're better off finding out this information before you distribute the report.

## When do you need to see this report, and when should it be distributed?

You should get into the habit of finding out the due date for activities assigned to you. The person requesting the report may want to see and approve the report before you send it out. Find out whether the report has a critical deadline.

## Is this how the report should look?

Before you start creating the new report, draw a picture of the report with all the titles, columns, groups, charts, maps, hyperlinks, and so on. Get the drawing approved. Then you'll have a guideline for creating the report. Here's a pattern for how you may want the report to look:

| Title | | |
|---|---|---|
| Header | | |
| Group | | |
| Field | Field | Field |
| XXXXXXXXXX | XXXXXXXXXX | XXXXXXX |
| | Summary Data | XXXXXXX |
| Footer | | |

## Finally, a test

One of the great fallacies of the computer era is that anything generated by a computer has to be correct. The truth is that the output of a report is only as accurate as the person who creates it. So, the last steps before sending your report to thousands of your fellow employees is to read it with great skepticism and retrace all your report-building steps to be certain that they're what you intended. Then, give the report to someone else familiar with the data and let that person examine it.

If you follow these steps, even in an oblique way, the stress and strain of creating reports is greatly reduced.

# Chapter 18

# Ten (Okay, Eleven) Tricks to Enhance Reports

*T*he purpose of a report often is to summarize and identify key information necessary to manage your enterprise. (Unless you work in government; then your purpose is to obfuscate and befuddle, thereby guaranteeing the need for more reports and securing your job!) So the following ideas are not tricks, really, just some guidelines for making your reports easier to understand and interpret.

## Use a predictable format

Being predictable doesn't mean being boring. Life is simpler for everyone if you and your readers can identify a report at a glance. Here are some suggestions:

- Be clear and consistent.

- Note selection conditions in the Report Footer. By adding the selection conditions in the Report Footer, you tell the reader what data you used to generate the report.

- Use standard formats for specific reports. By using standard formats for specific reports, you engender consistency so that anyone can then identify the type of report by its format.

- Use the same labeling format for the same type of report object, such as subtotals, summaries, and grand totals.

You can also record information regarding the report by entering the information in the Document Properties dialog box. To do so, follow these steps:

1. **Open the report.**

2. **Choose File⇨Summary Info to open the Document Properties dialog box with the Summary tab displayed.**

3. **In the Comments box, add any comments you want.**

   Figure 18-1 shows the Summary tab in the Document Properties dialog box for the Employee Sales sample report info.

4. **Click OK to close the dialog box.**

5. **Choose Insert⇨Special Field to open the Field Explorer dialog box.**

 6. **Select Report Comments and click the Insert to Report button on the toolbar.**

7. **Move the mouse pointer to the section of the report in which you want the Report Comments to appear.**

8. **Click the mouse button to insert the field.**

**Document Properties**

Summary | Statistics |

Application: Seagate Crystal Reports

Author: Allan

Keywords:

Comments: This report is used in Crystal Report for Dummies, version 8. Chapter 11

Title: A Brilliant Report

Subject: Customers and Sales

Template:

☑ Save preview picture

OK | Cancel | Help

**Figure 18-1:** Summary info for the Employee Sales sample report.

New to Version 8 is the Save Preview Picture check box. If this option is selected as part of adding the report summary, some of the information and a thumbnail sketch can be seen when you look for a report in the Open dialog box. Figure 18-2 shows the Open dialog box with the Properties button selected and the Report Summary information displayed. Figure 18-3 shows the Open dialog box with the Preview button selected and the Preview Picture displayed. With this capability, you can be certain that you're opening the correct report — a real time-saver if the report is large.

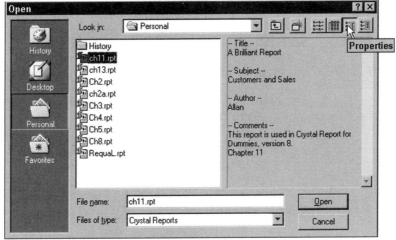

Figure 18-2:
The Open
dialog box
with the
Properties
button
selected,
revealing
the report
summary
information.

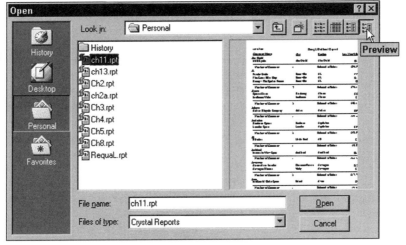

Figure 18-3:
The Open
dialog box
with the
Preview
button
selected,
revealing
the preview
picture of
the report.

## *Allow generous white space*

The acronym used to describe reports that are too busy and number-laden is MEGO, meaning My Eyes Glaze Over. Keep this fact in mind when you start adding detail to a report: Your report is only as good as the information the reader can easily receive.

Another way to add readability is to format every other line of the Details section in a different color. See Chapter 10 for the formula to do so.

## Position report headings and page numbers in the same place for every report

Many reports are generated on a regular basis. Therefore, their design should remain the same to avoid the need to re-create and edit the look of a report with each generation. So that your report reader can easily locate crucial information, display data in a predictable order.

Consistently paying attention to format makes the information in your report accessible.

## Make data easy to understand

Always avoid insider terms and jargon. If your report includes calculations, you may need a key to how they are constructed.

Here are a couple of suggestions that I've found make a report easier to understand:

- ✔ When using long text fields from your database, use the Can Grow format option to wrap the text onto another line rather than allowing the text to be cut off because the column is too narrow.
- ✔ Use standard terminology in the text objects you create.

All the field headings that Crystal inserts in a report are editable. If the field name that is copied from the database is cryptic, change the field heading to something that everyone can understand. If the field heading you require is too long for the width of the column, wrap the heading onto a second line and make the text field taller rather than wider.

## Place and align columns appropriately

Readers can easily become confused if the data isn't correctly labeled. Keeping the headings with the proper data and positioning data in a consistent, logical order is very important. See the steps in Chapter 3 for help with this.

The proper placement of columns and their headers can make all the difference in a report:

- ✔ List columns from left to right, consistent with the sort specification.
- ✔ If a Sort Order is required, use Ascending order. However, if you need to use Descending order, insert a note in the header to notify the report readers.
- ✔ Align data with the column header.

Keeping the data aligned with the accompanying headers and using a logical order is another way to make the report more understandable.

## Keep columns consistent

Arrange the columns of data on your report so that readers can easily determine where one set of data ends and another begins. Keep the following tips in mind:

- ✔ Space columns evenly to make boundaries obvious.
- ✔ Keep columns near enough so that a reader can scan a line.
- ✔ To eliminate the need to move back and forth to confirm column headings for the data, repeat the column headings on each page by inserting them into the Page Header section. See Chapter 9 for more on formatting.

## Use column headers strategically

Any numeric columns must have clear headings that define what the columns contain. Chapter 10 shows you how to combine a field with explanatory text. When creating column headers, keep the following in mind:

- ✔ Use meaningful column headers above each field space.
- ✔ Specify units (meters, units, millions of dollars) when not clear.
- ✔ Use abbreviations that readers understand in field labels.

## Visually group data

Reading a report that resembles a dictionary is quite tiring to the eye. Relieve eye fatigue by effectively using white space, as follows:

- ✔ When record information appears on more than one line, separate each record with a blank line.
- ✔ Leave a blank line between groups of data.

Crystal Reports does leave space between groups, but you may want to increase the distance for added clarity. Or you may choose to draw a box around the individual groups.

## Add charts and/or maps to make your reports more descriptive

Charts and maps are far superior to numbers when it comes to relating relationships or trends. The charting and mapping capabilities of Crystal Reports make presenting your data in a more visual way an easy task. You can find information about charts and maps in Chapter 6.

## Add graphics to make your report visually interesting

Although you do want to avoid graphic clutter, keep in mind that photographs, designs, or logos can convey a great deal of information.

What company report is complete without your photo adorning the title page? (On second thought, maybe you should save that idea for when you become company president.)

## Add hyperlinks to enhance your report or to direct readers to more information

With the ability to insert hyperlinks into a report, you have all the capabilities of the Web at hand. If you're the report creator, you can insert your e-mail address so that questions can be sent to you directly from the report. If you want an on-demand subreport (rather than one that's embedded), add a link to another report. Or, if the report contains customer data, you can create hyperlinks directly to the customer's Web site.

# Index

# Notes

# Notes

YOUR ONLINE RESOURCE

# WWW.DUMMIES.COM

# Discover Dummies Online!

The Dummies Web Site is your fun and friendly online resource for the latest information about *For Dummies*® books and your favorite topics. The Web site is the place to communicate with us, exchange ideas with other *For Dummies* readers, chat with authors, and have fun!

## Ten Fun and Useful Things You Can Do at www.dummies.com

1. Win free *For Dummies* books and more!
2. Register your book and be entered in a prize drawing.
3. Meet your favorite authors through the IDG Books Worldwide Author Chat Series.
4. Exchange helpful information with other *For Dummies* readers.
5. Discover other great *For Dummies* books you must have!
6. Purchase Dummieswear® exclusively from our Web site.
7. Buy *For Dummies* books online.
8. Talk to us. Make comments, ask questions, get answers!
9. Download free software.
10. Find additional useful resources from authors.

Link directly to these ten fun and useful things at http://www.dummies.com/10useful

SURF THE NET

WWW.DUMMIES.COM

For other technology titles from IDG Books Worldwide, go to www.idgbooks.com

Not on the Web yet? It's easy to get started with *Dummies 101*®: *The Internet For Windows*® *98* or *The Internet For Dummies*® at local retailers everywhere.

IDG BOOKS WORLDWIDE

Find other *For Dummies* books on these topics:
Business • Career • Databases • Food & Beverage • Games • Gardening • Graphics • Hardware
Health & Fitness • Internet and the World Wide Web • Networking • Office Suites
Operating Systems • Personal Finance • Pets • Programming • Recreation • Sports
Spreadsheets • Teacher Resources • Test Prep • Word Processing

# IDG BOOKS WORLDWIDE BOOK REGISTRATION

Register This Book and Win!

## We want to hear from you!

Visit **http://my2cents.dummies.com** to register this book and tell us how you liked it!

- ✔ Get entered in our monthly prize giveaway.

- ✔ Give us feedback about this book — tell us what you like best, what you like least, or maybe what you'd like to ask the author and us to change!

- ✔ Let us know any other *For Dummies®* topics that interest you.

Your feedback helps us determine what books to publish, tells us what coverage to add as we revise our books, and lets us know whether we're meeting your needs as a *For Dummies* reader. You're our most valuable resource, and what you have to say is important to us!

Not on the Web yet? It's easy to get started with *Dummies 101®: The Internet For Windows® 98* or *The Internet For Dummies®* at local retailers everywhere.

Or let us know what you think by sending us a letter at the following address:

*For Dummies* Book Registration
Dummies Press
10475 Crosspoint Blvd.
Indianapolis, IN 46256

™

BESTSELLING
BOOK SERIES